'Britain's leading thinker on contemporary European affairs . . . Garton Ash has produced a humane, democratic manifesto for our times'
Sunder Katwala, *Observer*

'Passionate . . . intelligent . . . admirably incisive' Ian McIntyre, *The Times*

'A fascinating book full of unfamiliar facts and piquant quotations'
Ferdinand Mount, *Sunday Times*

'Garton Ash's strength is his ability to marshal his formidable sources and knowledge to scatter received wisdoms . . . *Free World* could hardly be more timely' Andrew Mueller, *Time Out*

'We are blessed in this country to have intellectuals like Timothy Garton Ash . . . who can communicate complex ideas in beautifully clear language . . . [an] illuminating and stimulating book' Yasmin Alibhai-Brown, *Independent*

'Brilliant . . . [a] lucid and penetrating analysis' Richard Aldous, *Irish Times*

'This book manages to stir the soul at the same time as it challenges the intellect' Gerard DeGroot, *Scotland on Sunday*

'This is an important book, refreshingly positive yet without pulling any punches . . . Learn and be stimulated. You will enjoy the reading'
George P. Shultz

'Timothy Garton Ash is one of the most astute observers of Europe and its relationship with the United States. In this important book, he dissects the currently troubled Atlantic relationship, places it in a broader global context, and provides a sense of hope for the future' Joseph S. Nye, Jr., author of *Soft Power: The Means to Success in World Politics*

'This is a book that will inform, encourage and even inspire readers everywhere' Peter Singer, Professor of Bioethics, Princeton University

## ABOUT THE AUTHOR

Timothy Garton Ash is the author of seven previous books of political writing and 'history of the present', which have charted the transformation of Europe over the last quarter-century. They include *The Polish Revolution*, *The Uses of Adversity*, *We the People* and *History of the Present* (all published by Penguin). He is Director of the European Studies Centre and Gerd Bucerius Senior Research Fellow in Contemporary History at St Antony's College, Oxford, and a Senior Fellow at the Hoover Institution, Stanford University. His essays appear regularly in the *New York Review of Books* and he writes a column in the *Guardian* that is syndicated widely across Europe and the Americas.

TIMOTHY GARTON ASH

# Free World

*Why a crisis of the West reveals the
opportunity of our time*

PENGUIN BOOKS

## PENGUIN BOOKS

Published by the Penguin Group
Penguin Books Ltd, 80 Strand, London WC2R ORL, England
Penguin Group (USA) Inc., 375 Hudson Street, New York, New York 10014, USA
Penguin Group (Canada), 10 Alcorn Avenue, Toronto, Ontario, Canada M4V 3B2
(a division of Pearson Penguin Canada Inc.)
Penguin Ireland, 25 St Stephen's Green, Dublin 2, Ireland
(a division of Penguin Books Ltd)
Penguin Group (Australia), 250 Camberwell Road, Camberwell, Victoria 3124,
Australia (a division of Pearson Australia Group Pty Ltd)
Penguin Books India Pvt Ltd, 11 Community Centre,
Panchsheel Park, New Delhi – 110 017, India
Penguin Group (NZ), cnr Airborne and Rosedale Roads, Albany,
Auckland 1310, New Zealand (a division of Pearson New Zealand Ltd)
Penguin Books (South Africa) (Pty) Ltd, 24 Sturdee Avenue,
Rosebank 2196, South Africa

Penguin Books Ltd, Registered Offices: 80 Strand, London WC2R ORL, England

www.penguin.com

First published by Allen Lane 2004
Published in Penguin Books with a new Postscript 2005
2

Printed in England by Clays Ltd, St Ives plc

*For*
*Thomas and Alexander*

For Freedom's battle once begun,
Bequeathed by bleeding Sire to Son,
Though baffled oft is ever won.

*These lines from Byron's 'The Giaour' were written on a scrap of paper by an unknown hand, using a translation by Adam Mickiewicz, the Polish Byron, and pinned up outside the gates of the Lenin Shipyard in Gdańsk in August 1980, to support the nationwide strike that gave birth to the free trade union Solidarity. The unknown copyist omitted the word 'bleeding'. This ruined the metre but improved the sense.*

# Contents

# To the Reader

If we are free, we can work with other free people towards a free world. Nothing can stop us, except the walls of ignorance, selfishness and prejudice that divide free men and women from each other, and the free from the unfree. These walls are not outside and beyond us, like the Alps or the Rocky Mountains. Minds build them; minds can knock them down.

The mind-walls have grown higher and more forbidding since 11 September 2001, the '9/11' of fear that was the true beginning of the twenty-first century. But we can take heart from another 9/11, written European-style, with the day before the month. On the evening of 9 November 1989, citizens began to hack away at the roughcast concrete of the Berlin Wall with whatever they could lay their hands on – and the wall came down. That marked the effective end of the short twentieth century. It was our 9/11 of hope.

In Part One of this book, I examine the crisis that has engulfed Europeans and Americans at the start of a new century. I try to establish what has really happened and why. I weigh many sorts of evidence, to confront myths with facts. It turns out that much of today's disarray can be traced back to the impact of those two very different 9/11s, the fall of the wall in Berlin and the fall of the twin towers in New York. Now it seems we will have to add a third date, 11 March 2004, when the terrorist bombing of Madrid, exactly two and a half years after the 11 September attacks on the United States, gave Europe its own epiphany of fear.

Anyone who writes 'history of the present' knows that it will have to be revised in the light of such events. Because things keep changing, the experience of reading this kind of book can be less satisfying than, say, settling down with some annals of ancient Rome, but it can also be more exciting – because things may still be changed. As you read, you will know more about parts of this story than I do today, either because you have special knowledge of one of the many areas of world politics that I discuss or simply because you will know what has happened since. And, vitally, your own political voice will itself be a part of the unfolding story. You will affect the outcome, and therefore the way future historians write about our time. When you peruse those annals of ancient Rome, you are reading history; here, you're also writing it.

So please treat this as a joint work in progress. If we can agree to attack the mind-walls, then, like the Berliners during that unforgettable night of 9 November 1989, we shall have the encouragement of hearing others zestfully hammering away to left and right of us. As the walls come down, we shall discover a surprising prospect. For this crisis actually reveals a great opportunity. Today, more people in the world are more free than ever before. Despite all the frightening problems of our time, we have unprecedented chances to achieve a further enlargement of human freedom. In Part Two, I go beyond a history of the present to suggest some ways in which we can seize those chances over the next twenty years, leaving behind us the rubble of demolished walls. Even if you can't agree with all these suggestions, I hope we can share this starting-point: it's up to us.

*TGA*
*Oxford*
*25 March 2004*

# PART ONE

# Crisis

# A Crisis of the West

When you say 'we', who do you mean?

Many of us would start the answer with our family and our friends. Widening the circle, we might think of our town or region, supporters of the same football team, our nation or state, a sexual orientation, a political affiliation ('we on the Left', 'we Conservatives'), or those who profess the same religion – world-straddling fraternities these, with more than 1,300 million Muslims and nearly 2,000 million Christians, though fraternities scarred by deep internal divisions. Beyond this, most of us have a strong sense of 'we' meaning all our fellow human beings. Some would add other living creatures.

Yet these largest senses of 'we' are seldom what people really have in mind when they say 'we must do this' or 'we cannot allow that'. The moral 'we' of all humankind is today more important than ever, but it's not the same as our operational 'we'. So let us pose the question more precisely: 'What's the widest political community of which you spontaneously say "we" or "us"?' In our answer to that question lies the key to our future.

For me, an Englishman born into the Cold War, that widest political community used to be something called 'the West'. My friends and I didn't spend much time worrying about its boundaries. If you had asked us, we could not have said exactly where it ended. Was Turkey part of the West? Japan? Mexico? But we had no doubt that it existed, as Europe existed, or communism. At its core, we felt, were the free countries on both sides of the Atlantic ocean, in Western Europe and North America. This Cold War West faced a hostile power that we called 'the East'. The East meant, in the first place, the

Soviet Union, its Red Army, its nuclear missiles and its satellite states in what was then labelled Eastern Europe.

Occasionally, Western politicians or propagandists tried to persuade us that non-communist countries everywhere should be described as 'the free world' – even if their governments were torturing critics at home, gagging the press and rigging elections. My friends and I never accepted that claim. We did not think Chile under General Pinochet was a free country. Altogether, this tag 'the free world', with its strident definite article, implying that all inside are free, all outside unfree, has seldom been used in public without pathos or in private without irony. 'We're the most hated cops in the whole of the free world,' boasts a Los Angeles Police Department officer in the Jackie Chan film *Rush Hour*.

But the West – yes, that was real. Anyone who travelled regularly behind the Iron Curtain, to countries like Poland, was confirmed in this belief. My friends there talked all the time about the West. They believed more passionately than most West Europeans did in its fundamental unity and its shared values; they feared it might be weak and decadent. 'We', they said, 'are the West trapped in the East.' At the time, I felt these Polish, Czech and Hungarian friends were, so to speak, individual members of the West far more than I felt Turkey or Japan were collectively part of it. Others, with different personal experiences, saw things differently. Where you stand depends on where you sit. Everyone had his or her own West, just as everyone today has his or her own America,* France or Islam. There are as many Italys as there are Italians. None the less, Italy exists.

This political community of the West was, like all political communities, both real and imagined. At its military front line, it was as real as real can be. On a cold winter morning, Dutch, Belgian, British, German, Canadian and American soldiers stood shivering all the way down the frontier between West and East Germany, ready to die together – 'all for one and one for all' – in the event of an armed attack from the East. The community was imagined in the sense that behind these men and women prepared to die together in battle there

* I hope other inhabitants of the Americas will forgive me for using 'America' throughout this book as shorthand for the United States of America. It's what we usually say in Europe, and it is shorter.

stood another army of assumptions made by the people who put the soldiers there, but perhaps also by the soldiers themselves; assumptions about what united 'us' and what made 'us' different from the people on the other side of the barbed wire. A mental army of the West.

Many believed, for example, in what they called 'Western values'. The West stood for freedom, human rights, democracy, the rule of law. These good things, they thought, had grown mainly in the West and distinguished us from others. The (hi)stories we tell ourselves are also the history of our own times – and a sometimes unintentional account of our intentions. During the Cold War, generations of American school and university students were taught an inspiring story of Western Civilization, marching onwards and generally upwards from ancient Greece and Rome, through the spread of Christianity in Europe, the Renaissance, the Reformation, the Enlightenment, the English, American and French Revolutions, the development of capitalism, the bourgeoisie and universal suffrage, two World Wars and the Cold War, to the sunlit uplands of an American-led 'Atlantic Community'. In the grand narrative of 'Western Civ', the West began in Europe and ended in the hands of America. It went from Plato to Nato.

On a dusty bottom shelf in the library of Stanford University in California I once found an example of this story told at its most confident and simplistic. *Life's Picture History of Western Man*, published in 1951, began by asking 'Western Man – who is he and where did he come from?'[1] The identity of this 'most wonderfully dynamic creature ever to walk the earth' apparently became clear in Europe 'about 800 AD (earlier in some places, later in others) and he was ready to set out on his bright-starred mission of creating a new civilization for the world'. In those good old days, Western Man – always capitalized – was 'fair of skin, hardy of limb, brave of heart, and he believed in the eternal salvation of his soul'. Darker-skinned persons, not to mention women, hardly got a look in. Western Man 'worked towards freedom, first for his own person, then for his own mind and spirit, and finally for others in equal measure'. *Life's* handsomely illustrated picture history followed Western Man's progress 'from his first emergence in the Middle Ages to his contemporary position of world leadership in the United States of America'. 'A new vehicle called the Atlantic Community', it concluded, 'now carries Western Man on his way.'

At once fed by and feeding these assumptions about a shared future written in the past, there developed in the second half of the twentieth century an immense, intricate, close-knit web of special relationships between government and government, military and military, company and company, university and university, intelligence service and intelligence service, city and city, bank and bank, newspaper and newspaper, and above all, between millions of individual men and women, aided by the rapid growth in the speed and volume of air travel and telecommunications. On this teeming worldwide web, each kind of thread had a hundred bi- and multilateral variants, French-American, French-German, British-American, American-Polish, Portuguese-Spanish, Slovenian-Italian, New Zealand-Europe, Australia-America, the European Community, the North Atlantic Treaty Organization and so on and on. Ever more people met, telephoned, wrote or faxed each other ever more often for ever more purposes. And that was before e-mail. Start drawing these links in different colours on a map and the map would soon disappear entirely beneath the inky tangle. There was a proliferation of such ties all around the world – people had begun to speak of 'globalization' – but no strands were thicker than those between Western Europe and North America.

If I close my eyes and try to conjure a visual image of this West, I come up with something so mind-numbingly conventional that I immediately open them again. What I see are those endlessly familiar newspaper photographs of our leaders meeting each other, which they now do constantly, unlike leaders in most of recorded history, who met only on very rare occasions, if at all. Turning the pages of this mental album, I come first to the group portrait of a dozen or more heads of government on the steps of some palace or grand hotel, almost all of them middle-aged white men in dark suits. (Western Man in his Native Dress.) Next come those demonstratively bonhomous, back-patting, elbow-clutching bonding displays between French president and German chancellor. Here's a grainy old snapshot of four men in tropical wear sitting under a beach umbrella in Guadeloupe, talking nuclear missiles; then a newer, digital image of an open-shirt and jeans encounter at some country retreat, with the American president and British prime minister serving as unpaid fashion models for Levi's, GAP or Banana Republic. And finally there's the perennial buggy scene – in which, somewhere in America, two middle-aged men, grinning boyishly, snuggle close together in the front seat of a golf buggy. The closeness is the message.

'Friendship' is the name diplomatically given to these relations between statesmen or stateswomen and, by two-way symbolic extension, to relations between the states they represent. If the states are friends, their leaders had better be; if the leaders become friends, that helps relations between their states. These instant, speed-glued political 'friendships' are interesting to observe. You wonder how genuine they can possibly be. When Winston Churchill and Franklin Roosevelt met aboard a battleship off the coast of Newfoundland in August 1941, singing 'Onward Christian Soldiers' with their massed British and American crews, they made one of the great symbolic bondings of the twentieth-century West. In what sense were Churchill and Roosevelt ever really friends?

Yet in the modern world we're not condemned to stand around like peasants at the Field of the Cloth of Gold, wondering how the Great Ones are getting on inside the marquee. We're not swineherds nervously contemplating the quarrels of the gods on Mount Olympus. We make our own history. Whatever the truth about the 'friendship' between, say, Margaret Thatcher and Ronald Reagan, or Helmut Kohl and François Mitterrand, I know that, for me, Pierre in Paris, Helena in Warsaw, John in Washington and Michael in Bonn were, and remain, friends. These friendships were born in the particular circumstances of a time and place. What friendship is not? We stood for the same things and against the same things: not all the same things, all the time, but quite enough to make common cause. We wanted to preserve freedom in the West and win it for people in the East. We had that essential fellow feeling. We felt that we were 'we'. And so we were.

To be sure, I also had quite a few good acquaintances who thought of the West as 'them'. The bloody Americans, the fucking Tories, the *Scheissliberalen* – imperialist, oppressive, exploitative, corrupt, responsible for toppling Salvador Allende in Chile and napalming children in Vietnam. Yet these critics were often measuring the Cold War West against its own proclaimed moral standards. Even as they savaged the hollow, hypocritical rhetoric of 'the free world', they were confirming the West's existence. Unless you are Don Quixote, you don't attack a chimera. So the Cold War West was a reality. If enough people think a political community is real, it's real.

With the disappearance of the communist East at the end of the Cold War, this West slowly descended into crisis. There were omens of discord throughout the 1990s, like a gathering storm, as well as endless speculation about what the new world order, or disorder, might be. At the beginning of the twenty-first century, the storm broke. When a group of Islamist terrorists flew two aeroplanes into the twin towers of the World Trade Center in New York on 11 September 2001, it seemed that the most influential prediction for the shape of the post-Cold War world was coming true. Here, surely, was Samuel Huntington's 'clash of civilizations'. For those planes seemed to be aimed at the heart of the West, one of Huntington's 'civilizations', in the name of another, Islam.

At first, the rest of the West rallied to America's side, under a heroic motto proclaimed by the editor of Le Monde, 'We Are All Americans'.[2] But within a year this crisis *for* the West had become a crisis *of* the West. Faced with the problem of how to fight an abstract noun – 'Terror' – the nations of the West did not pull together as they had in the late 1940s against Stalin's Red Army; they fell apart in bitter disagreement. The administration of President George W. Bush decided that the 'war on terror' required a war against Iraq; most Europeans disagreed. By the spring of 2003 we had the unprecedented spectacle of France actively canvassing for votes against the United States in the Security Council of the United Nations, on a question of war or peace that the United States considered vital to its own national security.

The American neoconservative Richard Perle concluded that France was 'no longer the ally it once was' and therefore Nato 'must develop a strategy to contain our erstwhile ally'.[3] Many Europeans thought the United States was threatening world peace. 'Is this a free world or Bush's world?' demanded a banner at a million-strong demonstration against the Iraq War in London on 15 February 2003. This was just one of several massive demonstrations in European capitals that day. They seemed, for a moment, to unite the continent in a single European 'no' to America's proposed war.

So the West was divided between Europe and America. Or was it? Certainly, most Europeans opposed the war and most Americans supported it. Political writers on both sides of the Atlantic saw in this an expression of deep underlying differences. One liberal American writer averred that the coming 'clash of civilizations' could be not the West versus the Rest, but Europe* versus America.[4] 'Americans are from Mars and Europeans are from Venus' wrote the conservative American Robert Kagan in an influential one-liner, suggesting that Americans are at once Martian, martial and the real men.[5] The original book title to which his quip alluded was *Men are from Mars, Women are from Venus*. Many on the European left hastened to agree: yes, Europeans and Americans are from different planets; yes, Europe, scarred by so many wars – lovely Europa, remembering her bad experience with bulls – proudly represents the female virtues of peace.

On closer examination, things were not so fabulously simple. The West did not split neatly into a European and an American half, like a well-cracked walnut. A large minority of Americans opposed the war and a large minority of Europeans supported it. At least eighteen European governments gave some endorsement to the American-led action. Crucially, the four countries at the heart of any history of the modern West – Britain, France, America and Germany – were divided two against two. To put it another way, the states with the first and seventh largest economies in the world (America and Britain) lined up against the fifth and sixth (Germany and France).[6]

I was reminded of George Orwell's competing blocs in *1984*, 'Oceania' and 'Eurasia'. This Oceania of 2003 aligned the two major European countries that face the Atlantic ocean, Britain and Spain,

---

* In this book, I have reluctantly followed our confusing practice of using a single word, 'Europe', to mean at least five different things: a historical concept, a continent with unclear frontiers, a number of European states acting through their national institutions, the European Union, and a vision of what that Union should be. Wherever possible, I have tried to make it clear which is meant.

with the great power across that ocean. As they went to war against Iraq, their leaders met literally in mid-Atlantic, on the Azores islands, with Portugal as proud host. Eurasia comprised France, Germany and Russia, in what the French newspaper *Libération* called 'The Anti-War Axis'.[7] Yet this nice dichotomy of Oceania and Eurasia also breaks down, since most of the states in the central zone of Europe between Germany and Russia supported the American-led war.

Like the earlier 'friendships', these enmities were represented to us, almost in pantomime, by the symbolic acts and body language of our rulers. Word came down from Olympus that for months President Bush had not even spoken on the telephone to Chancellor Schröder of Germany. Senior officials fluttered about, giving a passable imitation of courtiers in the time of Louis XIV, telling you '*das Verhältnis ist sehr schlecht*' (the relationship is very bad) and 'Schröder's screwed it completely'. When the heads of the opposed groupings had to meet, at a long-scheduled multilateral summit, newspaper photographs showed Presidents Bush and Chirac looking tensely in opposite directions – for all the world like Prince Charles and Princess Diana as their marriage broke up.

Behind the pantomime, there was real emotion. What European leaders said about each other in private was poisonous. At No. 10 Downing Street, they called Dominique de Villepin, the French foreign minister, 'Vile Pin'. The prime minister of another major European state (not Britain) privately described Chirac and Schröder as 'a dangerous couple'. Nor were these emotions confined to politicians. A student at Yale University confided in his professor, 'I wake up every morning feeling furious at the French.' I met a man in California who told me he had cancelled his order for two of the latest Mercedes cars in protest at German opposition to the war. (He was not, you will gather, a poor man.) I went to my doctor in Oxford and he said 'that Bush is such a cowboy, isn't he?' At every level, from the president to the postman, there was this confusion, or elision, between a particular government or leader and the whole nation or group. Was it Bush you were angry with or 'the Americans'? Chirac or 'the French'? Romano Prodi or 'the Europeans'?

This confusion, or elision, is typical of nationalism. In the Iraq crisis of 2002/3 we again saw nationalism in the familiar form of the people of one nation getting angry with those of another. Many English people, for example, egged on by some of their newspapers and politicians, got angry with the French – something they had been doing, on and off, for more than 600 years. But we also saw nationalism in the larger, transferred sense identified by George Orwell in his 'Notes on Nationalism'. Orwell says that other 'isms' – his own idiosyncratic list includes communism, pacifism, Catholicism and anti-Semitism – share a common mental structure with nationalism. It is, he says, 'the habit of assuming that human beings can be classified like insects and that whole blocks of millions or tens of millions of people can be confidently labelled "good" or "bad"'.[8]

The broader nationalisms that found expression in this crisis of the West can be called, in crude shorthand, anti-Americanism and anti-Europeanism. How can we know when we are in the presence of these broader nationalisms? How can we distinguish them from the positive patriotisms of both Americans and Europeans? Well, it's never easy, but here's a rough and ready test. If we hear a voice generalizing angrily about '*the* Americans' or '*the* Europeans', the disease is close. And if that voice turns out to be our own? Then we should stop, and examine our assumptions.

I am writing soon after these events, when tempers have barely cooled. We don't yet know if the war of words over the war on Iraq was just another of those family quarrels that have regularly punctuated the life of the West, or something far deeper. Is this the last or merely the latest crisis of the West?

After all, many historians insist that what characterizes 'Western Civ' is its divisions: between Rome and Byzantium, between church and state, between monarchs and feudal lords, between self-governing town and surrounding country, between Protestants and Catholics, between each and every nation-state (the nation-state being one of modern Europe's most enduring and double-edged contributions to the world), between executive, legislature and judiciary, between the old world and the new. It is precisely these divisions, this diversity, that has made the history of Europe and America different from that of China. Inasmuch as there is a historic unity of the West, this is the shared fruit of its own incessant internal partings. Disunity may be the West's deepest unity.

As for the closer political unity of the Cold War West: that was only forged in the late 1940s after fierce disagreements about how to confront the new threat from 'the East'. Transatlantic solidarity was then shaken again and again by rows that have long faded into the history books – disengagement, Suez, de Gaulle's military withdrawal from Nato, the neutron bomb, Solidarity in Poland, the deployment of Cruise and Pershing missiles – crisis upon crisis, their very names now remembered only by old men and historians. Sleeping-pills for schoolchildren. I have in front of me as I write a yellowing pile of weighty articles, dating back more than fifty years, each averring that the latest crisis is unprecedented, worse than any before, insoluble, et cetera. If you look inside even the closest political partnerships of the West, such as the British-American 'special relationship', you find, documented in the diaries and secret papers, nasty purple rashes of mutual mistrust, resentment and contempt. Yet the Cold War West survived.

A few important things are, none the less, different at the beginning of the twenty-first century. The states of the post-1945 West are no longer held together by a single common enemy, with a massive Red Army deployed in the heart of Europe. The threats we now face are more diffuse, hidden, ill-defined. There is far more room for disagreement about who or what they are, let alone how best to deal with them. Following the collapse of the Soviet Union, America has become the world's sole superpower. It is much less clear to Americans that they require the partnership of Europe to secure their own freedoms.

For its part, Western Europe no longer needs the United States to defend it against the Red Army. Instead, most of the countries that used to be occupied by the Red Army are now members of the European Union. Europeans are struggling to find an emotional glue to hold together this extraordinary project of voluntarily associating twenty-five very diverse European countries in a single political community. Such emotional glue has traditionally been found, or manufactured, by identifying an alien and threatening 'them' – an 'Other', in the dread jargon of identity studies, or, in plain English, just a good old enemy – against which 'we' can warmly bond. With the fading of Europe's other Others, of which more below, Europeans are tempted to find that Other in the United States. We are to define ourselves by what we are not: America! And the wretched of the earth are to be saved not by the hard grind of Americanization but by the soft charm of Europeanization.

Like an electric storm, this crisis of the West has harshly illuminated a jagged landscape – with a question mark on every peak. Is the world now divided between the West and the Rest? Is the West now divided between Europe and America? Can the West be put together again and, even if it can be, should it be? What is the right 'we' for our time?

I begin my exploration of this jagged landscape at home, in Britain, which of all the heartlands of the West is the one most painfully torn between Europe and America. From this divided country, our journey will proceed outwards, first to Europe, then to America, and finally to the world beyond the West.

# I

# Janus Britain

## PUTNEY

If you take the Number 74 red double-decker bus from Baker Street you will eventually cross the River Thames at Putney. On the south bank of the river, immediately to your left as you come across Putney Bridge, you will spy a church, half-hidden behind trees. Most of your fellow passengers – their faces set in the tired, closed mask of the London commuter – will not spare it a glance. Yet in this Church of St Mary the Virgin, on 29 October 1647, one Thomas Rainsborough spoke words that have resounded through the modern history of the West.

At the height of the English Civil War, England's revolutionary army was debating who should have the vote in elections to the Westminster parliament. Radical 'Levellers' among the officers and regimental delegates were locked in fierce dispute with Oliver Cromwell. According to notes made at the time, Colonel Rainsborough said:

For really I think that the poorest he that is in England hath a life to live, as the greatest he; and therefore truly, sir, I think it's clear, that every man that is to live under a government ought first by his own consent to put himself under that government; and I do think that the poorest man in England is not at all bound in a strict sense to that government that he hath not had a voice to put himself under.[1]

The poorest she still did not get a look in, but this was nevertheless a revolutionary statement of the claim for government by consent and equal political rights for all citizens. Here in Putney, in 1647, a plain-spoken English gentleman described and demanded the essence of what we mean today when we say 'democracy'. His claim echoed around the old world – and into the new. Thomas Rainsborough's sister married John Winthrop, the Puritan governor of the Massachusetts Bay Colony who declared that New England should be 'as a City upon a Hill'.[2] His younger brother settled in Boston.[3] There are six towns called Putney in the United States.[4]

If you step inside St Mary's, you will find that only the original tower survives of the church where Rainsborough spoke. Yet in the nave, with its 'theatre in the round' seating, the radical democratic spirit of the Levellers is still carried forward by the vicar, the very unreverential Reverend Giles Fraser – stocky, bald-headed, pugnacious, dressed in T-shirt, jeans and trainers.[5] Leaving the church and turning left up Putney High Street, this is what you will see: Hot Wok Express, Il Peperone pizzeria, Enoteca (an Italian restaurant), the Odeon cinema (probably showing an American movie), Sydney (an Australian bar-restaurant), La Mancha (a Spanish tapas bar and restaurant), Pizza Hut, Blockbuster video, La Noche (another Spanish tapas bar and restaurant), Superdrug, McDonald's and right next to it the coffee place Costa, Caffé Nero (the Reverend Fraser's favourite observation post), Starbucks, United Colors of Benetton, Pret à Manger, Burger King, Rogerio's café, the Piccolo bar – and that's only up to the railway station.

In between are the old, sturdy British familiars: Thomas Cook's travel agency, Millets, British Home Stores, the Abbey National building society turned bank, Boots the chemist, Thornton's chocolate shop, the Halifax, W. H. Smith's. Halfway down the high street there is a pub called Ye Olde Spotted Horse, which features, amidst its faux-Elizabethan white-and-black half-timbering, a large and rather handsome nineteenth-century model of a black-and-white spotted dray horse. But the British horse, unlike the leopard, can change his spots. For inside this Victorian pub, blackboards above the bar now offer 'Wines of the Day: Merlot – Chile, Pinot Noir – NZ, Rioja – Spain, Shiraz Cabernet – Australia, Cotes du Rhône – France'. The menu promises 'Linguine with Ham and Goat's Cheese Sauce' and 'Crème de Menthe Ice Cream Bombes'. A Young's Brewery poster on the wall promotes not beer but wine, with this incentive: 'Win a Trip to Spain!'

You may say this is just the superficial, brand-and-chain Americanization and Europeanization that we now encounter everywhere in the developed world; what has been called the Euro-American shopping mall. But the internationalism of Putney goes a little deeper. Quite a few of the apartments in the riverside block that looms behind the church are rented by city firms for their foreign staff: 'A lot of Yanks,' says Reverend Fraser. The French community can be met in St Simon's Church in Hazlewell Road, and there was until recently a French bookshop in Lower Richmond Road. Nearby, there's the headquarters of Voluntary Service Overseas, which in 2002 sent some 1,600 British volunteers to work in forty three developing countries.[6] In Upper Richmond Road you can call on Longview Solutions, a software company promising to provide you with 'a single source of financial truth'.[7] Its other offices are in Toronto, Philadelphia, Chicago, Dallas, San Jose, Atlanta and Madrid.

Everywhere there are what a local estate agent snootily calls 'the Antipodeans'. Australians and New Zealanders – 'thousands of them' cries the estate agent, with a mixture of personal disgust and professional delight – pack into rented accommodation and cram the Sydney bar. No worries. The district of Southfields, a maze of small streets, is now a little South Africa. The local MP quotes an estimate that as many as 20,000 South Africans live there. People from the rest of the Commonwealth – that noble republican moniker of the Cromwellian revolution, now incongruously applied to Her Britannic Majesty's former Empire – from Pakistan, India, Africa and the Caribbean, are not yet so numerous as in neighbouring parts of London. Putney can nevertheless already boast a Sikh temple, an African Families Association, and, in Gressenhall Road, the world headquarters of the Ahmadis, a dissident Muslim sect originating in the Punjab and claiming millions of adherents in seventy countries. Finally, and resented by many local people, who believe they are taking scarce council housing, jobs and benefits, there are the asylum-seekers from every unhappy corner of the world.

What you glimpse here, in Putney, are the many faces of Britain at the beginning of the twenty-first century. Janus, the Roman god of doorways, passages and bridges, had two faces, usually depicted on the front and back of his head, pointing in opposite directions. Janus

Britain has four. The back and front faces can be labelled 'Island' and 'World'; the face on the left says 'Europe' and that on the right 'America'. No wonder Britain's head aches.

At the end of this chapter I shall examine the latest attempt to cure that national headache – the Blair bridge project – and ask what it tells us about the wider relationship between Europe and America. But it's a great mistake to divorce foreign policy from domestic reality. The high street is the place to start. So let's look first at the four faces of Britain's everyday life, and the competing narratives that go with them.

## ISLAND WORLD, WORLD ISLAND

'Island' is a face that the whole world knows: 'this scepter'd isle / This earth of majesty, this seat of Mars'.[8] Or, as a German newspaper once less flatteringly put it, 'the largest holiday island in the world'.[9] '*Messieurs*,' the French historian Jules Michelet used to begin his lectures on British history, '*l'Angleterre est une île*.'[10] He thus perpetuated in four words two hardy continental myths – that Britain is the same as England and that it is just one island. In fact, the history of Europe's largest group of offshore islands has been shaped by the workings of four nations, the English, the Scottish, the Welsh and the Irish. But 'Island' will serve as fitting shorthand for a face that looks back with pride at a version of the British past which, like all national(ist) (hi)stories, blends fact and myth, memory and forgetting, true continuity and invented tradition.

'Island' is the Britain, but more especially the England, of the parish church, the pub, the club, the college; of the retired colonel (no Rainsborough he) reading the *Daily Telegraph* and the gardener reading the *Daily Mail*; of country lanes, cricket, warm beer and shepherd's pie. Here is an England that sees itself still in the mirror of Orwell's often quoted and imitated sketch *The Lion and the Unicorn*, and reassures itself with that gruff celebration. In 1993, the Conservative prime minister, John Major, declared that 'fifty years from now Britain will still be the country of long shadows on country grounds, warm beer, invincible green suburbs, dog lovers and pool fillers and – as George Orwell said – "old maids cycling to Holy Communion through the morning mist"'.[11]

This Britain, understood largely as an extension of England, prides itself on an exceptional history of continuous freedom, self-government and the rule of law. The British, another historian remarks, 'have a genius for the appearance of continuity'.[12] Yet, stripped of all sentimental mythology and invented tradition, the facts are still remarkable. There has been an England, and a people who have called themselves the English, continuously since at least 937, when King Alfred's grandsons defeated a Northumbrian coalition, including Danes and Scots, in the battle of Brunanburh.[13] The county or shire – a term now made familiar to hundreds of millions of cinema-goers as the bucolic homeland of the hobbits – is one of the oldest continuous units of territorial self-government in the world.

What people call 'the law of the land', that is, English common law, was there already when the Normans came, and still survives. From Magna Carta in 1215 to the English revolutions of the seventeenth century, the human and civil rights – including individual property rights – that would come to be seen as characteristic of 'Western Civ' advanced furthest and fastest in England. The English parliament *was* the mother of parliaments. These things are true. They distinguish Britain, and especially England, from continental countries shaped by the legacy of Napoleonic administration, devastating wars on their own territory, and successive occupations. It is not a mere chimera that generations of continental Europeans, from Montesquieu to Jean Monnet, and generations of Americans have admired. The legacies of these things live on, in what British people say and do every day.

'World' seems, at first glance, the opposite of 'Island'. Certainly a Rastafarian evening in Neasden or an Eid-ul-Fitr among the converted cotton mills and new-built mosques of Bradford is a very long way from the rural England of weekend cricket, church and pub. But the historical connection between 'World' and 'Island' is direct and simple. The world has now come to the island because the island first went to the world. England expanded, initially absorbing all the other parts of these offshore islands in an internal empire, then scattering across the high seas, to every corner of the earth, its own language, goods, customs and people – now including the Scots, Welsh and Irish as well as the English. In the process, Britain became already by the nineteenth century a 'world island'. While remaining an 'island world' it was also an island engaged throughout the world, at once stubbornly insular and relentlessly international.

In the second half of the twentieth century, as Empire folded into that ever vaguer Commonwealth, the peoples of the former Empire came, in growing numbers, to live on the island. Roughly one out of every twelve people now living in Britain belongs to what are awkwardly classified as 'minority ethnic groups'.[14] There are well over two million 'Asian or Asian British', mainly from India and Pakistan, more than one million 'Black or Black British' and a quarter of a million Chinese.[15] They have brought their own languages, religions and customs to the British, as the British once exported theirs to them. They strengthen old ties and create new ones, with India, Pakistan and the rest of Asia, with the Caribbean and Africa, with the Middle East, with every corner of the world.

I am writing this page in Oxford, less than a mile from where J. R. R. Tolkien penned his romantic agrarian fantasy of the shire. Our local newsagent is Mr Mansha, who was born in Pakistan, our pharmacist is Mr Ahmed, who was born in Pakistan and worked for years in Saudi Arabia, our grocer is Mr Ayyub, who was born in India, married a Czech and has a flat in Prague, and our dentist, Mr Sapsford, is a cheery New Zealander. Were you to retrace Orwell's road to Wigan Pier, nearly seventy years on, you would find yourself staying often in Asian neighbourhoods. When the Indian state of Gujarat was hit by an earthquake in 2001, thousands of families among Britain's estimated 650,000 people of Gujarati descent were directly affected.[16] At the same time, there were some 75,000 Iraqis living in London.[17] A careful study has found that more than 300 languages are spoken in the capital.[18] Only New York can seriously compete with London for the title of most cosmopolitan city in the world.

These back and front faces of Janus Britain, 'Island' and 'World', make a strong contrast: between past and future, and, to some extent, between country and city. There's also an uncomfortable tension between the two. 'We Can't Keep Them Out' shrieks a headline in the conservative *Daily Express*, over a photograph of asylum-seekers running for a Britain-bound train in northern France.[19] Many Islanders do not want more World. Not in their 'neck of the woods' anyway.

## JANUS BETWEEN EUROPE AND AMERICA

The contrast between Britain's left and right faces, 'Europe' and 'America', is less extreme; both are, after all, faces of Western modernity. Yet politically it's the conflict between these two that has been tearing Janus Britain apart.

If a Londoner went to sleep in 1939 and woke up today, what would strike him most forcefully is the degree to which the old island has become both Europeanized and Americanized. The first shock would await him already on Putney High Street, with Starbucks to his right and Caffè Nero to his left. Our once famously awful British food has been transformed: pizza and panini are on sale at every corner, while you must hunt to find a suet pudding or a Spotted Dick. In Ye Olde Spotted Horse, and 60,000 pubs across the land, the British now drink twice as much continental lager as they do traditional British beers.[20] The once distinctive British crowd is hard to distinguish in dress and physical appearance from the everyday shopping crowd on a high street in Germany or a mall in Wisconsin. People from Seattle to Sheffield to Sarajevo wear the same brands of T-shirt, jeans and trainers. To judge merely from outward appearance, the Reverend Fraser could as well be a Canadian software specialist or a Slovenian journalist.

As soon as our visitor from 1939 works out how to turn on the television, he will find himself transported to America. One teenager of my aquaintance concludes that *all* the entertainment programmes he and his friends have watched regularly, as they grow up, are American imports. *Friends*, *West Wing*, *Frasier*, *Star Trek*, *The Simpsons*, *Buffy the Vampire Slayer*, *Fresh Prince of Bel Air*, *ER*: they permeate British popular culture. The head of one television channel explains that he and his fellow executives make an annual journey to

Los Angeles to purchase these programmes. Their trip to LA is, he says, 'like the *haj*'.

Together with the prevalence of American films and music, this has led to the Americanization of British English. British teenagers use 'like' as a verbal link in the same way as their American counterparts: 'he was, like, "shall we go to Caffé Nero?" and I was, like, "oh no . . ."'. (Their parents would have said 'um' or 'er', or nothing at all.) Another teenager tries to convince me that the American 'butt', as in 'kick butt', is an English word for bottom, bum or arse, which of course it was – in the seventeenth century. In 2002, John Major was asked on the radio about the first Gulf War. It was, said Mr Major, all too easy for 'Monday morning quarterbacks' to be wise after the event.[21] He obviously assumed that his invincibly British old maids, preparing to cycle to Holy Communion through the morning mist, would at once understand the meaning of a phrase from American football.

Faced with this tsunami of Americanization, our visitor from 1939 might turn with an expectation of relief to proper football – association football or soccer – the game England gave to the world. Then he would be startled again to find that leading British clubs routinely field teams composed largely of foreign players.* For an early twenty-first-century Englishman, the heroic names 'familiar in his mouth as household words',[22] to quote the most famous of all Shakespeare's patriotic speeches, are no longer 'Harry the King, Bedford and Exeter'; they are Arsène Wenger (the French manager of Arsenal football club), Ruud van Nistelrooy (the Dutch striker for Manchester United), and Sven-Göran Eriksson (the Swedish manager of the England team). At a pub in Aldershot, I talk to English private soldiers – 'squaddies' – who are ferocious English nationalists. They are just back from holidays in Spain and drinking many litres of Stella Artois, the Belgian beer. As we speak, Eriksson's face

---

* At a match against Southampton in December 1999, Chelsea played the following team: Ed De Goey (Holland), Albert Ferrer (Spain), Celestine Babayaro (Nigeria), Emerson Thome (Brazil), Frank Leboeuf (France), Dan Petrescu (Romania), Gustavo Poyet (Uruguay), Didier Deschamps (France), Roberto Di Matteo (Italy), Tore Andre Flo (Norway) and Gabriele Ambrosetti (Italy). So far as I can establish, this was the first time a British team took the field without a single British-born player.

comes up on a large television screen in the corner. 'That man,' roars a half-drunk squaddie, 'that man has done more for England than Tony Blair!'

Yes, there is still the very English football star David Beckham, but he has moved to Spain, to play for Real Madrid. Beckham is not alone. At least 100,000 British people live in Spain. Some stand for office in local elections. In the popular British gangster film *Sexy Beast*, Spain is portrayed as a land of found content, replete with sun, wine, sex and emotional ease; Britain, by contrast, is all rain, discomfort and repressed anger. In total, some half a million British people live or work in the European Union, while perhaps three quarters of a million continental Europeans live or work in Britain.[23] At Boots the chemist one morning, I hear a German student asking nervously for a 'recipe' for her inflamed eye. 'You mean a *prescription*,' the pharmacist patiently explains. The pharmacist is Spanish. It could equally well have been a Ugandan Asian pharmacist correcting the English of a Polish building worker. At the same time, perhaps one million British people live in the United States, and more than a quarter of a million Americans live in Britain.[24]

The famously insular British took more than 56 million trips abroad in the year 2000, when the total population was just under 60 million. Spain was the top holiday destination, receiving 28 per cent of all British visits, then France, with 18 per cent, then the United States, with 7 per cent.[25] Some 4 million British people go to the US each year.[26] If you are clever in booking your flight with Ryanair or Easyjet, you can fly to Rome for £4.99. On the front page of the *Daily Telegraph* you find a horror story about the European Union right next to an advertisement for these cheap flights to European destinations. Inside there will probably be a feature about some middle-class English couple who are making a wonderful new life restoring a farmhouse in Provence. But this is not just a cosmopolitanism of the prosperous middle class. One melancholy autumn day, a London taxi driver is complaining, as usual, about the weather and the traffic. He now plans, he says, to spend half of each year abroad. Where? He answers without a moment's hesitation: 'Florida or Spain.' Spain is close, sunny and he has a brother-in-law running a bar in Alicante. Equally sunny Florida is not so close but 'they speak the language'.

'Florida or Spain' – there, in a single throwaway line, you have Janus Britain.

Britain's everyday intimacy with continental Europe is nourished by physical proximity; that with America – and with the other 'English-speaking peoples', especially in Canada, Australia, New Zealand and South Africa – flourishes in spite of distance. In business, the media and academe, the transatlantic interchange is incessant. British and American professors rotate in and out of jobs in their respective universities. British magazines, such as *Granta* and *Encounter*, have been edited by Americans; American magazines, such as the *New Yorker* and *Vanity Fair*, by British journalists. The *New York Review of Books* sometimes seems to have more British contributors than the *London Review of Books*. *Newsweek* has identified a new city called NY-LON, inhabited by a privileged transatlantic elite who live and work in *both* New York and London.[27] The sixty-seven British dead in the 9/11 attacks on the World Trade Center bore solemn witness to that intimacy. Then the altar in St Paul's Cathedral was draped with the Stars and Stripes, Her Majesty the Queen sang 'The Battle Hymn of the Republic', and, emerging, was seen to wipe away a tear.

Three thousand miles are reduced to thirty yards in the phrase British people often use to locate America: 'across the pond'. At one semantic stroke, the Atlantic becomes narrower than the Channel. In 2003, the proposition 'that the Channel is wider than the Atlantic' was put to a well-heeled, somewhat conservative London audience in a public debate. A majority voted in favour, although a large minority disagreed.[28] On the European side, there is geography; on the American, language. With America, there is shared culture, history, economics and politics. With Europe . . . shared culture, history, economics and politics.

The British, writes a former American ambassador in London, 'seem to know mainly what they used to be'.[29] But even that history keeps changing. Until well into the 1970s, most English schoolchildren were told a charming story about what the bestselling popular historian G. M. Trevelyan memorably called 'a strange island anchored off the Continent', and how that Island became a great Empire.[30] This Island-to-Empire story was transmuted by Winston

Churchill into a grand narrative of what he christened 'the English-speaking peoples', with the United States as part of the same political community as the United Kingdom, together with its Commonwealth and Empire. By the end of the twentieth century, you could fill a small library with books chronicling, dissecting and often celebrating the shared history of what was now called 'the Anglosphere' – with, at its heart, Britain, America, and their common 'language of liberty'.[31]

Then, in the 1990s, a new wave of historians came with an alternative story: that of Britain's long, shared history with continental Europe. We were now reminded that Britain has only been physically separated from the continent for a mere seven to eight thousand years, and is already joined to it again, by a tunnel under what is no longer called the English Channel, just the Channel or *la manche*.[32] For a millennium, the people of these islands were Catholic Christians, like most other Europeans; when we became Protestant, we were far from being the only Protestants in Europe. Many of our kings and queens were by origin French, Dutch or German. Britain was for centuries part of a single 'trans-channel polity'.[33] In short, we British are not half so unique as we think we are.

This alternative story is not arbitrary or invented; the facts it assembles are generally true. It would not be equally possible to write the history of Britain as, say, an Asian country. You cannot make bricks without straw. But how historians combine the straws and arrange the bricks reflects their personal preferences, and the circumstances of their own time. Clearly, this rewriting of the history of Britain as a European country has something to do with the fact that Britain is now more closely involved with its continental neighbours than at any time since the English lost possession of Calais in 1558. To say 'we have always been a European country' is not just to explain a new present, it's also to point to – or at the very least, to hint at – a likely future. So the battle over Britain's unpredictable past is also about Britain's future.

Economically, more than half Britain's trade is with the European Union and slightly less than one sixth with the United States. Roughly half its foreign investment is in or from Europe, but another third is in or from the United States.[34] Some three million British jobs depend on trade with Europe; more than a million depend on American-owned companies.[35] Britain's version of capitalism is somewhere in between those of continental Western Europe and the United States. The way British industry relies on the stock market to raise capital, with an increasingly frenetic emphasis on 'shareholder value', is more like America, but the way the government redistributes national income through the welfare state is more like France or Germany. Britain has created more new jobs than France, but less than America; those jobs are often worse paid and less secure than in France, but there is still not the large underclass of 'working poor' that you find in America.

Politically, Britain shares great chunks of its formal sovereignty and effective power with the European Union. In many fields, EU legislation takes precedence over English or Scottish law. British citizens routinely appeal from the highest British courts to both the European Court of Justice and the separate European Court of Human Rights. This makes truly 'history' – in the dismissive American usage of the word – Henry VIII's Act in Restraint of Appeals of 1533, with its seminal statement 'this realm of England is an empire'. Empire, that is, in the sense of sovereign authority from which there is no appeal. If you have to put a new level of fire insulation in your office door, or modify the way you package your apples or computer parts, this is probably as a result of a British regulation implementing some EU directive. Britain, one of the great trading nations of the modern world, no longer negotiates its own trade agreements. That is done by the responsible European Commissioner, most recently a Frenchman. Senior British officials spend much of their time in Brussels, trying to shape decisions that will directly affect British citizens and consumers.

Britain is also formally committed by Article 5 of Nato's North Atlantic Treaty to go to the assistance of any one of twenty-five other countries, most of them in Europe, if they are attacked. For sixty years, this country has had troops continuously stationed on the continent of Europe. In theory, the United Kingdom still retains its unlimited sovereign right to make war or peace. In practice, it could not have won the last war it fought on its own, the Falklands War of 1982, without the overt and covert assistance of the United States.

Scattered across East Anglia are bases with signs outside saying RAF Lakenheath, RAF Alconbury or RAF Mildenhall; these are, for all practical purposes, US Air Force bases, from which planes are despatched to foreign military engagements on orders from American commanders. An American military website for RAF Lakenheath describes it as 'England's largest US Air Force-operated fighter base'.[36]

Britain prides itself on possessing an independent nuclear deterrent, but its nuclear missiles cannot function properly without American support.[37] In 2002, £1.5 billion worth of Apache attack helicopters were reportedly sitting useless in sheds in Shropshire, because the US Congress had held up the transfer of software for a pilot-training simulator.[38] As the British public discovered during the Iraq War of 2003, the British and American intelligence services are virtually married to each other, exchanging operational intelligence at all levels almost every day. A former head of the CIA has said he thinks the CIA is much closer to Britain's Secret Intelligence Service (MI6) than it is to the FBI; and American naval intelligence, he went on mischievously, is probably closer to British naval intelligence than it is to American army intelligence.[39]

In government, different jobs bring different tilts. If you are a civil servant dealing with the environment, trade or immigration, you spend much of your life working with other European officials, and trying to implement EU decisions. If you sit in the Ministry of Defence, you spend your life trying to keep up with the Americans, as they leap financially and technologically ahead of all other military powers. If you are prime minister, you keep turning from one side to the other, like a man who can't get to sleep in an uncomfortable bed. So the duality of Europe–America is replicated at every level of British life, from the taxi driver to the prime minister.

## FOUR STRATEGIES AND A PELTING FARM

Does any of this matter to anyone except the British? If the Janus dilemma were unique to Britain, it would still matter a little to the rest of the world because Britain – with the world's seventh largest economy,[40] a permanent seat on the UN Security Council, a big member state's influence on any EU decision and a tradition of worldwide military and diplomatic engagement – still matters a little in the world. But Britain's dilemma is not unique; or rather, unique only in its intensity, and in the banal sense that each national case is always unique.

Every other European country has its own version, though usually less extreme, of Island vs. World, if one takes 'Island' to mean not the mere condition of being land surrounded by water (a physical fact of ever diminishing importance) but the nurtured peculiarities of a real or claimed exceptionalism. France, with its 'cultural exception', Germany, with its historical 'special path' (the *Sonderweg*), Spain, Italy, Poland – all have their own version of Island. And all have a growing portion of World, whether Muslim Turks in Germany, Muslim Algerians in France or Muslim Moroccans in Spain. All will therefore be directly affected by any 'clash of civilizations', such as some have seen looming between the West and the Islamic world since 11 September 2001. All are torn between Europe and America. Most European countries have more Europe in their hearts than Britain; none has as much America. But they are all getting more of America, whether they like it or not, and they are all, in some measure, facing both ways.

The writer Robert Musil said wonderfully of his native Austria after 1918 that it was 'an especially clear case of the modern world'.[41] Today, Britain is an especially clear case of the modern world. It is a place where the impact of one great potential conflict of the early twenty-first century – the West versus the Rest – is clearly visible, and another – Europe versus America – is most sharply felt.

Throughout the Cold War, Germany was the world's central divided country. Germany, and especially divided Berlin, was a thermometer of the worldwide struggle between the two blocs known as 'East' and 'West'. Limited though Germany's sovereignty was, everyone looked with interest (and some nervousness) to see what new ways, if any, the Germans themselves might find to lower the Berlin Wall. Now Britain is the divided country – divided not by a concrete wall, of course, but by what Germans call the *Mauer im*

*Kopf*, the wall in our heads. Britain is a thermometer – or is it a seismograph? – on whose trembling needle you can measure the improvement or deterioration of relations between Europe and America. Limited though Britain's effective sovereignty is, everyone looks with interest (though also with much weariness) to see if the British may yet develop new ways to resolve a dilemma with which we have wrestled so ineffectually for more than fifty years.

First impressions are not encouraging. The British have no less than four different answers to their Janus dilemma – and therefore none. 'The trouble with this country', says a Canadian friend who lived in Britain for many years, 'is that it doesn't know what story it wants to tell.' Exactly so. These competing answers are at once attempts to formulate a national strategy, projected forward from a version of the national story, and stories projected backwards from a chosen strategy. The four competitors are: 1. regain independence; 2. choose America; 3. choose Europe; and 4. try to make the best of our intimate relations with both America and Europe.

The strategy of regaining independence builds on the old island story. It says: we have an exceptional history; we have been a free and independent country longer than anyone; personal freedom and national independence go hand in hand; our freedoms and independence are now under threat, mainly from Europe; as so often in the past, we must fight to defend them. This narrative draws on an immensely powerful self-image: that of Britain fighting heroically on, led by Winston Churchill, after France had fallen to Hitler's armies in the summer of 1940. 'Very well, alone' – as the cartoonist David Low captioned that famous picture of a British soldier defiantly shaking his fist at bomber-filled skies, from the cliffs of an island almost engulfed by storm waves.[42]

This story speaks with great emotional force to many British people, and by no means only to the dwindling number of those old enough to remember 1940. It is also shamelessly exploited by Britain's tabloid newspapers. When the European Union was to be presented with a new constitution, in the summer of 2003, the country's most popular newspaper, *The Sun*, produced an unforgettable front page. Under the slogan 'Save our country', with a Union Jack waving behind, it said: '1588 – WE SAW OFF THE SPANISH [photograph of Queen Elizabeth I], 1805 – WE SAW OFF THE FRENCH [photograph of Nelson], 1940 – WE SAW OFF THE GERMANS [photograph of Churchill], 2003 – BLAIR SURRENDERS BRITAIN TO EUROPE [unflattering photograph of Blair].'[43] 'Tony Blair', began the story inside, 'is about to sign away 1,000 years of British sovereignty . . .' Papers like *The Sun* and the *Daily Mail* feed upon the simplistic version of 'Our Island Story' that many British people have grown up with, and daily reinforce and coarsen it. 'We appear', an agonized reader wrote to the *Daily Mail* in 1997, 'to be one tick of the clock away from losing our sovereignty, our independence and not just 1,000 years of history but history from when the first man fought to protect this country from an invader.'[44]

Logically, the advocates of 'independence regained' should be as much opposed to sharing Britain's sovereignty with the United States as they are to sharing it with the European Union. But only a very few still uphold that consistent defence of sovereignty – 'Come the three corners of the world in arms, / And we shall shock them'[45] – which was enunciated with classical lucidity by earlier politicians such as Enoch Powell, on the old British right, and Peter Shore, on the old British left. Instead, most now make a sharp distinction between bonding with the US (good) and with the EU (bad).

The story-strategy of 'independence regained' therefore shades into the second one: choose America. Britain, says this school, cannot go on doing the splits between an emerging federal superstate, a United States of Europe run from Brussels, and the only remaining superpower, the United States of America. It has to choose; it should choose America. 'Britain's final choice: Europe or America?' was the title of a lecture given in 1998 by Conrad Black, then the proprietor of the country's bestselling conservative broadsheet, the *Daily Telegraph*.[46] Britain, argued Black, should loosen its bonds with the EU and instead join the North Atlantic Free Trade Area with the United States. Britain must plump for its 'common Atlantic home'.[47] This was emphatically the view of the country's most influential prime minister since Churchill, Margaret Thatcher. In her lifetime, she said – and if she said it once, she said it a thousand times – all the problems had come from across the Channel and all the solutions from across the Atlantic. For this school, as for the first, the prime witness, role model and adopted patron saint is Winston Churchill.

Language, they say, trumps geography. The Anglospherist poet and historian Robert Conquest imagines an 'English-Speaking Union' as an alternative to the abhorrent European one.[48] The American option is extended to embrace the whole of the Anglosphere, identified as 'the set of English-Speaking Common Law nations',[49] including Canada, Australia and New Zealand as well as Britain and America. These five countries also happen to be partners in a worldwide electronic intelligence-gathering operation known as Echelon. Yet it's Anglo-America that remains at the heart of Echelonia. As the old Anglo-American military alliance of 1941 was self-consciously reforged in the Iraq War of 2003, one usually sober British commentator described America and Britain as 'the most reliable axis of good in the world for many years'.[50]

It's a political fact of the first importance that some combination of these two positions, which are together known in British political shorthand as 'Eurosceptic', is emphatically supported by the country's most widely read newspapers. Every day, more than 22 million people – nearly three out of every four readers of a national daily – pick up a dose of Euroscepticism.[51] Papers like *The Sun*, the *Daily Mail* and the *Daily Telegraph* advance these positions not only in their editorial and comment pages but, more importantly, on their news pages. The iron distinction, still upheld by some of the quality press in continental Europe and North America, between news reporting and commentary – 'fact is sacred, opinion is free' – has long since disappeared. Their daily news stories are linked across the weeks and years in a kind of meta-story, an implicit grand narrative in which plucky Churchillian Britain, small yet Great, ably assisted by our English-speaking cousins across the seas, holds out once more against a threatening, invasive, bad old Europe.

This is partly because two major clusters of these papers have for years been the personal property of two of Britain's Anglosphere cousins – testimony, in itself, to the openness of the world island. The Australian-American Rupert Murdoch owns, among many other media, *The Sun, The Times* and the *Sunday Times*. Until his spectacular fall from grace in 2004, the Canadian-British Conrad Black owned the *Daily Telegraph*, the *Sunday Telegraph* and *The Spectator*, an important gadfly weekly. Eurosceptics both, Murdoch and Black have chosen their editors to suit. However, there is also a distinct, domestic history of two generations of conservative journalists who, deeply influenced by Margaret Thatcher, and traumatized by the pound sterling's bad experience with the European Exchange Rate Mechanism, found in opposition to the EU their new great fight after the end of the Cold War. For them, Brussels was, and perhaps still is, the new Moscow. Then there's the intense commercial competition between British newspapers. Good 'knocking copy' sells well, and knocking the French is the oldest British pastime of all.

Whatever the precise mixture of causes, the result is plain to see on any news-stand almost any day of the year. It's strictly impossible to prove how much these 'Eurosceptic' papers shape popular views, and how much they merely echo and reinforce them, but it seems reasonable to assume that what some 22 million people read every day in their newspapers does influence their politics.[52] In any case, one essential point is clear: British governments have, for more than a decade, ceased to believe that they can safely defy these papers on the issue of Europe.

The third story-strategy – choose Europe – is the exact mirror-image of the second. Starting from the same premiss, that Britain faces a fundamental choice between Europe and America, it comes to the opposite conclusion: Britain must plump for Europe. The key political question of our time, wrote the *Guardian* columnist Hugo Young, one of the most eloquent advocates of this view, was 'could Britain . . . truly accept that her modern destiny was to be a European country?'[53] While 'Eurosceptics' lament that Britain is in thrall to the European Union, 'Europhiles' lament that Britain is in thrall to the United States. In the last column Hugo Young wrote before his untimely death in 2003, he despairingly reflected on the way in which Tony Blair's attachment to the 'special relationship' with the United States had led his country into the Iraq War. 'What does this mean?' he asked, and answered himself: 'That we have ceased to be a sovereign nation.'[54] Which is exactly what Eurosceptics say about Britain's relations with the EU.

So all of the first three schools – 1. regain independence, 2. choose

America, 3. choose Europe – echo, in their different ways, the words that Shakespeare put into the mouth of the dying John of Gaunt. For that famous speech about 'the scepter'd isle' descends to these despairing lines:

> This land of such dear souls, this dear, dear land,
> Dear for her reputation through the world,
> Is now leased out – I die pronouncing it –
> Like to a tenement or pelting farm.[55]

The three schools just cannot agree who owns the pelting farm.

In British parlance, the competing tendencies are sometimes called (by Anglospherists) 'anti-Americans' and 'pro-Americans', or (by Eurospherists) 'pro-Europeans' and 'anti-Europeans'. Both sets of terms are inherently prejudicial. The first implies that those who are against the current trajectory of the European Union must be against Europe; the second, that those who oppose the policies of a particular US administration must be against America. Of course there are people in Britain who are genuinely anti-European and genuinely anti-American. You don't have to go far to meet them, in pub or club, disco or demo. (To find both in one person – to find, that is, a consistent British or English nationalist – is now a rarity.) Yet to use these terms implies that the person thus tagged is guilty of nationalist prejudice until proven innocent. Intellectual justice, like the old English common law, requires us to make the opposite assumption.

Anglospherists say Britain should loosen its ties with Brussels and tighten those with Washington; Eurospherists say Britain should loosen its ties with Washington and tighten those with Brussels. Eurospherists say it should join the single European currency, the Euro; Anglospherists say 'never'. If you press both sides to explain what exactly the 'final choice' means, answers became fuzzy, even evasive. Does the Anglospherist consider that Britain should leave the European Union? Well, not yet, not necessarily; but it must change it. Does the Eurospherist think Britain should leave Nato? Well, not exactly; but it must change it.

Both sides agree, however, that this choice is not just about foreign policy. It's also about domestic policy, about values, about what kind of country we want Britain to be. 'Choose America' mingles with 'regain independence' as the mantra of Britain's majority right-wing newspapers; 'choose Europe' is most often heard from those of the left, especially *The Guardian* and *The Observer*. The *Observer* columnist Will Hutton, a passionate spokesman for the 'choose Europe' school, claims that Britain shares far more features of its social and economic life with Europe than with the United States. Britain, he maintains, is 'unambiguously European'.[56] It merely needs to 'rediscover and reassert the European value system at its core'.[57] To choose Europe is to place a premium on social justice, solidarity, the environment, the welfare state and the quality of the public sphere. Many on the right agree: to choose America means, for them, to prefer the free market, an enterprise culture, the American business model, low taxes and the minimal state.

Others on the left argue that to choose Europe means to 'modernize' Britain's constitutional arrangements: to introduce a written constitution and specified, appealable rights, such as most continental European countries enjoy, to devolve power from Westminster to Scotland, Wales and Northern Ireland, and perhaps even to abolish the monarchy. Roll on the Federal Republic of Britain. During the Iraq crisis, another sense came to the fore: to choose Europe is to favour peaceful solutions to international disputes, multilateralism, respect for international law and aid to the developing world.

So the geopolitical options are also ideological ones. Nothing in Britain is ever quite simple. It's a columnist of the left, Jonathan Freedland, who wrote a sparkling book arguing that Britain should 'bring home the [American] revolution' and become more like the United States.[58] The Labour Chancellor of the Exchequer, Gordon Brown, is fascinated by American solutions. None the less, as a general rule, 'choose Europe' is now a story-strategy of the left and 'choose America' is a story-strategy of the right.

Finally, there is the fourth option: to try to preserve what can still be preserved of British independence in an increasingly interdependent world, maintain close ties with America *and* be fully in Europe. Here is an attempt to reconcile all the four faces of Janus Britain, both Island and World and, more especially, Europe and America. I might be tempted to call this the fourth way, were it not for the fact that the idea of a 'third way', as revived by ideologists of the post-Cold War liberal left, and popularized by Tony Blair, has met such widespread scepticism, mounting to derision. Unlike the 'third way' this fourth option is not some vague ideological construct. It is what most British governments have in practice more or less consciously attempted to do ever since, in 1961, Harold Macmillan made what he called the 'grim choice'[59] to apply to join the European Economic Community.

Some prime ministers have leaned more to the European side, like Edward Heath, others more to the American, like Margaret Thatcher, but all have attempted to do both. This is what the Blair government has tried programmatically to do; what most senior officials pronounce 'sensible'; what representatives of many larger businesses, with interests across the Atlantic and the Channel, urge upon them. It is what a great many British people, perhaps even a silent majority, will privately agree that Britain should do, if they are pressed beyond their first reactions. Its advocates can call in aid the holiest of all British household gods: Common Sense.

The combination option has eloquent apostles in journals such as the *Financial Times* and *The Economist*, but it is less prominently represented than any of the others in the newspapers that most British people read. In a fiercely competitive press, strong, dramatic, simple views trump mild, complicated ones. 'EU to hijack our economy' (*The Sun*), 'A vote to save our country!' (*Daily Mail*), 'Queen: Is Blair Out To Axe Me?' (by accepting a European constitution, that is, according to the *Sunday Express*) and 'Blair losing battle over United States of Europe' (*Daily Telegraph*) are all more exciting than 'US and EU agree a moderately useful initiative'.[60] The British, famous around the world for understatement, have always had an appetite for overstatement. To be sure, centrist, pragmatic conclusions can be heard on the BBC. But even the BBC, facing constant accusations of 'bias' from the Anglospherist right, and concerned to retain listeners and viewers by livening up its programmes, will generally prefer – in the name of 'balance' and the cause of entertainment – a lively, polarized debate betwen a militant 'Eurosceptic' and a passionate 'Europhile'.

The result is curious. A strategy that is the official policy of the government is the one least represented in the British media. This is obviously better than the position in totalitarian states, where nothing but the government's policy is represented in the media; it's still a little odd.

Moreover, the strategy that the government has actually tried to implement is the only one without an emotive story to support it. Tony Blair has endeavoured to tell such a story in successive speeches and interviews since he came to power in 1997. His is a story about how the world island has become a 'bridge' between Europe and America; a rather active bridge, since it also tries to pull Europe and America closer together. But this story, unlike the other three, is not underpinned by history, myth, literature or popular imagination. Unlike Churchill, with his *History of the English-Speaking Peoples*, Blair has not penned a magnificent, widely read, four-volume 'History of the Bridge'. Nor has anyone else. The imaginative firepower of historians, writers and journalists has fusilladed in other directions. There are no poems to the bridge. There are no songs about the bridge. As Europe and America clashed over Iraq, commentators of both Anglospherist right and Eurospherist left gleefully agreed that Blair's bridge had collapsed. Yet in the minds of most British people, the bridge has probably never existed in the first place. They have no idea they are supposed to be in, of, over or under a bridge. It is, in this very important sense, the bridge that never was; or at least, never yet has been.

Before we examine Blair's bridge, however, we must reflect for a moment on the legacy of the giant who looms above all these competing story-strategies.

## CHURCHILL AND CHURCHILLISMS

All British foreign policy since 1940 has been footnotes to Churchill. The British are still living with the consequences of his strategic choices between America and Europe. Most of their ongoing dilemmas are anticipated in his speeches. His black-and-white photograph on the wall as you ascend the staircase at No. 10 Downing Street is no bigger than that of Neville Chamberlain or Clement Attlee, but he is the only former prime minister to have another, large portrait photo (the famous one by the Canadian photographer Karsh) prominently displayed on the ground floor. In a moment of national extremity, every prime minister asks, 'what would Churchill have done?' Tony Blair, in the Iraq crisis, was measuring himself against the defining hero as much as Churchill's immediate successor, Anthony Eden, had done in the Suez Crisis of 1956. Churchill was still around to say, privately, that Eden had got it wrong over Suez. He is no longer around now, so everyone can answer 'what would Churchill have done over Iraq?' in their own way.

After Churchill came not just Churchillism but Churchillisms. Every side in the national argument makes its Churchillian case. His own inspirational, protean, often deliberately vague and sometimes self-contradictory words furnish a memorable quotation for every school: Churchillism against Churchillism. No one can conclusively adjudicate these rival claims. We can never know what Churchill himself would have done. What Churchill actually did – the subject already of more than 3,000 published works[61] – can only be understood in its full, dense historical context. None the less, there are a few things that need to be said here about the real Churchill and the competing Churchillisms.

'We shall defend our Island, whatever the cost may be, we shall fight on the beaches, we shall fight on the landing grounds, we shall fight in the fields and in the streets, we shall fight in the hills; we shall never surrender . . .'[62] Churchill's most famous words defined the British to themselves in the summer of 1940; turned their worst into their finest hour. This was his greatest moment, but it was not the state he wished the British to be in. That is so obvious in the historical context that it would hardly need pointing out, were it not for the fact that a Churchillian stance of solitary defiance is endlessly replayed on the front pages of *The Sun* and the *Daily Mail*, as if every new directive from Brussels were one of Hitler's Messerschmitts. An island standing alone was the last thing Churchill wanted Britain to be. No one could have been less of a Little Englander.

What Churchill most wanted was for Britain to remain the centre of a glorious, world-straddling Empire and Commonwealth, if possible 'for a thousand years'.[63] Even after the Second World War he still pictured world politics as three intersecting circles: the United States, an emerging United Europe and the British Commonwealth.

Again, it is so obvious, yet so widely overlooked, that the vision dearest to Churchill himself is the only one that features not at all in early twenty-first-century Churchillisms. No one in their right mind now thinks Britain should centre its national strategy on the Commonwealth.

In fact, Churchill's hope was doomed as soon as Hitler's own perverted version of 'thousand-year empire' brought Britain to war with Nazi Germany. Faced with that challenge, Britain had to look for help, either to Europe or to the United States, or to both. Europe meant, above all, France. Although he always bore America firmly in mind, and heart, Churchill looked first to France, a country he loved and admired. He was, noted the diarist Henry 'Chips' Channon, 'a fanatical Francophile'.[64] When he spoke in April 1939 of 'a solid identity of interest between the Western democracies,' he meant Britain and France.[65] 'The French', he said a month later, 'have the finest, though not the largest, army in existence at the present time.'[66] Only when that army was so shockingly defeated in June 1940, only when his last, extraordinary offer of a complete political union between France and Britain failed to forestall Pétain's capitulation to Hitler, did he turn all his efforts to the United States.

The way he then conjured the British Empire's tenuous, tense pre-war relationship with America into an enduring Special Relationship (with, for the British if not for Americans, a capital S and R) was to prove the most enduring Churchillism. If you want a glimpse of the great conjuror at work, read the eyewitness account by H. V. Morton of Churchill's August 1941 meeting with Roosevelt in Canada's Placentia Bay. Morton shows him rehearsing, like a film director, the joint church service at which the assembled British and American crews would sing 'Onward Christian Soldiers' and 'O God, our Help in Ages Past' on the deck of the battleship HMS *Prince of Wales*: 'Mr Churchill walked about inspecting every detail, often taking a hand by moving a chair an inch one way or another and by pulling out the folds of the Union Jack.'[67]

Then, in a radio broadcast, he interpreted his own theatrical production to the world, evoking 'that densely packed congregation of fighting men of the same language, of the same faith, of the same fundamental laws, of the same ideals, and now to a large extent of the same interests, and certainly in different degrees facing the same dangers'. They represented 'two major groupings of the human family, the British Empire and the United States, who, fortunately for the progress of mankind, happen to speak the same language and very largely think the same thoughts, or anyhow think a lot of the same thoughts'.[68] Notice how the essential qualifications, 'very largely', 'a lot of', 'certainly in different degrees', are scattered like foam in the wake of a battleship advancing at full speed. In fact, America was not at war with Hitler in August 1941 and, to the disappointment of the British, did not come in as a result of that Atlantic meeting. 'Why not now?' Morton asked.

After the fall of France, the political marriage with the United States always came first for Churchill. He had grown to adulthood at a time when Britain and America were first cautiously contemplating a shared 'Anglo-Saxon' supremacy to supplant their long nineteenth-century rivalry. (On the British side, this impulse already reflected a sense of declining relative power.[69]) Inspired by the Anglo-American comradeship in arms at the end of the First World War, he had spent part of the inter-war years working on his *History of the English-Speaking Peoples*, discovering a common future in the shared past. Everything had prepared him to be the Shakespeare of Anglo-Americanism. If he were born again, he told a companion on his way to deliver his 'iron curtain' speech at Fulton, Missouri, in 1946, he would like to be born an American.[70]

Yet he never forgot Europe, and especially France. The maxim of British policy expounded by a conservative commentator in 2002 – 'Love America, Hate France'[71] – would have been abhorrent to him. He loved both. He admired Charles de Gaulle as much as he was exasperated by him. He fought fiercely for the restoration of France as a great power after the war. Behind Churchill's back, his 'friend' Roosevelt made fun of this to Stalin, in a private meeting at the Yalta summit in February 1945. According to the official American record, Roosevelt confided to Stalin that 'the British were a peculiar people and wished to have their cake and eat it too'.[72] But Churchill persisted and won, for de Gaulle, France's seat at the top table.

Voted out of office by the British people in 1945, he devoted much time in opposition to advancing the cause of a United Europe. 'The first step in the re-creation of the European family must be a partner-ship between France and Germany,' he declared at Zurich in 1946.[73] As 'ten ancient capitals of Europe' disappeared behind the Iron Curtain, those European peoples who could still unite in freedom should do so.[74] He was feted like Charlemagne at the Hague Congress of Europe in 1948. He was a founding father of the Council of Europe, the original pan-European organization of democracies, and spent weeks actively involved in its debates. During its meeting at Strasbourg in 1949, he addressed – 'Prenez garde! Je vais parler en français' – the largest, most enthusiastic outdoor rally that city had ever seen in the cause of European union.[75]

He was, however, grandly ambiguous and inconsistent about Britain's role. Would the British Empire be a benign external 'friend and sponsor', like the United States, as he explained at Zurich, or was it for 'France and Britain to take the lead', as he declared in the Albert Hall in 1947?[76] Generally, he stuck with the less committed stance, frustrating practical enthusiasts of European integration such as Jean Monnet. When France and Germany went ahead, without Britain, to develop the Schuman Plan for the European Coal and Steel Community, he moved a motion in the House of Commons criticiz-ing the Labour government for not joining in. But when he became prime minister again, in 1951, he did nothing to reverse that decision. He poured scorn on the planned European Defence Community, call-ing the proposed multinational army 'a sludgy amalgam'.[77] 'We shall', he said, reaching new heights of inspirational vagueness, 'work in true comradeship for and with United Europe.'[78] The German Chancellor Konrad Adenauer came to No. 10 Downing Street to dis-cover what on earth this meant. Churchill sketched on a card his map of three circles, marked 'United Europe', 'USA' and 'Br Com' (British Commonwealth), with fairly small areas of intersection. A decade later, Adenauer reproduced the map in his memoirs, commenting drily 'nothing has changed in this posture of Great Britain's'.[79] It was the self-styled 'good European' Churchill who declined for Britain the role of leading a European union.[80]

Instead, he went with America. The 'Special Relationship' shaped by Churchill's two premierships was, as one of its best historians writes, a British diplomatic strategy.[81] Its goals were, first, to save

Britain from defeat; then to preserve as much as possible of Britain's fast failing power, by sticking close to its hegemonic successor; and to keep America engaged in Europe in ways that Britain thought best, for Britain of course, but also for Europe and the world. In January 1953 President Eisenhower noted irritably in his diary that his old wartime comrade 'had developed an almost childlike faith that all the answers are to be found merely in British–American partnership'.[82] As Churchill completed his great memoir-history of the Second World War, he worried about offending the Americans: 'If I am going to die, then I can say what I like . . . but if I live and am still Prime Minister, then I must not say things which will anger Ike.'[83] So in the very writing of the book that indelibly lodged in British minds a horror of appeasement (appeasement of Hitler, that is, or Nasser, or Saddam Hussein), Churchill was himself practising a kind of literary appeasement – of the American president. For self-censorship is the political writer's appeasement.

Here, then, was the Churchillian legacy: unambiguous commitment to the United States, ambiguous commitment to Europe. Joint action sustained by a shared language on the one side; fine words often unmatched by deeds on the other. For all that had changed over the intervening fifty years, many on the continent of Europe, contemplating the stance taken by Tony Blair in the war to depose Saddam Hussein, would mutter: *plus ça change, plus c'est la même chose.*

## THE BLAIR BRIDGE PROJECT

At the turn of this century, between 1997 and 2003, Tony Blair became the most prominent and articulate spokesman, among serving politicians, of the proposition that Europe and America must work together, for their own advantage and for that of the wider world. An acute Bulgarian observer wrote that in the conflict over Iraq, central and east Europeans 'supported Tony Blair rather than George W. Bush'.[84] In Washington, American Democrats had tears in their eyes when Tony Blair unfolded this vision before a joint meeting of both houses of Congress in July 2003. If Europe and America work together as partners, he said, 'then the other great nations of our world, and the small, will gather around in one place, not many'.[85] No one else made this argument with the same clarity, authority and evangelical certainty; not his counterparts in any of the capitals of Europe, not the president in the White House. Atlanticists every-where looked to Blair, just as opponents of American hegemony and supporters of a rival European superpower looked to the French pres-ident Jacques Chirac, with his doctrine of 'multipolarity'.

Yet by the end of Blair's first six years in office many, even among the supporters of his vision, felt that he had failed. Blair's bridge, they said, was buried somewhere in mid ocean: an Atlanticist Atlantis. That harsh judgement might still prove premature, but self-evidently he had not succeeded in preventing a crisis of the West, the most pro-found since the end of the Cold War, which left France and the United States facing each other more like enemies than friends. To ask 'why did Blair's bridge fall down in 2003?' is thus a way of asking 'how, if at all, could those who share his strategic vision of partnership between Europe and America do better in future?'.

You might think we do not yet have enough evidence to answer the first, historical question, let alone the second, speculative one. On the contrary. Even as the story unfolded, participants spoke with remark-able if partisan frankness about what was going on behind suppos-edly closed doors. Within weeks, we had eyewitness accounts of what was said in the Oval Office in Washington and across the Cabinet table in London. Within months, we were reading the internal e-mails of the most senior officials in British government, including their debates about the public presentation of secret intelligence. This new openness of Western government is only partly intended. It's a kind of market-led glasnost. It horrifies officials and places strains on the smooth workings of government, since nobody can be sure that any-thing they say will remain confidential for long. Yet that's a price worth paying for the democratization of political knowledge; and only with this democratization of political knowledge can we begin to build a free world.

Doubtless there are still a few secrets left, but the historian's prob-lem – as so often with very recent history – is not a drought but a flood of evidence. A rich alluvial crop of 'instant histories' has already told, with ever more first-hand detail, a story whose stages were soon familiar: Blair's first summit with George W. Bush in February 2001 (known as the 'Colgate summit' because, asked what he and Blair had in common, President Bush said, 'well, we both use Colgate toothpaste'[86]); the emotional response to the 9/11 attacks ('thank you for comin', friend'[87] declared Bush to the pale-faced British leader standing tall in the gallery of the US Congress); a crucial discussion on Iraq at the president's ranch in Crawford, Texas, in April 2002; an angry face-off with Jacques Chirac at an EU summit in October 2002, dubbed by the British '*le row*'; what British and American diplomats called the 'de Villepin ambush' at the UN on 20 January 2003; Donald Rumsfeld's dismissal of France and Germany as 'old Europe' two days later, soon followed by the 'Letter of Eight' pro-Atlanticist European leaders; Chirac's neo-Gaullist '*non*' to a second UN resolution on 10 March, answered by Blair's neo-Churchillian speech to the House of Commons on 18 March, and so on.

What conclusions can be drawn from this already familiar story? Unsurprisingly, many have blamed the collapse of Blair's bridge on Blair himself. They have charged him with 'amateurism' in foreign policy, with 'hubris' and with becoming 'Bush's poodle' – that is, preferring a subordinate relationship with a right-wing administration in the United States to a partnership of Social or Christian Democratic equals in Europe. Carefully examined, the grain of truth in each of these charges soon opens out into a larger truth about something more than just the character of a singular politician.

Take 'amateurism', for a start. When Tony Blair came to power in May 1997, he had no experience of foreign policy. Shortly before his election, he invited a small group of academics to tell him about Europe over a mug of tea in the garden of his Islington home. He introduced the discussion by saying frankly that he did not know so much about the subject; he had spent his whole political career trying to make the Labour party electable; he had not had time to travel around the continent like Denis Healey (a veteran Labour politician), getting to know the people and the politics there. He therefore had to learn on the job. This was difficult, even when you had first-rate diplomatic advisers sitting just down the corridor in No. 10 Downing Street. So he made mistakes. For example, it was a mistake to publish, in a 'dossier', British intelligence guesswork about weapons of mass destruction in Iraq, as the justification for a war towards which the Bush administration was advancing for diverse reasons of its own.

Yet he was not alone in this occasional callowness. The democratic politics of our time are full of career politicians in early middle age, who come to office as accomplished experts in all the techniques of winning power at home – but complete amateurs in the exercise of power abroad. George W. Bush and Gerhard Schröder were two others. They all learned on the job; they were all unduly influenced by their personal relations with each other; they all made mistakes. The diplomacy of the Iraq crisis of 2002/3 was a case study, on all sides, in how not to run a world. In its blunderings – though not, fortunately, in its results – it was justly compared with the months leading up to the outbreak of the First World War in 1914.

Then take 'hubris'. Tony Blair, like most people who get to the top, had an extraordinary drive and self-belief. This helped him to do bold and admirable things. Without it, for example, he would not have held out in 1999 – ahead of and angering the then American president – for the deployment of ground troops to halt an ongoing genocide in Kosovo. By the autumn of 2002, however, a touch of hubris, the occupational disease of all human beings in power, was detectable. In one conversation with a group of journalists he uttered these unforgettable words: 'I've fought two wars – or three, if you count Sierra Leone.' 'I've fought' – as if he personally had marched through the mud of Kosovo and the rocky mountains of Afghanistan. He seemed to believe at this time that his personal charm and leadership could keep Europeans and Americans together, as the Bush administration advanced towards a war to depose Saddam Hussein. He did not anticipate that France and Germany would combine to plot a very different course.

Yet this hubris was not just a personal trait, nor simply a *déformation professionelle* of all powerholders. It was a recurrent characteristic of a certain British approach to the world. Even before he became prime minister, Blair's speeches were full of the need for Britain to play a leading 'role', to have 'influence', to 'lead' in Europe. Under the slogan 'We will give Britain leadership in Europe', the New Labour election manifesto in 1997 showed Jacques Chirac looking wonderingly at a youthful, well-thatched Blair. A caption read 'Tony

Blair takes the lead in talks with President Jacques Chirac of France.[88] When he came to power, he began by lecturing other centre-left leaders about how they must 'reform' the EU. This preoccupation with 'leadership', with your country's role and status in the world, was shared, in this acute form, by only one other European country: France.

The leitmotif of the bridge appeared early in his premiership. It is intrinsically hubristic. Why should a German chancellor go via Britain if he wants to talk to Washington? Why should an American president, if he wishes to reach Madrid, Rome or Warsaw? It mixes a general proposition – that Europe and America should stick together – with a particular claim for Britain's special role, which Blair elsewhere described as 'pivotal'.[89]

That claim is part of a long-running attempt, from Churchill on, to maximize the declining influence of a former world power. France has been doing exactly the same since 1945, although by a different route. Blair, the neo-Churchillian, and Chirac, the neo-Gaullist, are brothers under the skin. Both countries share this obsession with what de Gaulle called 'rank', as if nations were ambitious army officers or rival football teams. So France will certainly never walk over a British bridge to Washington. But the hubristic metaphor irritates others in Europe too. Chancellor Schröder once sarcastically remarked that the traffic over the bridge seemed to be all in one direction.[90]

What, then, of the charge that Blair became 'Bush's poodle'? In his attitudes to Europe and America, Blair is a child of Janus Britain. He likes both. He speaks passable French and once spent a summer working as a barman in Paris. 'The first time I voted',[91] he recalled in 1999, was to vote 'yes' in the 1975 referendum. This asked 'Do you think that the United Kingdom should stay in the European Community (Common Market)?' While seeking election to parliament in the early 1980s he trimmed to the Labour party's line, which then called for Britain to leave the European Community. But he stood for the party leadership in 1994 on a moderately 'pro-European' platform. The Guardian's Hugo Young, who talked to him often at this time, concluded that Blair had become 'a proper European'.[92]

'A *proper* European' – but what did that very English phrase, at once lofty and prim, really mean? It meant, to be sure, that the new prime minister liked the continent of sunshine, French wine, *polenta* and wonderfully chic women. It meant that he had none of the hang-ups about Europe of an older generation of politicians, both Labour and Conservative. It meant he was convinced that Britain must be fully involved in the European Union – 'at the heart of Europe', in the plangent phrase of his predecessor John Major – for at least four reasons: to secure trade, investment and jobs for Britain, to 'lead' Europe to internal economic and political reform, to maintain Britain's influence in the world, and to secure the eastern plinth of his transatlantic bridge between the United States and Europe. It meant he wanted to overcome, once and for all, a half century of British ambivalence about the European project. It meant all these things. But did it mean he liked the European Parliament or Commission? Did it mean that he was steeped in European history, as Churchill was, and heard the subterranean melodies that moved Germans or Italians or Spaniards to act as they did? Did it mean that he could, in this deeper sense, 'speak European'? It did not.

Like many British 'Europeans' before and alongside him, like Roy Jenkins, Edward Heath and Kenneth Clarke, Blair was a very British pro-European. He genuinely wanted to be in there. His government joined the 'social' chapters of the Maastricht Treaty, which the Major government had rejected. He tirelessly sought ways to strengthen Britain's connections with her major partners: a joint 'third way' paper with Chancellor Schröder of Germany, the St Malo initiative on European defence with President Chirac of France. When it became clear that the single currency was going ahead, he privately resolved to take Britain into the Eurozone if he possibly could, for political reasons. But in private he could be distinctly sceptical about the actual mechanisms and institutions of European integration. His main idea, he told one small meeting of advisers around the Cabinet table, was 'a Europe of nation-states'. Mandarin knights coughed discreetly and explained that this would have a disastrous impact in Europe, since it would make him sound like Margaret Thatcher. 'So why is it,' he asked, 'that Chirac can say that and I can't?'

His keynote European speeches, even when they were delivered on the continent, tended to turn into speeches about why Britain had to be in Europe rather than about Europe as Europe. The 'island story' myths of a conservative British household in the 1950s, and the history lessons of an English public schoolboy in the 1960s, kept breaking through. In a speech in Warsaw in 2000, he described Britain as 'the victor in World War II, the main ally of the United States, *a proud and independent-minded island race (though with much European blood flowing in our veins)*' (my italics).[93] Island race! After a subsequent Blair speech in Warsaw, I asked the first prime minister of independent Poland, Tadeusz Mazowiecki, a Catholic baptized in the deepest waters of European history, how he liked it. 'It was good,' he said, 'but I don't know, there was something missing . . .' And when Blair explained his European commitment to a joint session of Congress in Washington in July 2003, it came out like this:

You know, people ask me after the past months, when, let's say, things were a trifle strained in Europe: 'Why do you persist in wanting Britain at the centre of Europe?' and I say 'Well, maybe if the UK were a group of islands 20 miles off Manhattan, I might feel differently. But actually, we're 20 miles off Calais and joined by a tunnel.[94]

Although he immediately went on to say 'we are part of Europe, and we want to be', it rather sounded as if he wished Britain were twenty miles off Manhattan.

This was more than just a politician trimming to his audience of the day. In America, unlike in Europe, Blair had perfect pitch. Standing where Churchill and Margaret Thatcher had stood before him, he played all the right Anglo-American chords: a hint of the King James Bible, a touch of the Shakespearean ('11 September was not an isolated event / but a tragic prologue, Iraq another act / and many further struggles will be set / upon this stage before it's over'), a dash of *Friends* ('I know this is kind of late, but sorry,' he said, apologizing for the British having burned the Congressional library in 1814 in colloquial language that one star of the American sitcom *Friends* might use to another), and whole buckets of the Churchillian. From start to finish, the speech was soaked in that 'language of liberty' which had made a common Anglo-American political discourse for almost four centuries. The words 'freedom', 'free' or 'liberty' appeared twenty-seven times. The speech climaxed in this astonishing hymn to America:

Tell the world why you're proud of America. Tell them when the Star-Spangled Banner starts, Americans get to their feet, Hispanics, Irish, Italians, Central Europeans, East Europeans, Jews, Muslims, white, Asian, black, those who go back to the early settlers and those whose English is the same as some New York cab drivers I've dealt with, but whose sons and daughters could run for this Congress. Tell them why Americans one and all, [sic] stand upright and respectful. Not because some state official told them to, but because whatever race, colour, class or creed they are, being American means being free.

Small wonder a group of Americans launched a 'Blair for President' campaign. It's hard to imagine him ever finding such words for a hymn to Europe.

Blair's eloquent pro-Americanism, his emotional Anglospherism, was heartfelt and culturally deep-rooted. It was also the expression of a strategic choice. In the Clinton years, things had been easy. Blair and his colleagues had made pilgrimages to Washington to learn from the 'New Democrats' how 'New Labour' (as it then became) might win an election. He and Clinton were ideological soulmates. Once elected, he could repair the damage done to Britain's relations with Washington by the Major government's feebleness over Bosnia, while also repairing its frayed ties with Europe. The 'third way', that capacious, woolly poncho, would envelop them both.

Suddenly he was faced with a very different president, George W. Bush. Blair and his advisers made a most deliberate choice: to get close to him and stay close to him. Their first grappling hook was Churchill. Having learned that Bush was a fan of Churchill, the British ambassador to Washington chose as Blair's present for the 'Colgate summit' a facsimile of the Atlantic Charter, agreed by Churchill and Roosevelt in Placentia Bay in August 1941, including Churchill's handwritten corrections. Shortly before the meeting, Bush's political adviser Karl Rove rang up to say that the president was looking for a bust of Churchill. The Blair team flew over with a bust of Churchill by a contemporary British artist in their plane, but decided it wasn't good enough. A few months later, the British ambassador proudly presented the president with a handsome Jacob Epstein head of Churchill, taken from the British government art collections. On loan, to be sure. Churchill would surely have approved this use of his graven image, in the kind of minutely choreographed political wooing that he himself began on the deck of the HMS *Prince of Wales*. His bust now stood in the Oval Office. President Bush said Churchill seemed to him 'like a Texan'. 'Sometimes', he reported, 'Churchill will talk back, sometimes he won't, depending upon the stress of the moment, but he is a constant reminder of what a great leader is like.'[95]

Blair then immediately grasped how the 9/11 attacks changed everything for America. All the Churchillian bells rang. He went to Ground Zero, where Mayor Giuliani was himself drawing inspiration from Churchill's conduct during the Blitz; he received his first standing ovation in Congress ('thank you for comin', friend'); he dashed around the world, covering more than 40,000 air miles, having fifty-four meetings with other leaders in the course of eight weeks, trying to help the US to respond wisely to the challenge.[96] Britain had once again appointed itself Athens to America's Rome.

As the Bush administration's agenda moved from destroying al-Qaeda in Afghanistan to regime change in Iraq, Blair stuck to his strategic choice. He seemed genuinely to believe that the combination of terrorism, rogue or failed states, and weapons of mass destruction was the great new challenge of our time – comparable, in scale if not in kind, to fascism in the 1930s or Soviet communism in the 1950s. But he also argued that Britain must 'remain the closest ally of the United States'[97] to try to prevent Washington from overreacting, to bring it back to multilateralism, and to 'broaden its agenda' to include, for example, a peace process between Israel and Palestine. 'I tell you that we must steer close to America,'[98] he admonished the British Cabinet in March 2002, according to the diaries of a former foreign secretary, Robin Cook, who was at the Cabinet table. By the autumn of 2002, Blair had almost become an internal player in the factional infighting of the Bush administration. There was, one experienced Washington observer told me at the time, a 'Cheney–

Rumsfeld faction' facing a 'Powell–Blair faction'.[99] Journalists joked that the British government was 'the provisional wing of the State Department' (by sarcastic analogy with the provisional wing of the IRA).[100] When Blair was wondering how to begin his broadcast on the outbreak of hostilities in Iraq, one of his closest aides suggested 'My fellow Americans'.[101]

This was the personal choice of a particular Englishman in his late forties; it was also the characteristic choice of a British prime minister. 'Tony's default position is to go with the Americans,'[102] concluded one of his senior advisers. That could have been said of every British prime minister since Churchill, except for Edward Heath. It came at a price. A letter drafted for Churchill to send to Roosevelt in 1940, asking urgently for support, said that the partnership between Britain and America could not flourish after the war if either country 'should be placed in the position of being the suppliant client' of the other.[103] Churchill deleted the phrase 'suppliant client', yet found himself in that position. 'What do you want me do?' he once angrily asked, when discussing a loan arrangement with Roosevelt. 'Get on my hind legs and beg like Fala?'[104] Fala was Roosevelt's dog.

Now that America was the world's only superpower, and Britain an empireless medium-sized European power, Blair accepted a subordinate role. 'Newest US Ambassador', said a headline in the *Wall Street Journal Europe*, 'is Prime Minister of the United Kingdom'.[105] A former foreign secretary, Douglas Hurd, commented that the Special Relationship was like a pennyfarthing bicycle in which Britain was the farthing – the tiny wheel at the back. It was all very well 'standing shoulder to shoulder' with Washington, but what if your shoulder only came up to the other man's knee?[106] 'I know that we used to be a colony of Britain,' a student at a small liberal college in Kansas said to me at this time, 'but what I want to know is: when did Britain become a colony of the United States?'

That was only half the price; the other half was paid in Europe. In 1963, an agreement between Harold Macmillan and President Kennedy to give Britain an American nuclear missile system had been taken by de Gaulle as the pretext for rejecting Britain's application to join the European Community.[107] Instead, de Gaulle signed the Elysée Treaty with Konrad Adenauer – the founding charter of France's special relationship with Germany. (Their Placentia Bay had been a dramatic *tableau vivant* of reconciliation in the Cathedral of Reims, with de Gaulle taking the Churchillian role as stage manager.) Forty years later, as Britain again went with America, Germany again lined up with France. And the coordinated Franco-German '*non/nein*' to the Anglo-American war on Iraq coincided, not accidentally, with the solemn reaffirmation of the Franco-German political marriage in celebrations to mark the fortieth anniversary of the 1963 Elysée Treaty, in January 2003. This was a piece of political theatre every bit as emotional, and as calculated, as the Anglo-American replays of Placentia Bay.

So the two key political couples of the Cold War West faced each other across a Channel that seemed wider than the Atlantic. Except that more than a million British people marched through London one bright winter Saturday – 15 February, a date to remember – to show that on this issue, at least, they felt more like their fellow Europeans across the Channel. This, in turn, increased Blair's suppliant dependency on Washington. It was precisely because much of British public opinion, and his own party, was in this sense 'European' that Blair had to go cap in hand to Washington, begging the president to support British efforts to achieve a second UN resolution sanctioning military action against Iraq. One of Blair's closest advisers told me he felt like a man hanging on by his fingertips to one side of a crevasse and his toes to the other. When that last diplomatic attempt failed, they fell into the crevasse.

It is often overlooked that the attempt and then failure to win a second UN resolution sanctioning war on Iraq resulted from an unbridgeable difference between the old European rivals Britain and France, not between the United States and France. And it was, characteristically, at the European end that Blair's bridge fell down. Whether by more skilful European diplomacy his government could have prevented Germany and France from lining up together so forcefully against the American–British position is an interesting speculation. Blair's own conclusion was that it would only have been possible if the Bush administration had itself been prepared to woo at least one of these two countries to its cause, which it was not.[108] Yet certainly the Blair government did not devote anything like the same political and diplomatic effort to the European side that it did to the American one.

At this point, however, we have to broaden the picture to include the whole of Janus Britain. For had Blair been able to do what he wanted over the previous six years, Britain might have drawn, in this crisis, on deeper wells of solidarity with and from Germany and France. It would, for example, have been close to sharing a single currency with them. But he had been frustrated in this by his own Chancellor of the Exchequer, Gordon Brown, who preferred American ways and the security of his own domestic political position to a European economic gamble, whose political justification was more clearly seen from No. 10 than from No. 11 Downing Street. Blair now had a foreign secretary who was lukewarm about Europe and a Cabinet from which many of the enthusiasts for the European cause had departed.

Beyond that friendly front bench he faced a Conservative opposition and a coven of newspapers stoking all the popular doubts and prejudices about Europe that I have already described. Blair had come to power by wooing these newspapers and he was frightened of taking them on. At the very moment of his first election, in 1997, he had made a Faustian bargain with Rupert Murdoch's *The Sun*, coveting its matchless access to millions of potential swing voters.[109] His political adviser Philip Gould records that, worried about Conservative attacks on Blair's openness to Europe, 'we got *The Sun* to run an article by Blair the next day, promising that he would "Slay the Euro-dragon".'[110] Those that live by *The Sun* will die by *The Sun* – or at least, must always fear that they will. In the autumn of 2003, Murdoch made no secret of the fact that he disliked the European constitution as much as the Euro, and indicated that *The Sun* could again give its support to the Conservatives.[111]

## SO NOW?

The Blair bridge project has been based, instinctively but also rationally, on the very nature of Janus Britain. It is, so to speak, Putney made policy. Britain's connections with both Europe and America are so thick and vital that to 'choose Europe' or 'choose America' would be to cut off the country's left or right leg. So it must keep trying to pull America and Europe together. This would be a complex and ambitious strategy even if the country were united behind its prime minister. But the country has not been united behind its prime minister; instead, it has been torn apart in a bitter, unending argument between four competing national strategies, of which Blair's bridge is the one least vividly represented in the media and least effectively underpinned in the popular imagination by a story blended from history and myth.

There is a real question whether even a master statesman – a Palmerston, Bismarck or Churchill – could successfully implement such a complex game-plan with such a divided country behind him – and especially under the intensely volatile conditions of television democracy, twenty-four hours a day, seven days a week. All democracies have arguments about foreign policy, otherwise they are not democracies. But if a country is successfully to follow any sort of national strategy then it does require a minimal consensus about what it is and where it would like to be. It needs to have some idea 'what story it wants to tell'. Many European countries have such a minimal consensus at the beginning of the twenty-first century; Britain does not.

So a second possible conclusion from this story has to do with Britain, and its need for such a minimal consensus, rather than with Tony Blair and the failings of his own highly personal diplomacy. However, we also have to consider a third hypothesis: that the forces pushing Europe and America apart are so powerful that any attempt to hold the two together, by however skilful a British prime minister, however strongly supported by a nation however united, would still be doomed to certain failure. In that case, the whole project is futile. Whatever the cost, Britain will have to choose. A man standing astride two oil tankers that are moving apart, and trying to hold them together with just the strength in his legs, is not a statesman – he's an idiot.

Yet the things we call 'Europe' and 'America' are not oil tankers. They are political assemblages of millions of individual human beings. It's time to look at them more closely.

# 2

# Europe as Not-America

## A NATION IS PROCLAIMED

'On Saturday, 15 February, a new nation was born on the street. This new nation is the European nation.'[1] Such was the conclusion drawn by Dominique Strauss-Kahn, a former French finance minister, from the simultaneous demonstrations across Europe on 15 February 2003, protesting against the Bush administration's advance to war with Iraq. Europeans already knew, wrote Strauss-Kahn, when they strolled down the high street of a European town or watched a European film, that they were in Europe. Anyone who was ill, old or unemployed appreciated the value of that social security which characterized the European model, and distinguished it from the prevailing models in the United States, Japan, India and China. But this was something more: 'the birth of a European nation. On one and the same continent, on one and the same day, and for one and the same cause, the peoples rose up. And suddenly we realize that these peoples are one.' 'We' – but who exactly were 'we'? – realized too that 'the Europeans have a common view of the organization of the world: far removed from solitary decisions in an Oval Office, instead preferring collective decisions in the framework of international institutions'. At the invitation of the President of the European Commission, Dominique Strauss-Kahn was at this time chairing a round table of eminent Europeans searching for a new project or, as he put it, 'myth' for tomorrow's Europe.[2]

That summer there appeared in many European newspapers an appeal for 'the rebirth of Europe', co-signed by Jacques Derrida and Jürgen Habermas, two of the continent's most famous living philosophers. In an introductory note, Derrida said they felt it to be both 'necessary and urgent' for 'German and French philosophers to raise their voice together'.[3] The text, written by Habermas, began by rhetorically contrasting two recent moments. First, there was the publication in various newspapers of the 'Letter of Eight' pro-Atlanticist European leaders, described by Habermas as a 'declaration of loyalty to Bush', which, he claimed, the Spanish prime minister had invited 'those European governments bent on war' to sign 'behind the backs of their EU colleagues'. Then there was 15 February 2003, 'when the demonstrating masses in London and Rome, Madrid and Barcelona, Berlin and Paris, reacted to this surprise attack'. While acknowledging the divisions within Europe, and the existence of a larger West as a 'spiritual contour', Habermas, like Strauss-Kahn, argued that what happened on 15 February can help to catalyse the formation of a European identity – if we Europeans want it to. We can forge this identity by consciously 'making our own' some parts of our historical heritage, while rejecting others.

He went on to list what he called six 'candidates' for building a European identity. First, there is the European separation of religion from politics: 'in our latitudes it's hard to imagine a president who begins his daily business with public prayer and relates his momentous political decisions to a divine mission'. Then there's the European belief in the 'formative power of the state' to correct the failures of the market. Thirdly, since the French Revolution Europe has developed a political party system – composed of conservatives, liberals and socialists – which continually confronts the 'sociopathological consequences of capitalist modernization'. The legacy of Europe's labour movements and its Christian-social tradition, meanwhile, is an ethos of solidarity, an insistent demand for 'more social justice' against 'an individualist performance ethos which accepts crass social inequalities'. A moral sensibility, informed by the memory of the totalitarian regimes of the twentieth century and the Holocaust, is reflected 'among other things in the fact that the Council of Europe and the EU have made the renunciation of the death penalty a condition of entry'. Finally, the way Europe has overcome its warlike past in forms of supranational cooperation has strengthened Europeans' conviction that 'globally, too', the domestication of the state's use of force requires a mutual limitation of sovereignty. Having lived through the rise and fall of empires, Europeans can now carry 'the Kantian hope of a world domestic policy'.

What Habermas argues with philosophical density, and Strauss-Kahn with eloquent political hyperbole, is that Europe is *different* from the United States, that in these differences Europe is, on the whole, *better* than the United States, and that a European *identity* can and should be built upon these differences – or superiorities. Europe, in short, is the Not-America. This triple claim is quite popular in Europe today. You hear and see it made repeatedly, often in cruder forms, but always with some of the same themes: solidarity and social justice, the welfare state, secularism, no death penalty, the environment and international law, peaceful solutions and multilateralism, transcending sovereignty, counterbalancing the US. Moving the motion 'This House would rather be European than American' at the Oxford Union, a university debating society, one student charmingly summed up the advantages of being European thus: 'You're less likely to get shot. This is a good thing. And if you are going to get shot, you're going to have social provision in hospital.'[4]

The arguments for Europe as Not-America can be heard at every turn in Paris, but they are also the stuff of pleas by British authors such as Will Hutton for Janus Britain to 'choose Europe'. Even before George W. Bush came to power, a senior and respected German journalist, Claus Koch, was admonishing Europe to face up to the fact that 'the American empire must be declared the enemy'.[5] More sophisticated protagonists of the Not-America school, like Habermas, do not deny the existence of an overarching West. But, says the most agile dialectician of German foreign policy, Egon Bahr, there are two Wests: a European West and an American West.[6] Responding to the US Defense Secretary Donald Rumsfeld's famous dismissal of France and Germany as 'old Europe',[7] the German philosopher Peter Sloterdijk wrote: 'Old Europe, honourably represented by France and Germany, is the advanced faction of the West, which, learning the lessons of the twentieth century, has turned to a post-heroic cultural style, and a corresponding policy; the United States, by contrast, is stuck in the conventions of heroism.'[8]

This emerging European self-image was dramatically reinforced from America itself. According to the American writer Robert Kagan, Americans still operate in 'an anarchic Hobbesian world' where individual nations have to use military might, while Europeans are moving on to a world 'of laws and rules and transnational negotiation . . . a post-historical paradise of peace and relative prosperity, the realization of Immanuel Kant's "perpetual peace"'.[9] What came to be known as 'the Kagan thesis' appeared, with perfect timing, just as America was gearing up to go to war on Iraq, and made a large impact in Europe. 'Yes,' excited Europeans exclaimed, 'that's who we are: systematic peace-loving Kantians!' (Derrida and Habermas also invoked Kant.) The fact that this confirmation came from a right-wing American – indeed, one of the fabled, demonized cabal of 'neo-conservatives' – doubled the impact. It was as if the devil had just certified the status of the angels.

Europeans had already derived their two biggest political ideas of the post-Cold War era from the United States: Francis Fukuyama's 'End of History' and Samuel Huntington's 'Clash of Civilizations'. Like Kagan's *boutade*, both had started as journal articles with a striking, deliberately overstated thesis. The authors' subsequent caveats and qualifications in the longer, book versions passed largely unnoticed. But this was something more. For here, Europeans were getting their own idea of themselves played back to them by an American, in an exaggerated form. We come from different planets! Americans are from Mars! And it must be true, because an *American* tells us so . . .

But which Europeans are we talking about? To leap from a scrap-book of quotations to a sweeping generalization about 'Europeans' or, worse still, '*the* Europeans', is to make precisely the mistake I've already criticized. In fact, it would take a whole essay to do justice to the views of a single European intellectual such as Jürgen Habermas.*

---

* The evolution of that profound thinker is curious: here is the intellectual high priest of German post-nationalism and 'constitutional patriotism' now pleading for an emotional identification with Europe, presented as distinct from and superior to America, in a fashion strongly reminiscent of the old-fashioned identity nationalism of European nation-states. So is it a case of German nationalism – bad, European nationalism – good?

It would call for a whole book to describe the variety of German approaches to this problem, another for France, yet another for Poland – and in geographical Europe there are at least forty countries, so we would need as many books. If you were serious, you would have to consider the governments, which change, the intellectuals, who write and talk so much, and the peoples, whose views may (we fondly imagine) be tracked in opinion polls and referendums. Combine those three levels, over time, in more than forty countries, and you have a moving matrix impossible to draw.

On both sides of the Atlantic there is plainly a felt need for simplifying generalization. To analyse is always to simplify, but here, the unavoidable simplifications of analysis are mixed up with other kinds of simplification: those of distance, ignorance and caricature, those for political and commercial effect, and those of an attempt to construct identity. In this chapter, I will look briefly at the European quest for identity, and some of the specific, national reasons for the 'Euro-Gaullist' stance taken by France and Germany in this crisis of the West. After stepping back to explore the reality of the alleged civilizational differences between Europe and America, I will examine what I call Euroatlanticism, the countervailing tendency to Euro-Gaullism. I make no apology for the fact that this part of our journey is like a winding path through a tangled wood. Europe *is* a tangled wood, and any cruder simplification does unacceptable violence to the reality. My conclusion, none the less, is simple: the whole of the new, enlarged Europe is engaged in a great argument between the forces of Euro-Gaullism and Euroatlanticism. This is the argument of the decade. On its outcome will depend the future of the West.

## FIVE HUNDRED MILLION CHARACTERS IN SEARCH OF AN OTHER

Two alternative explanations were widely offered for the vehemence of European criticism of the United States in the early twenty-first-century crisis of the West. Some said it was caused by the provocative, high-handed, unilateralist behaviour of the Bush administration;

others, that it was an expression of deep-seated, almost genetic European 'anti-Americanism', a phenomenon comparable to (and, some suggested, in part motivated by) anti-Semitism. If it were the former, it could be burned away like morning mist by the sun of a different administration; if the latter, it would not disappear so easily.

The truth is, of course, that it depends which Europeans you are talking about. There are Europeans without a scintilla of anti-Americanism in their being, who were deeply worried by what they saw as the arrogant, clumsy, militaristic unilateralism of the Bush administration, and especially that part of it represented by Defense Secretary Donald Rumsfeld and Vice President Dick Cheney. So were many Americans. Were they anti-American Americans? However, it's also true that prejudicial stereotypes of America, which can be traced back in European political culture through most of the twentieth century, were given new vigour by a president who seemed to fit an old stereotype so well: the brash, philistine Texan cowboy. Behind my Oxford doctor's throwaway remark – 'that Bush is such a cowboy, isn't he?' – there lay a world of cultural assumptions, reinforced by images that America had projected of itself, on the big and small screen, in a thousand Westerns. Some of the matching assumptions about Europe's embattled moral and cultural superiority are also very old. A French school textbook, published in 1904, lamented that 'America is becoming the material pole of the world' and asked wistfully 'for how long will Europe remain its intellectual and moral pole?'[10]

Both these explanations, the short-term, contingent (anti-Bushism) and the long-term, endemic (anti-Americanism), contain elements of truth. But the most important part of the explanation lies in the historical shift following the end of the Cold War. Europe and America are no longer held together by a single, clear common enemy. The United States is now both absolutely and relatively more powerful, and needs Europe less than it did when the old continent was the central theatre of its confrontation with the Soviet Union. But the shift is even more profound and unsettling for Europe. For the United States, it poses the question 'what should the United States' role now be in the world?' It does not compel Americans to ask 'What is America?', let alone 'Where is America?' or 'Why do we have

America at all?' Yet it forces Europeans to ask precisely those fundamental questions: 'What is Europe?', 'Where does Europe end?' and
'Why Europe?' – meaning, what is the project of European Union
ultimately for?

In the Cold War, the case for the European project was easy; or at
least, so it appears with hindsight. A relatively small number of West
European countries, which already had a great deal in common, were
brought together by two overwhelming imperatives. First, never
again should the nationalistic competition between nation-states
reduce the continent to the horrors of total war and Holocaust, to
that bestiality, humiliation, penury and rubble which everyone in the
1950s and 1960s still remembered. And second, a European community must be built as a bulwark against the threat of Soviet
communism. So what was this Europe for? To save us Europeans
from ourselves, who had made that bloody past, and from the Red
Army; from the barbarians at the gate and the barbarian within us.
These two themes sounded, like Wagnerian leitmotifs, through all the
early debates about European integration. They grew fainter, more
confused, in the music of the 1970s and 1980s, when enlargement
from six to twelve member states made the European orchestra more
polyphonous, and détente softened the conflict between communist
East and anti-communist West; but they were still there in the minds
of the men and women who shaped the European project.

Then came Europe's 9/11 of hope,* the fall of the Berlin Wall and
that year of wonders, 1989, which saw the threat of Soviet communism softly and suddenly vanish away. What an opportunity – and what
a crisis! Fifteen years later, the European Union comprises twenty-five
enormously diverse European states, including, incredibly, three Baltic
republics which in 1989 were still part of the Soviet Union. It stretches
from the Atlantic to the River Bug, from the North Cape to Cyprus.
The continent has never been so close to a dream of unity in freedom.
These countries share a common market, a common legal framework,

---

* '9/11 of hope' may be easier to say on this side of the Atlantic because we don't
instantly associate 9/11 with the telephone number for emergencies, which is 911 in
the United States but 999 in Britain, and a bewildering assortment of different numbers in other European countries, as well as the standardized but little-known 112
across the European Union.

common political institutions; twelve of them have a single currency. The political project called 'Europe' goes both wider and deeper than it ever has before. But where on earth will it end, both geographically and politically? What is it ultimately *for*?

Not, obviously, to defend us against Soviet communism. That old, simplifying, uniting enemy has gone, and with it much of the enthusiasm of the United States for supporting European integration. Is it still to defend us against ourselves, against the European barbarian within? After all, European barbarism has just shown itself again, for a whole decade in the Balkans, with neighbour butchering neighbour, in fratricidal wars that cost more than 200,000 lives, and with the attempted ethnic cleansing of several million human beings, mainly Muslim Bosnians and Kosovars but also Christian Serbs and Croats. Once again, the West's 'intellectual and moral pole' has needed American help to stop Europeans murdering each other. So this is still a very good reason for 'making Europe'. However, it does not seem to be a compelling one for the majority of Europeans today. Most Europeans under the age of fifty now take peace and relative prosperity for granted. In this sense, Europe is a victim of its own success. And the fool's paradise is not just inhabited by West Europeans: in the 1990s, most Czechs were as indifferent to the plight of besieged Sarajevo as most Germans had been to the sufferings of Prague a decade before.

One much older account of Europe's purpose has been given a new lease of life since the 11 September 2001 terrorist attacks, and through the debate about Turkey's possible membership of the European Union. Shortly after the 9/11 attacks, the Italian prime minister Silvio Berlusconi made some typically crass remarks about the West's mission to civilize backward Islamic peoples.[11] The veteran Italian journalist Oriana Fallaci fulminated wildly against 'our Muslim invaders', engaged in a 'Reverse Crusade' to conquer and profane Europe.[12] In such remarks we see a garish resurrection of the original, medieval definition of 'Europe' as Christendom defending itself against militant Islam. The first known mention of 'Europeans' comes in a chronicle describing an eighth-century battle against the Arab heirs of Muhammed, who were by then advancing across the Pyrenees from what is now Spain into what is now France.[13]

'Europe' first became established as an alternative term for Christendom in the writing and preaching that the great Renaissance Pope Pius II directed against the encroaching Muslim Turks.[14] Habermas and other writers of the European left may trumpet secularism as a defining feature of contemporary Europe, but you have only to hear European Christian Democrats talking about Turkey and Islam to understand that the equation of Europe with Christendom is still far from dead.

Yet this old equation cannot be the basis of a viable political identity for Europe in the early twenty-first century. For a start, Europeans are now among the most secular people on earth. Many of those most directly engaged in the European project see it as a secular, humanist application of the Enlightenment. They ensured that Christianity did not even receive explicit mention as part of Europe's heritage in the preamble to the draft European constitution.[15] Moreover, those Europeans who are religious are increasingly likely to be Muslim rather than Christian. While no one knows exactly how many Muslims live in the European Union, legally or illegally, a minimum realistic estimate is 12 to 13 million.[16] There are perhaps another 7 million in Balkan countries such as Albania and Bosnia, which will sooner or later join the European Union. The EU has in principle accepted Turkey as a candidate for membership. Although Turkey is a secular state, its rapidly growing population of around 70 million people is largely Muslim. And this is not to count Russia, with perhaps as many as 20 million Muslims. The populations of Europe are ageing fast, so more immigrants will be needed to support the pensioners, and these will largely be Muslim immigrants. For this increasingly Muslim Europe to define itself against Islam would be ridiculous and suicidal.

The lifting of the Iron Curtain has therefore revealed a stage on which Europe must confront its own radical indeterminacy. In a sense, Europeans are now face-to-face with Eratosthenes, the Greek geographer who in about 220 BCE drew 'Europe' on a map, covering roughly the area we still know as Europe today.[17] This purely geographical delineation, though arbitrary, has at least the sanction of great antiquity. Yet according to Eratosthenes, Europe stopped at the Bosporus. In the Roman and Byzantine periods, what is now western Turkey was part of a single Mediterranean world; but when Europeans started to draw proper maps again, in the fifteenth century, they followed Eratosthenes and drew the frontier on the Bosporus. Now, partly as a result of promises made during the Cold War, the European Union has crossed even that ancient line, explicitly recognizing Turkey as a European country. So what on earth is to bind this far-flung group of twenty-five going on forty enormously disparate countries together? As the French historian Jacques le Goff once remarked: 'Europe has had a name for twenty-five centuries, but it is still in the design stage.'[18]

Sophisticated answers can, of course, be found about the need for larger units than the nation-state to meet 'the challenges of globalization'. These will not provide what I have called the emotional glue to keep this sprawling Union together. Traditionally, in all human communities, that glue has been found in the celebration of difference from (and usually superiority to) some other human community. Often, this 'Other' was an enemy fought in wars. These differences are both real and 'constructed' – evoked, imagined, dramatized by politicians, playwrights, poets, historians and songwriters. Britain, for example, a peculiar nation composed of four nations, was forged in real wars against France; but Britain also, to sharpen its own sense of what it was, 'created in France its opposite'.[19] Such identities are usually 'forged' in both senses of the word: beaten into shape while heated, and falsified.[20]

Europe, the German historian Rudolf von Thadden has argued, will not be made without an Other.[21] But what Other remains? America is one thing all Europeans – now so broadly defined – have in common. Since the United States is the most powerful country in the world, most Europeans share that mixture of fascination and resentment which dominant powers have always attracted. 'Anti-Americanism' is in this sense less like anti-Semitism than it is like anti-Britishism in the nineteenth century, anti-Frenchism in the eighteenth, anti-Romanism throughout the Roman empire, and, no doubt, anti-Mesopotamianism in the third millennium BCE. Henry Kissinger has interestingly compared attitudes in the EU to those in other contemporary regional groupings, such as the Association of Southeast Asian Nations (ASEAN) and Mercosur in South America. He argues that each grouping defines itself 'sometimes subconsciously, often deliberately . . . in distinction to the dominant powers in its region. For ASEAN, the foils are China and Japan (and, in time, probably India); for the European Union and Mercosur, the foil is the United States, *creating new rivalries even as they overcome traditional ones*'[22] (my italics).

This is not to say that the differences discovered by Habermas, Strauss-Kahn and other European writers don't exist. That remains to be examined. It is to say that there's a powerful temptation for anyone who believes in the project of European union to highlight and accentuate such differences: to define Europe by contrast with, if not outright opposition to, America. And the line between Europe as Not-America and Europe as Anti-America is not clearly marked on any map.

## GAULLISM VERSUS CHURCHILLISM

'Euro-Gaullism' is a convenient label for this view of European identity. French intellectuals and politicians are its most frequent proponents. Yes, a French Gaullist parliamentarian agreed with me during a discussion in Paris, 'the West' certainly exists, but there is also, he insisted, something specific to Europe, 'and if I had to sum it up, I would say *l'intelligence européenne*'. The French Gaullists Jacques Chirac and Dominique de Villepin led the opposition to America's war on Iraq, in the name of 'old Europe' and a 'multipolar world'. However, it was Blair's Britain, not Bush's America, which insisted on the second UN resolution that Chirac's France then successfully blocked. At the finishing line, the diplomacy of the Iraq crisis came down to a clash of two old-European strategies, Gaullism and Churchillism. In the French case, as in the British, an overall approach to international relations was inextricably bound up with a national diplomatic strategy to preserve as much as possible of a former world power's dwindling status and influence.

The relation of Gaullisms to the historical Charles de Gaulle is as complex as that of Churchillisms to the real Churchill. We need to distinguish sharply between Gaullism at home and abroad. The former is a domestic political tendency of the centre-right, the latter an approach that can count on much wider support. Nor can we ever know what de Gaulle himself would have done. For all his pursuit of independence from the Americans, de Gaulle showed unstinting solidarity with the administration of John F. Kennedy during the Cuban missile crisis. Perhaps, contemplating Chirac's defiance of the United States over another matter that Washington considered vital to its national security, de Gaulle might have muttered 'surtout, je ne suis pas Gaulliste'. In two separate imaginary conversations with the General in 2003, de Gaulle's French biographer and a distinguished British historian of France both came to the conclusion that he would have acted differently.[23]

Yet certainly the origins of these divergent strategies can be traced back to those two grand old sparring partners, Churchill and de Gaulle, and to one year: 1940. Nineteen-forty was, as David Reynolds has written, the fulcrum of the twentieth century.[24] For Churchill, that great Francophile, the traumatic fall of France meant launching Britain on the only path that remained available to preserve its greatness: conjuring a special relationship with the United States, however subordinate Britain's role might at times become. For de Gaulle, it meant launching a crusade to restore the greatness of France from the ashes of total defeat. In the first place this involved convincing the French that their true national spirit lay in the anti-Nazi Resistance, and in securing recognition for France as a great power during and immediately after the war.

When he returned to office in 1958, de Gaulle was smarting from another blow to French pride, this time delivered by the United States over Suez. Again, Britain and France drew very different conclusions. Britain would stick closer than ever to Washington while de Gaulle set out to bolster French greatness through what he called a 'European Europe'. This meant a warm embrace of Germany, cultivating relations with Russia and China, demonstrating independence from the United States by withdrawing from the military structures of Nato, and his famous 'non' to British membership in the European Community. When Paul Reynaud, the prime minister of 1940 whom both de Gaulle and Churchill had urged to go on resisting Hitler's advancing armies, dared criticize de Gaulle's 'non' to Britain in 1963, de Gaulle sent him a letter. Or rather, an empty envelope – but on the back was written, in a familiar hand, 'if absent, forward to Agincourt or Waterloo'.[25] The ancient rivalry with England is as much a constituent part of Gaullism as the modern differences with the United States.

Unlike the British, the French are generally quite happy to speak for Europe and to adjudicate which Europe is or is not truly 'European'. This comes the more easily because there is an old French tradition, dating back at least to the eighteenth century, of regarding Europe as an extension of France. In 1777 an Italo-French man of letters, Louis-Antoine Carracioli, even published a book entitled *Paris le modèle des nations étrangères ou l'Europe française* (Paris, the Model for Foreign Nations, or French Europe).[26] 'He talks of Europe, and means France,' Macmillan commented on de Gaulle.[27] With just a little exaggeration we might say that the British are in-capable of identifying themselves with Europe and the French are incapable of distinguishing themselves from it.

Having suffered that shattering defeat in 1940, and German occu-pation, and many changes of constitution (the country is now on its *Fifth* Republic), the French are also less inclined than the British – more particularly, the English – to fetishize formal sovereignty. Even French conservatives have usually concluded that national power and influence may be maximized through the institutions of European integration. De Gaulle himself was more reserved than many of his compatriots in this regard. He was reluctant to share more sover-eignty than was strictly necessary in the European Community, and provoked its first great internal crisis by his attitude. His Europe was to be, so far as possible, intergovernmental rather than supranational. He wanted to make Europe *à l'Anglaise*, but without the English. None the less, France's 'rank' was to be secured through the institu-tions of Europe, with French political leadership supported by Germany's economic weight. It's no accident that at the beginning of the twenty-first century, de Gaulle's grandson, Pierre de Boissieu, sat in Brussels, pulling the strings at the intergovernmental heart of the European Union.[28]

Other French politicians – not domestically Gaullists, indeed anti-Gaullists – have been prepared to go much further towards a supranational or 'federal' Europe. But for them, too, the specifically French motivation is almost invariably present – just as the specifically British motivation is rarely absent among British advocates of Atlanticism. A classic example is Jacques Delors, the French socialist who, as head of the European Commission, presided over dramatic advances in European integration, from the completion of the single market to the Maastricht Treaty, which paved the way for European monetary union. In 1988 Delors published a book entitled *La France par l'Europe* – the very title is eloquent. It contained this sentence: 'Creating Europe is a way of regaining the degree of liberty necessary for a "certain idea of France".'[29] A 'certain idea of France' was, of course, de Gaulle's signature phrase.

The fall of the Berlin Wall plunged this strategy into crisis. With the enlargement of the European Union to include the new democracies of central and eastern Europe, Germany, not France, would be at its centre. Germany, soon united and fully sovereign, would no longer be prepared to play the horse to France's rider – a simile that de Gaulle himself is alleged to have used. However skilful its diplomacy, France would not be able to shape European policy in a Europe of twenty-five member states as it had in a Europe of twelve, or, better still, the original six.

The French language, too, would be further marginalized. Once the universal language of European civilization and international diplomacy, French is now used less and less: vanquished by American English and even overtaken by Spanish. In vain do French politicians attempt to restrict the amount of American music on the radio, American films on television, and Franglais everywhere. When the European Court of Justice ruled that EU governments could not require all foodstuffs on sale in their countries to be labelled in the national language, a furious article in *Le Monde* denounced this treacherous manoeuvre of the 'Anglophone party in Europe', and 'the programmed hegemony of Anglo-American'. However, the author concluded, the French with their 'cultural exception', now rebaptized as 'diversity', will fight back. Adapting Marx, he proclaimed a fighting slogan: 'Cultural and linguistic minorities of all countries, unite!'[30] Here was a fine example of the universalization of a national dilemma. The French have become an endangered minority – therefore they will be the spokesman of all endangered minorities.

You can't begin to understand the emotions behind the French position in the early twenty-first-century crisis of the West unless you appreciate the full trauma of this loss of political and cultural centrality – in the world, in Europe, and now even in the European Union. The French Gaullist foreign minister, Dominique de Villepin, personified the Euro-Gaullist resistance to American policy when he spoke 'in this temple of the united nations' (that is, the UN Security Council chamber in New York) on 14 February 2003. Making an obvious allusion to Donald Rumsfeld's dismissal of 'old Europe', he concluded 'this message comes to you today from an old country, France, from a continent like mine, Europe, which has known wars, occupation and barbarity'.[31] In a rare gesture, the multinational audience in the UN chamber applauded.

It must have been an intoxicating moment for de Villepin, a forty-nine-year-old professional diplomat and man of letters who had recently published an 823-page book entitled *Éloge des voleurs de feu* (Hymn to the Thieves of Fire), evoking the glorious if fated role of the French poet in a nasty world. A year earlier he had produced *Le cri de la Gargouille* (The Cry of the Gargoyle), a plangent appeal to France to rouse itself 'from the temptation of resignation [that] threatens a nation as it feels torpor overcoming it'. 'For many abroad,' he wrote, 'the French funeral has already been held!'[32] And before that, he published *Les Cent-Jours ou l'esprit de sacrifice* (The Hundred Days or the Spirit of Sacrifice), which celebrated, in equally purple prose, Napoleon's last, heroic, doomed attempt to regain power – ending at the battle of Waterloo.

It would be absurd to suggest that all his compatriots embraced this particular political aesthetic of glorious if doomed resistance, let alone that all Euro-Gaullists share the French national complexes. But Euro-Gaullism is unimaginable without the contribution of French Gaullists, and Americans have not been wrong to see in France the political leader of Europe as Not-America.

# GERMAN EMOTIONS

France is the leader, but it was Germany that made the difference over Iraq. Without German involvement there would have been no Paris–Berlin–Moscow axis in 2003. The West would not have split down the middle. In defying America, France was continuing the foreign policy tradition of its Fifth Republic; Germany was abruptly departing from the foreign policy tradition of its Federal Republic. Since the 1960s there had always been German Gaullists, but the golden rule of (West) German foreign policy was always to stay as close as possible to both Paris and Washington. This meant that the German position was usually somewhere between the French and the British ones. Knowing that American support was vital to the Federal Republic and West Berlin in the Cold War, Konrad Adenauer had never gone with de Gaulle against the US. Every federal chancellor since Adenauer had maintained this line. Grateful to America for its wholehearted pursuit of German unification – by contrast with the hesitations of Britain and France – Helmut Kohl and, in his early years as chancellor, Gerhard Schröder, continued the tradition. It was also well accepted at home. In a 1995 poll, 50 per cent of those asked said the United States was Germany's best friend.[33]

When he came to power in 1998, Chancellor Schröder was concerned that unified Germany should behave, and be treated, as a 'normal' grown-up European nation-state, not a hunchback of history.[34] This 'new normality' meant that he would send German troops to help bring peace and freedom to Kosovo, and take a leading role in the reconstruction of post-Taliban Afghanistan. But for him, it also meant that he would on occasion say 'no' to the United States. His 'no' over Iraq came in a very messy way. In the spring and early summer of 2002 he gave Bush to understand that Germany would not publicly oppose an action to 'do' Iraq. Then, faced with the prospect of losing an election, he suddenly came out on the hustings against any war on Iraq. He would not, he said, 'click his heels' and say 'yes' to whatever America decided.[35] President Bush felt personally betrayed. Germany was then cold-shouldered by Washington in a way unimaginable during the Cold War, thus in turn deeply offending the German chancellor. Umbrage was given, taken, and given again.

There are a couple of general lessons to be learned here. One is about the danger of political opportunism, such as Schröder's, which allows even basic tenets of a nation's foreign policy to be abandoned in the cause of re-election. Another is about the folly of making the relations between major states dependent on the personal relations between stubborn middle-aged men.

It is, however, as important to understand the specific German emotions to which Schröder appealed and by which, at least to some extent, he and his colleagues were also swayed. American observers were quick to spy 'anti-Americanism'. Of course there was a seam of anti-Americanism in Germany, as there was in every European country. 'What we hold against the American nation', said a German government press statement in 1942, 'is in the first place [its] complete lack of culture.'[36] The signatory was Adolf Hitler. In revulsion against that perverted notion of German 'culture', and as a result of American occupation and support, West Germany after 1945 became one of the most Americanized and pro-American societies in Europe. 'Germans may make bad Germans,' America's viceroy in Germany, General Lucius D. Clay, is supposed to have said, 'but they make damn good Americans.'[37]

At West Berlin's Tegel airport they erected a solitary signpost: 'Los Angeles 9684 km'. An arrow helpfully points in the right direction. In the mental geography of the West Germans, it often seemed that Los Angeles was closer than Leipzig, the Atlantic narrower than the River Oder. However, the protest generation of 1968 was, to say the least, highly critical of 'American' imperialism – partly in reaction to what they saw as the excessive and even slavish pro-Americanism of their parents, whom they also charged with complicity in Nazism. Gerhard Schröder and his foreign minister, Joschka Fischer, both belonged to Germany's class of '68. That matters. But two other sources of emotion matter at least as much.

First, the Germans, much more than the British or the French, have a deep and vivid revulsion from all and any war. In 2002/3, the country was going through an intensive phase of collective 'recovered memory', relating particularly to the horrors of the wartime bombing of German cities, which had recently been evoked in television programmes and bestselling books.* We must do everything to avoid a war over Iraq, said Germany's defence minister during a television discussion in February 2003, 'because millions of innocent people will die in it'.[38] Millions? French opposition to 'America's war' was mainly about America; German opposition was about both war and America, in roughly equal parts.

For a second source of deep frustration was that Germans very much wanted their country to be treated by America as a grown-up. France had been trying to restore its 'rank' as a great power since 1945, but it had at least been a fully sovereign country – or if it surrendered sovereignty, it did so voluntarily, trading *de jure* sovereignty for *de facto* power. Germany, by contrast, had until 1990 been a divided country, its sovereignty involuntarily limited by treaty, its once and future capital city divided by a concrete wall and cut into sectors still humiliatingly controlled by Soviet, American, British and French military administrations. Its 'normality' as a sovereign nation-state was brand new and precious. Germans wanted to be wooed with the promise of being 'partners in leadership', as President George H. W. Bush had done in 1989.[39] They hated the way they were being treated by his son. Phrases like 'not a colony', 'not to be treated as a vassal' and 'the need for emancipation' surfaced again and again in the German debates.[40]

Beyond political opportunism, this was, I believe, the dominant emotion in Schröder's case. Nor was it absent in the German foreign minister, Joschka Fischer. I had a memorable conversation with Fischer in the summer of 2003. We met on a Sunday afternoon at a café in central (formerly East) Berlin. He was dressed not in one of his formal three-piece suits but in T-shirt, jeans and trainers: American uniform. He said wise and mature things about mending the rifts in the West. He illustrated with two glasses and a sugar bowl on the café table how Germany was almost invariably somewhere between France and Britain: closer to London on some issues, closer to Paris on others.

* I say 'recovered memory' because no one under the age of fifty-seven could possibly have remembered the wartime bombing, since they would not have been born in 1945. Still, they sometimes talked as if they did: 'we remember', 'we, who suffered'. Another interesting example of the uses of 'we'.

For the foreseeable future, he observed, Europe would oscillate between the Gaullism of Paris and the Atlanticism of London. The arguments with the United States were 'all in the family'. But then, as I pressed him on the detail of his government's troubled relations with the Bush administration in Washington, he leaned forward conspiratorially and muttered 'don't we want to make a Boston tea party?'[41] It was a joke, of course. Perhaps it was meant to tease an Englishman about Blair's too servile proximity to Bush. The Boston tea party, he added, had done both Britain and America good. None the less, this was an astonishing thing for a German foreign minister to say. The clear implication was that Europe (or who else were 'we'?) was in some sense a colony of the United States. When he got up to leave, he completed his all-American uniform by putting on a black baseball cap inscribed 'American Eagle'. 'Yes,' he smiled, 'I bought it in Boston.'

The leader of the opposition Christian Democrats, Angela Merkel, used a motherly metaphor to describe these German emotions. With its constant talk of 'emancipation', Schröder's Germany was, she said, like a thirteen-year-old child going through puberty – and revolting against the American dad.[42] These emotions were strong and widely shared. Combined with revulsion against war as such, hostility to Bush as the stereotypical Texan cowboy, and an eminently reasonable scepticism about the actual case for military action to depose Saddam Hussein, they produced a dramatic swing in German public opinion – from America to Europe. The proportion of people who thought America was Germany's best friend fell from that 50 per cent in 1995 to just 11 per cent in March 2003.[43] Those who thought France was Germany's most reliable partner rose from 23 per cent in 1996 to 56 per cent in 2003.[44] In another poll, people were asked whether the European Union or the United States was more important to the vital interests of their country. In summer 2002, 20 per cent of Germans said the US and 55 per cent said the EU; a year later, just 6 per cent said the US and 81 per cent said the EU.[45]

It would be very premature to deduce from these startling results a permanent shift from German Atlanticism to German Gaullism. What they do show is the extreme volatility of opinion in Europe's central power. For though Tony Blair might like to describe Britain's role as 'pivotal', Europe's real pivot is Germany.

## IS EUROPE BETTER THAN AMERICA?

We could go on exploring the different mix of motives in, say, Italy, Spain, Greece or the Netherlands, and every case would be interestingly different. But I've probably said enough to indicate why a view of Europe as Not-America has been so vigorously propagated by political intellectuals and intellectual politicians in Europe at the turn of this century. We now have to step back and ask: is the claim of Europe's civilizational difference from America true? And is it believed by enough Europeans to forge a sustainable political identity? The answers to these two questions are quite distinct. Something can be true but not believed, or believed but not true. Most national identities have a large dose of the latter. A nation, it has been said, is a group of people united by a common dislike of their neighbours and a shared misunderstanding of their own past.

Let's start with the question 'is it true?' The claim is that Europe is a) different from and b) better than the United States. The claim of difference has to mean, if it's serious, that European countries have important things in common that also distinguish them – each and all – from the United States. Or, to rephrase it as another question: do all Europeans have more in common with each other than they do with Americans? How, beyond personal impressions, can we measure significant difference between such vast assemblages of individual human beings? The best that scholars can come up with is to look, over time, at the policies of states and groups of states, at economic and social statistics, and at opinion polls that try, with some sophistication, to get at attitudes and underlying values.

The most salient European–American differences seem to cluster around six things: religion, the role of the state, inequality, the environment, national sovereignty, and, last but not least, the ownership of guns and capital punishment for using them. Americans are, in aggregate, much more religious than Europeans. A few striking results from recent opinion polls illustrate this clearly: 83 per cent of

Americans say they regard God as important or very important, compared with 49 per cent of Europeans; 47 per cent of Americans say they attend church at least once a week, as against less than 20 per cent of Europeans;[46] 58 per cent of Americans say you have to believe in God in order to be moral.[47] Four out of every five Americans believe in life after death, and one in three thinks the Bible is 'God's word, literally true'.[48] In its religiosity, America is the great exception: the one country in the world to be both rich and religious.

Americans, in aggregate, also think it more important that government should leave them free to pursue their own goals, whereas Europeans think it more important that governments should guarantee that no one is in need.[49] Correspondingly, Americans feel that success or failure depends more on the individual's own efforts.[50] Europe consequently has more of the 'welfare state' than the United States. The federal tax burden in the United States is under 30 per cent, whereas the average tax burden for the fifteen member states of the European Union in 2003 was just over 40 per cent.[51]

In the distribution of wealth, America is more unequal than most European countries. The richest tenth of the population earns nearly six times more than the poorest tenth; in Germany and France, the ratio is just over three to one. The United States also has the largest proportion of its people in long-term poverty.[52] Meanwhile, it boasts some three million millionaires. The richest 1 per cent of the population hold nearly two fifths of the country's wealth.[53] So middle-class America is sandwiched between a chronically poor underclass and a super-rich overclass. As we shall see in a later chapter, America also stands out from other developed countries in its gas-guzzling environmental profligacy, a product of the distinctive 'American way of life'.

Most Americans are more patriotic than most Europeans. Even before the surge of emotion prompted by the 9/11 attacks, 72 per cent of Americans said they were 'very proud' of their country, compared with just 49 per cent of the British and 40 per cent of Germans.[54] Americans, unlike most Europeans, also own guns; lots of them. There are some nine guns in private hands for every ten Americans, compared with less than three for every ten Europeans.[55] The homicide rate in the United States is more than quadruple those in Britain,

France and Germany, despite what many Europeans regard as the barbaric deterrent of capital punishment.[56]

So Habermas's catalogue of European–American difference is not based on nothing. From the other side of the Atlantic, the American social scientist Seymour Martin Lipset has summarized these differences as 'American Exceptionalism'.[57] Yet such aggregate figures only tell part of the story. For a start, which Europe are we talking about? Habermas's European vision immediately struck another leading German political thinker, Ralf Dahrendorf, as an evocation of the old West Germany before unification.[58] Habermas's generalizations may hold to some extent for the original six member states of the European Community, but even in the European Union of fifteen member states, at the time Habermas was writing, and certainly in today's European Union of twenty-five, let alone in the geographical Europe of forty-plus, the divergences between European countries are immense.

For example, it is not empirically serious to talk of a single 'European model' of democratic capitalism. A major academic study comparing 'Varieties of Capitalism' identifies two major types of capitalist economy: the liberal market economy and the coordinated market economy.[59] It classifies Britain and Ireland, along with America, as liberal market economies; Germany, Belgium, the Netherlands and the Scandinavian countries are placed among the coordinated market economies. The authors find that France, Italy, Spain, Portugal and Greece occupy 'more ambiguous positions', possibly constituting 'another type of capitalism, sometimes described as "Mediterranean", marked by a large agrarian sector and recent histories of extensive state intervention'.[60] All vary in their labour markets and social policies. The tax burden in Sweden is more than 50 per cent of its gross domestic product, whereas in Britain the figure is less than 38 per cent.[61]

So that is three sorts of capitalism among just fifteen EU states. This picture does not begin to consider the new capitalist economies of central and eastern Europe, very different again, that are now inside the EU; let alone those European countries, such as Ukraine, which are not yet capitalist democracies heading towards EU membership. Does the life of a lawyer in Hamburg more closely resemble that of a lawyer in Kiev or in Boston? The answer must surely be Boston. The same would be true of a teacher, a plumber or a bus driver. Like nation-builders of old, Habermas and others are *attributing* to a very diverse human community commonalities that do not yet exist, in the hope that this will help those commonalities to emerge. The 'European model' is a prescription presented as a description.

Even on the indicators that seem most clearly to reveal a transatlantic gulf, the differences across the wider Europe can be very large. Take patriotism, for example. Three out of every four people in Ireland say they are 'very proud' of their country – more than in the United States – and the Poles are nearly as proud, while only one in five of the Dutch confess to such an old-fashioned sentiment.[62] Or take religion: more Ukrainians than Americans say it is necessary to believe in God to be moral, and a staggering 84 per cent of Turks agree – though most of them would know that God as Allah. Even between France and Germany there is a large gap on that question: 33 per cent of Germans agree, against only 13 per cent of the French.[63] Habermas says it is unimaginable that in Europe a president would begin his daily business with public prayer, but this is exactly what the British parliament does. The United States has never had an established church; Britain still has one, and progressive, welfarist Sweden only disestablished its Lutheran Church in 2000. It's undoubtedly true that European societies are generally more secular, and the gap between religion and politics is becoming wider in Europe even as it narrows in America. Yet, as we've seen, the afterlife of Christendom still has a powerful influence on the self-definition of Europe.

The generalizations about America may seem more securely founded. But here, too, we face a puzzle. There's an old joke from the time when European dictatorships, of left and right, were in the habit of declaring 99 per cent 'yes' votes on a 99 per cent turnout: 'Why is it that I only meet the 1 per cent?' Quite a few Europeans feel this way when they try to compare their own, personal American encounters with the poll results. Why? Perhaps because they spend their time on the more liberal East and West coasts rather than in the conservative Midwest and South.

In fact, polling analysis shows consistent, deep differences between these two Americas – tagged, rather confusingly to a European ear, 'blue America' (for the more liberal states, especially those on the two coasts) and 'red America' (for the big L of the conservative heartlands and the South). If one disaggregates 'blue' and 'red' America, then 'blue' America often turns out to be a quite European shade of pink. On several of the key social issues claimed as defining Europe, American Democrats turn out to be closer to Europeans than they are to Republicans. And this 'blue' America is not a small, embattled minority. If you add up the votes cast in the 2000 presidential election for the Democrat Al Gore and the left-wing maverick Ralph Nader, they outnumber by more than three million those cast for the conservative Republican George W. Bush.

The profusion of guns is a real difference between America and Europe – except for parts of Europe's 'Wild East', in the Balkans and today's eastern Europe (Ukraine, Belarus, Moldova), where handguns are still freely toted. It's tempting to extrapolate from this American domestic phenomenon to foreign policy: cowboys at home, cowboys abroad. The American satirist Michael Moore does this vividly in his film *Bowling for Columbine*, drawing an imaginative connection between the shootings at Columbine High School in Colorado and the Clinton administration's bombing of Serbia. A slightly more serious version of this argument is advanced by Robert Kagan: Americans retain a readiness to use military force in a dangerous 'Hobbesian' world.

Except that, from the end of the Vietnam War to the 11 September 2001 terrorist attacks, France and Britain were generally more willing to send their soldiers into dangerous action than the United States. It was Tony Blair who urged the American president to deploy ground troops in Kosovo, while French troops repeatedly intervened in Africa. It was American governments that were petrified of their boys coming home in the notorious bodybags. On this record, the two most important military powers in Europe, the British and the French, are at least as much 'from Mars' as the Americans. After 9/11, many Americans felt their country was under attack, so a majority supported the wars in both Afghanistan and Iraq. Only time will tell how lasting this shift in attitudes will be. On 15 February

2003 – that birthday of the 'European nation' – an estimated 200,000 people in San Francisco and 100,000 people in New York protested against President Bush's proposed war on Iraq.[64] Presumably that made them Europeans too?

Some 200,000 people also demonstrated in Sydney, Australia, which brings us to a further problem with the stylization of difference between Europe and America. What about the other capitalist democracies of the developed world? Are they not wrestling with the same problems of balancing wealth-creation and distribution, individual enterprise and social cohesion? Are they not confronting the same difficult dilemmas of war and peace? The Australian government, for example, sent troops to participate in the Iraq War, but only half the population supported it.[65] If you add Australia, Canada, Japan and the other developed countries in the Organization for Economic Cooperation and Development (OECD) to the scatter charts, America and Europe look less than ever like two distinct and discrete blocks.[66]

Thus, in the considered view of the comparative political economists, Canada, Australia and New Zealand join America, Britain and Ireland as liberal market economies. In economics, the Anglosphere is an empirical reality. Meanwhile, Japan joins Germany as a coordinated market economy, and Turkey sits somewhere with France and Spain as a Mediterranean one.[67] In respect of the welfare state, Canada and Australia are somewhere in between America and continental Europe – along with Britain. America is, in Seymour Martin Lipset's phrase, the 'welfare laggard' of the developed world.[68] But even that contrast is not as stark as many Europeans believe.

Take healthcare, for example. America actually spends a larger proportion of its gross domestic product on health than any European country – 13.9 per cent in 2001. The nearest European country was Switzerland, with 10.9 per cent, while Britain spent just 7.6 per cent.[69] Yes, the larger part of this was private healthcare, for those Americans who could afford it. But remarkably, the figure for *public* expenditure on health was exactly the same in Britain and the United States: 6.2 per cent of GDP. America's Medicaid programme alone spends more on caring for 40 million poor Americans than Britain's cherished National Health Service does on looking after all the country's 60 million people.[70] Spends it badly, to be sure: if I were old, poor and sick, I'd rather be in Britain. None the less, except for its worst inner-city slums, America is not the primitive capitalist jungle of European imagination, where human beings slink away like wounded animals to die in bloodstained holes.

Altogether, America's public spending priorities are less different from those of European welfare states than you might think. The US budget distinguishes between National Defense and Human Resources, in which it includes education, training, employment, social services, social security and healthcare – in short, the 'social' functions of the state, broadly conceived. It is interesting to track the ratio between them over the last sixty years. In 1945, the ratio was 89 per cent on defence to 2 per cent on social spending (the balance is accounted for by other budget categories). As late as 1970, America spent more on national defence than on social welfare. By the end of the Cold War, however, the ratio was roughly 24: 49 (defence: social), and in the last year of the Clinton administration it had fallen to 16: 62. All the huge hikes in military spending under George W. Bush only pushed that up to an estimated 20:65 in 2004.[71] As the country's ageing and often overweight baby-boomers move into retirement, either that ratio will increase still more to the advantage of domestic social spending or the system will go bust. Just like Europe.

Ah, you may say, but what about the underlying *values* that inform the whole European approach? Surely these are different? Values are tricky things to measure, but there's a group of professional pollsters and analysts who have spent more than twenty years trying to do exactly that. Consolidating and cross-checking the responses of more than 120,000 people in 81 countries, in the latest round of the World Values Survey, Ronald Inglehart has drawn a 'cultural map' of the world along what seem to be two key axes.[72] The result is printed on page 257 below. As you will see, there is no single, solid bloc of Europe versus America. Instead, Inglehart identifies distinctive though adjacent groupings of Catholic Europe, Protestant Europe, English-speaking, and ex-Communist countries. On the Inglehart values map, France is closer to Australia than it is to Sweden, let alone to Bulgaria. Of course, the methodology and choice of criteria can be disputed. But if we were trying to build a European identity around, say, hair colour or vegetables, and the experts in hair colour or vegetables told us there is no distinctive European hair colour or vegetable, we would surely take notice. Why not with values?

The Euro-Gaullist claim is not just that Europe is different; it's that Europe is better. (Hard to build a European patriotism around the idea that Europe is worse.) In what sense is this true? The economic historians find no clear evidence that one variant of capitalism has produced a better long-term economic performance than another. Different models have different advantages – and disadvantages. For example, a liberal market economy gets more people into paid employment, while a coordinated market economy has lower income differentials and makes more welfare provision for those out of work.[73] But is it better for someone to have badly paid work, as in America, or, as in Germany, slightly better-paid long-term unemployment? It's a matter of opinion which of the two is more debilitating for the human spirit. After all, the European Union's own charter of rights includes the 'right to engage in work'.[74]

You can be fired more brutally in the US; you can also be hired more easily. Americans work more and more; most West Europeans work less and less. In 1999, the Germans worked on average just over 1,500 hours per year against the Americans' nearly 2,000.[75] Almost three quarters of the population of working age in the United States was employed, compared with less than two thirds of the Germans and French.[76] (The British were once again in between, with just over 1,700 hours worked on average per year and more than 70 per cent of the working-age population in employment.) However, those Europeans lucky enough to have a job are generally guaranteed a higher minimum wage and more job security. This is what we call 'social' Europe – and it's a choice. Especially in the 'Mediterranean' societies, it leaves more time for the other good things of life: family, friends, food, recreation, *la dolce vita*. However, that comes at a price; one that is paid most painfully by the long-term unemployed, including a disproportionately large number of young people from Europe's Muslim immigrant communities.

America spends far more money on research and development than Europe: not just military but also medical. So Americans work out the newest, most original ways to take human lives but also to save them, to kill and to cure. Primary education is excellent in Scandinavia; higher education is better in America – unsurprisingly, since the US spends 2.7 per cent of its gross domestic product on it, compared to 1.0 per cent in Britain and Germany.[77] Europe might still like to think of itself as 'the intellectual and moral pole' but the top American universities are the best in the world. Europeans redistribute more money to the poor via the state, but Americans give far more in private philanthropy.[78]

Many European societies, especially Britain and France, still suffer the curse of class, but American society still has the curse of race – the legacy of slavery. On the other hand, America is better than Europe at making new immigrants feel at home. The German government famously offered long-term residence to 20,000 Indian IT specialists, but the Indians preferred Silicon Valley.[79] Comparative polling shows Americans taking a far more positive view of their ethnic minorities than Europeans do.[80] How, then, will Europe cope with the massive inflow of Muslim immigrants? Might it, perhaps, learn from America?

Inevitably, all that I can offer here is a small scattershot of examples, to chip away at the mind-walls of prejudice and constructed difference between Europe and America. Yet most of us can add to these more or less scientific findings our own personal impressions of Europe and America, Europeans and Americans. Taking all in all, we may emerge from this tangled jungle of claims and data with two alternative conclusions:

a) 'America and Europe are two different, strongly contrasting civilizations, and one is better.' (For 'one' insert Europe or America according to taste.)

b) 'America and most of the diverse countries of Europe belong to a wider family of developed, liberal democracies. America is better in some ways, Europe in others.'

Statement b) is less interesting, less galvanizing, but it has the boring old merit of being true.

## EUROATLANTICISM

To be sure, Europeans can believe the claim of civilizational difference and moral superiority even if it is not true. In a poll conducted in the summer of 2003, 79 per cent of Europeans said they thought Europeans and Americans have different 'social and cultural values'.[81] Whether or not the facts bear out that belief, the belief is itself an important fact. Yet overall, the polls present a more contradictory and volatile picture than this one spectacular finding would suggest; and polls, like X-rays, only capture one black-and-white slice of an intricate reality. The reality is that Europeans are deeply divided about the United States and Europe's relationship to it. The divisions run through political parties, social classes and intellectual milieux; they also run through individual hearts and minds. Many a European can exclaim, like Goethe's Faust, that two souls contend in his troubled breast.

In fact, Europeans spend far more time talking about America than they do talking about Europe. The Convention on the Future of Europe, which met throughout the period of the Iraq crisis to produce a draft European constitution, was supposed to generate a Europe-wide political debate. Jürgen Habermas hoped that intensive communication between Europeans about the constitution would help create a European public sphere.[82] Perhaps this would even be the embryo of a European *demos*. Instead, most Europeans spent the year of the Convention debating American policy and the Iraq War. The president they argued about was not the proposed president of Europe but the president of the United States. As we've seen, Habermas himself ended up seeking Europe's intercommunicative identity not in the constitutional debate but in opposition to Bush's war and the American 'Other'. It's not just in Britain that your attitude to the United States is a defining feature of your political identity. Of all Europeans, we can say: tell me your America and I will tell you who you are.

Typically, even Europeans' characterization of their own divisions is borrowed from America. On 22 January 2003, as the entire parliaments of France and Germany were meeting in Versailles to reaffirm their countries' special relationship, the American Defense Secretary

Donald Rumsfeld was asked at a press conference about European reluctance to join his war against Iraq. 'You're thinking of Europe as Germany and France,' he replied. 'I don't. I think that's old Europe.'[83] The centre of gravity of 'Nato Europe' was shifting to the east, he said, and there were lots of other countries in Europe who were 'with the United States' and not with France and Germany. Eight days later, an article appeared in the *Wall Street Journal Europe*, and a number of European newspapers, which seemed to bear out this contention. Signed by the leaders of eight European states – Spain, Britain, Italy, Denmark, Portugal, Poland, Hungary and the Czech Republic – what became known as the 'Letter of Eight' was not, as Habermas claimed, a 'declaration of loyalty to Bush', but more a general reaffirmation of a Western community of values and transatlantic solidarity in the war against terrorism.[84] Shortly thereafter, following some behind-the-scenes drafting by a forceful American advocate of Nato enlargement, the leaders of ten central and east European countries that were applying to join Nato (the 'Vilnius Ten') signed an open letter with even more explicit support for the United States.[85]

Europeans, having obsessively discussed two American big ideas, the 'end of history' and the 'clash of civilizations', and then seized on the American Robert Kagan's essay to characterize their own elusive identity, now went around clucking about 'old Europe' and 'new Europe' in a thousand conferences, speeches and commentaries, as if Donald Rumsfeld were some Michelet, Gibbon or Ranke, speaking with profound authority on the deep divisions of European history. (Couldn't Europeans have a big idea of their own for a change? Or did intellectual hegemony inevitably go with political hegemony?) This fascination with Rumsfeld's crude distinction was justified only in so far as his comment reflected an attempt by part of the Bush administration to 'divide and rule' in Europe.

As analysis, the dichotomy between 'old Europe' and 'new Europe' has somewhat less value than a cartoon-strip. Poland, Spain and Britain are hardly 'new'. When Dominique de Villepin criticized American policy at the UN Security Council on behalf of his 'old country' and continent, the British foreign secretary Jack Straw replied that he also came from a very old country, 'founded in 1066 by the French'.[86] The implication of Rumsfeld's distinction was that there was a group of European countries who were solidly pro-American and another group who were solidly anti-American. This was completely wrong. In all these countries, the majority in public opinion polls was consistently against Rumsfeld's war. Political and intellectual opinion was also divided, and even the governments had many doubts. Tony Blair and José Maria Aznar may have been convinced of the case for war against Iraq, but many of their ministerial colleagues were not. Silvio Berlusconi of Italy told Bush he thought the war was ill-advised, but said he would support it out of solidarity with the United States. A change of government in Italy or Spain could rapidly have produced a different stance; as it might have done in Germany, but in the other direction.

Against the motley array of constituencies and individuals that I've called 'Euro-Gaullist' there's another motley array that can be labelled 'Euroatlanticist'. Britain is a traditional bulwark of Atlanticism, but divided, as we have seen, between those who reject the European side of the Blair bridge project, those who reject the American side, and a few who still reject both. Spain and Portugal are also torn. Both countries have their own historic Atlanticisms. These connect them more directly with Spanish- and Portuguese-speaking Latin America, although North America too is becoming increasingly Spanish-speaking. However, the Spanish right, with a long memory, still recalls how the Americans robbed Spain of the remains of its transatlantic empire at the end of the nineteenth century; the Spanish left has not forgotten how the US supported General Franco. Ireland – to stay with the countries of Europe's Atlantic rim – is deeply conscious of its ties to 34 million Irish-Americans,[87] but it is also a traditionally neutral state that strongly identifies with Roman Catholic Europe, and with the European Union in which it has so visibly prospered.

The most unambiguous voices of Euroatlanticism come from the new democracies of central and eastern Europe, and especially from the largest of them, Poland. Poland, like Ireland, is tied to the United States by a history of immigration. There are some 10 million Americans of Polish origin and, unlike Americans of German origin, many of them keep lively connections with the motherland. A Woodrow Wilson Square in Warsaw reminds Poles of America's part in resurrecting independent Poland after the First World War. Despite Polish resentment of the American (and British) 'betrayal' at Yalta in 1945, most Poles feel a debt of gratitude to the United States for helping them win their own liberation from communism during the Cold War. In France and Germany, the student protest of 1968 was directed against the authorities at home and the United States; in Poland, the student protest of 1968 was directed against the authorities at home and the Soviet Union. The Polish '68ers, who went on to participate in their country's liberation movement, Solidarity, discovered how much Americans cared for the cause of freedom in their country through first-hand, direct experience – visits by American human rights activists, US diplomats exceeding their brief, writers' declarations of solidarity and smuggled dollars for underground printing presses.

From the grey, costive reality of a battered concrete apartment block under martial law, the American dream, as seen in a hundred Westerns, seemed even more fascinating than it was to Italians or Spaniards (and they were fascinated too). Sometimes, Polish Americanophilia took rather extreme forms. At a time when millions were protesting against the deployment of American Cruise and Pershing missiles in Western Europe, a graffito appeared in Warsaw. It read: 'I kiss your Pershings.' The Polish romance with an American dream of freedom and courage was perfectly captured by the placard with which Solidarity campaigned for support in the country's first semi-free election for more than forty years. It showed Gary Cooper wearing a Solidarity badge, and it said 'Solidarity – at High Noon, 4 June 1989'. The designer of this famous poster obviously assumed that a reference to the American Western *High Noon* did not have to be explained to an ordinary Polish voter.

After the end of communism, Poland set out on its 'return to Europe', but some of its key economic advisers and strongest supporters came from the United States. Thanks to American policy, it was Nato, not the European Union, that first welcomed Poland into membership – along with the Czech Republic and Hungary. Most of the new democracies of central and eastern Europe, and the Baltic states above all, continue to feel threatened by an unstable, resentful Russia. Understandably, they believe that the US is the most effective guarantor of their security. Poland bought American F-16 fighters to strengthen its own defences, sided with the Bush administration in the controversy over the Iraq War, and even agreed to head an occupation zone in Iraq.

For some in France, this is the final proof that Poland – for so long France's soulmate in the other Europe, and the only European country that still praises Napoleon in its national anthem – has become a fifth column for America. This is another complete misunderstanding. Most educated Poles, like their counterparts in other central and east European countries, believe passionately in Europe; more passionately than most west Europeans. The Czech dissident and post-liberation foreign minister of Czechoslovakia, Jiří Dienstbier, entitled a book he wrote while he was compelled for political reasons to work as a stoker, *Dreams of Europe*.[88] When I was travelling through the Iron Curtain in the 1980s, to and fro between what were then called Western and Eastern Europe, I concluded that Cold War Europe was indeed divided into two halves: the West, which had Europe, and the East, which believed in it. These true believers have, to be sure, been disillusioned by the grudging welcome given them by the European Union over the long fifteen years it has taken to get from liberation to membership. They thought they would be welcomed like long-lost cousins into the bosom of a family; they found themselves treated as provincial applicants to an exclusive metropolitan club. Dienstbier's sequel, a decade later, was entitled *From Dreams to Reality*.[89]

Still, they have no doubt that their future lies in Europe. So they believe in both Europe and America. In other words, they believe in the West – the more so, because for nearly a century they have felt themselves to be not fully part of it. Oswald Spengler, when he published his *Decline of the West* in 1918, defined the 'culture' whose demise he portentously prophesied as 'the *west*european-american' (my italics).[90] In the Cold War these countries were cut off from the West by the Iron Curtain. Rather as German or Hungarian nationalism was most pronounced among the minorities outside the frontiers of the nation-state, so Westernism was most emphatic along the West's excluded periphery, in what the Czech writer Milan Kundera memorably called 'the kidnapped West'.[91] 'When we said West,' recalls the Romanian philosopher and politician Andrei Pleşu, 'it never crossed our minds that . . . Western Europe and Northern America were divergent entities.'[92]

Yet this was not a blind passion. In the writings of Václav Havel, both as dissident essayist and after he became president, you can find the most considered reflection on the values that Europe and America have in common. It was Havel, and other leaders of post-communist central and eastern Europe, who introduced into the post-Cold War debate the word 'Euroatlantic', often in the slightly clumsy form 'Euroatlantic structures'.[93] So far as I can establish, this term had not been used before. People in the West had talked about 'the Atlantic alliance', 'transatlantic relations' (a notion that itself did not exist before 1945), and 'the Atlantic community', but the prefix 'Euro' is significant. The point was precisely to combine, in equal measure, the European and the American. No one talked more eloquently of the deeper meaning of the *European* project than Václav Havel did. A new balance was implicit in the new word.

These central and east European leaders were, in this sense, Blairite long before Blair. When, in the crisis of the West, Europe seemed to come into conflict with America, they were as torn as the British were. Poland's negotiator with the European Union, Jan Kułakowski, described their feelings: 'We're asked, "Are you for America or Europe?" It's like choosing your mother or your father.'[94] But this very Blairite refusal to choose was, in the eyes of at least some Gaullists, tantamount to a choice: the wrong one. After the 'Letter of Eight' and that of the 'Vilnius Ten', President Chirac angrily commented that these countries were proving themselves to be *'pas très bien élevés'* (not very well brought up) and that they had 'lost a good chance to remain silent'.[95] Far from being grateful for this lesson in European etiquette, from a past master of *politesse*, central and east Europeans were furious. Was it only the French who were allowed to speak for Europe? For them, Chirac's rebuke seemed to be a new version of a famous slogan from Orwell's *Animal Farm*, which they had read with fascination in smudgy samizdat editions. Someone had again repainted the motto on the end of the farm barn, at the behest of a pig called Napoleon. It now read: All Europeans are equal, but some Europeans are more equal than others.

None the less, we must beware of oversimplifying. Havel, for example, was not typical of his compatriots. The Czech prime minister did not sign the 'Letter of Eight' and Czech public opinion was strongly opposed to the war on Iraq. Young Polish students happily joined with their Italian peers in anti-globalization protests. There is a strong chance that, as these countries become more closely integrated into the European Union, so their peoples will identify more with Europe than with America.

Meanwhile, Chirac did not go uncriticized in his own country. He reached intoxicating heights of personal popularity during his Napoleonic hundred days of glorious if doomed opposition to Bush's war. Yet even some Parisian intellectuals – traditionally among the most anti-American people on earth – were quick to criticize his arrogant assumption that he could speak for Europe. 'With the European community divided and Nato splintering,' commented the philosopher André Glucksmann, 'the Franco-German duo calls itself "Europe" and says it speaks for 25 nations, but represents only three (thanks to Belgium). The "old Europe" couple criticizes American "arrogance" and "unilateralism", compliments that can easily be turned back on them. Is there a more insane way to saw off the branch you're sitting on? Is there a less productive path to European unity?'[96] Glucksmann went on to write a sharp, short book entitled *West Against West*, in which he also pilloried French and German appeasement of Putin's Russia.[97] Instant books with titles like *France Falls*, *French Disarray* and *French Arrogance* excoriated the hubris of the Chirac regime.[98]

Bernard-Henri Lévy, perhaps the most famous living Parisian intellectual, came to speak at a debate in London on the motion that 'the American empire is a force for good'. He spoke *for* the motion. While he had opposed the war on Iraq, he said, he was fed up with the US being blamed for all the misery of the world and he was fed up with anti-Americanism – which, he added, he knew well as a Frenchman, 'because we invented it'.[99] Two distinguished French academics published books analysing and criticizing French anti-Americanism.[100] This French anti-anti-Americanism is not the same as Euroatlanticism, but it does mean that Euro-Gaullism is eloquently challenged in its very capital. Long-time Euroatlanticist political writers such as Pierre Hassner, who for years have ploughed a somewhat lonely furrow in the footsteps of Raymond Aron, now enjoy belated recognition. A Paris-based 'republic of ideas', both a network and a journal, is devoted, among other things, to narrowing the intellectual Atlantic. To be sure, this is still an intellectual minority, in quantity if not in quality.

If French intellectuals are divided about Euro-Gaullism, the French business community is more Euroatlanticist. A former American ambassador to France, Felix Rohatyn, says he finds business people to be America's best friends in France.[101] That is even more true in Germany, although in both countries you have to distinguish between more cosmopolitan big business and more defensive smaller companies. Even the more outward-looking French and German business leaders don't necessarily favour the 'American business model' and the kind of deregulation pioneered by Ronald Reagan and Margaret Thatcher. Some do; others think their own varieties of capitalism can compete quite well.

What all European business leaders see, however, is the huge and growing interdependence between the American and European economies, and the damage that can be done to their businesses by political disputes. This is not just a matter of the rich Californian cancelling his order for two Mercedes. The much-publicized trade disputes between the US and the EU over steel tariffs, genetically modified foods or corporate tax breaks are more important. Yet according to an incisive study by Joseph Quinlan, transatlantic trade comprises just 20 per cent of all transatlantic commerce, and trade disputes have affected less than 1 per cent.[102] What has really transformed the transatlantic economic relationship is investment, meaning that American companies own European ones and vice versa, selling goods and services through their respective foreign affiliates. American firms invested more capital overseas in the 1990s than in all the previous four decades combined – and half of it went to Europe. Accordingly, in 2001 half the total foreign earnings of US companies came from Europe. The United States had more assets in Germany than in the whole of Latin America; in the year 2000, its foreign affiliate sales in Germany were ten times those in China.

Europe has an even larger stake in the United States. European firms hold roughly two thirds of all foreign-owned assets in the US, and sales by European-owned companies in the US were worth $1.4 trillion in 2000 – four times the value of European exports to the United States. To illustrate these figures with a few familiar brand names: American Chrysler is owned by German Daimler, American AirTouch by British Vodafone, American Arco and Amoco by BP. The American publisher of this book, Random House, is owned by the German company Bertelsmann.

This also means jobs. If you add together direct and indirect employment, then by Quinlan's reckoning nearly 6 million Europeans owe their livelihoods to American investors and some 7 million American workers depend on European investors – who, he adds, 'on average pay higher wages and provide greater benefits than domestic US employers'.[103] So the 'European social model' is right there, in America, and the 'American business model' is right here, in Europe. In the business world, Euroatlanticism already exists, without a hyphen.

Transatlantic economic interdependence grew spectacularly after the end of the Cold War, in precisely the period when the transatlantic political community was heading for crisis. Economics and politics moved in opposite directions. The political West is no longer cemented together by the threat of Soviet communism, but a surviving Soviet Marxist would predict a political solidarity of bourgeois states arising from these huge shared material interests of capitalists on both sides of the Atlantic. However, a Soviet Marxist might yet again be wrong. The very high degree of economic interdependence in Europe before 1914 did not stop the old continent tearing itself apart.

Last but not least, there is the Americanization of everyday European consumer life. Even on Jean Monnet Square, named after the founding father of the European Union, in the heart of the smartest quarter of Paris, the 16th arrondissement, there is a McDonald's – although it's the most elegant McDonald's in the world, with cream and crimson painted woodwork, *fin-de-siècle*-style lamps, and a glass cabinet displaying works by Victor Hugo. Around the corner, a bust of Voltaire looks down from the wall of the Lycée Janson on to a shop called USA Concept Sport. A little further up the Rue de la Pompe, Racine and Molière gaze stony-eyed at another sportswear shop, Compagnie de Californie. The *lycée* students wear trainers, baseball caps and T-shirts proclaiming I ❤ NY.

Europeans across the continent enjoy American movies and music.[104] If you ring the office of Jacques Delors's think tank, Notre Europe, and they put you on hold, the canned music down the line is 'All that Jazz', sung in American English. What the French called '*l'Amérique dans les têtes*', the America-in-the-head, is everywhere. Of course it's entirely possible to love *Ally McBeal* and hate George W. Bush, to enjoy a Big Mac before going out to demonstrate against American foreign policy. That's what a great many young Europeans do. If they are anti-American, they are deeply Americanized anti-Americans. But most Europeans are well able to make the distinction between an administration and a nation. Asked in summer 2003 'what's the problem with the US?', nearly three quarters of those in France and Germany registering a negative view of America said 'mostly Bush', against less than a quarter saying 'America in general'.[105] Even when they are critical of the United States, Europeans retain a favourable view of Americans as people.[106]

## A POWER FOR WHAT?

Euroatlanticists and Euro-Gaullists generally agree on one thing: Europe should play a bigger role in the world. So, apparently, do most Europeans. More than two thirds of those asked in a poll in the summer of 2003 said the European Union should become a superpower.[107] After all, this enlarged EU of twenty-five states has far more inhabitants than the United States, and a combined economy of comparable size. The draft European constitution envisages a European foreign minister, and a common foreign and security policy, 'including the progressive framing of a common defence policy'.[108] But a power for what?

At one end of the spectrum, there are those who want the European Union to become a second 'world nation', in the words of the former French foreign minister, Hubert Védrine.[109] Very few of these European nationalists (that is, protagonists of a European nation) say outright that they want it to be a rival to the United States.

The senior German journalist who wrote 'the American empire must be declared the enemy' is an exception.[110] This is not considered politic – or polite. After all, did not the French intellectual Jacques Attali observe, in a defence of 'old Europe', that politeness is a European invention?[111] (The Chinese of Confucius' time might have been surprised.) So the Gaullist president of the Convention on the Future of Europe, Valéry Giscard d'Estaing, pleaded for Europe to acquire 'the power to take on the giants of this world'.[112] Euro-Gaullists talk of *l'Europe puissance* and, at their most explicit, of the EU as a counterweight to the US. Americans are not wrong to suspect in this more than meets the eye.

However, the European nationalist or Euro-Gaullist aspiration is not simply directed against the United States. There are also Euro-Gaullists, especially among the elites of the former European great powers, for whom aspiring to be a world power is an end in itself. De Gaulle expressed this almost as a syllogism when he said that France 'because she can, because everything invites her to do so, *because she is France*, must carry out in the world policies that are on a world scale' (my italics).[113] Churchill would have said much the same for Britain. And I will never forget hearing the passion with which a distinguished, white-haired former president of Germany spoke of how Europe might one day become a *Weltmacht* (a pre-1945 German term for world power). In this view, France, Britain and Germany can no longer be world powers on their own – but together, as Europe, perhaps they might. An aspiration that is both unrealistic and discredited for individual European nation-states is somehow considered realistic and respectable for Europe as a whole.

Then there are Europeans who want Europe to play a larger role in the world for almost the opposite reason. Europe, they feel, has learned from its terrible history of competing nation-states, each aspiring to mastery. After giving the world the curse of the nation-state, Europe should now offer the global antidote. The European Union is a model of how nation-states can overcome their differences, in a law-based transnational community of peaceful cooperation. That model is now ripe for export. It's already embracing many post-communist democracies of Europe. It exercises a benign magnetism in the Balkans and in Turkey. In this spirit, one senior and liberal German diplomat confesses that his ultimate ideal would be 'the Europeanization of the world'. If America has a universalist aspiration, born of the Enlightenment, so do France and Germany.

In the same spirit, such patriots of transnational Europeanism emphasize Europe's contribution to promoting 'global public goods'. Europe gives nearly three times as much as the United States in foreign development aid.[114] Europeans are involved in peacekeeping operations and reconstruction after conflict around the world. They support the International Criminal Court. They wish to implement the Kyoto Protocol on climate change, and are altogether more solicitous of the environment. Here the claim of difference from, and even superiority to, the United States does not amount to hostility; it is, so to speak, friendly rivalry in a good cause.

Finally, there are those who believe, like Tony Blair, that in shaping its own foreign and security policy Europe must always stay close to the United States. Its goal should be to try and broaden Washington's agenda by neo-Churchillian engagement. Those global public goods can only be achieved by Europe and America working together.

You will typically hear more French and German voices at one end of this spectrum, and more British and Polish ones at the other. When the French commentator Bernard Guetta challenged the Polish writer Adam Michnik to agree that Europe should become a world power as a counterweight to the United States, Michnik crisply replied: 'Power, Yes. Counterweight, No.'[115] But the division is not simply along national lines. If Americans are confused about Europe's intentions, they have every reason to be, because Europe is itself confused. Millions of Europeans are swinging between the two poles of Euro-Gaullism and Euroatlanticism, in the argument of the decade.

Which of the two positions is more realistic, in the sense of 'capable of being realized'? The crisis of 2002/3 showed that the Chiracian version of Euro-Gaullism is a hiding to nowhere. An attempt to unite Europe around a rival policy to the United States ended up splitting Europe down the middle. France and Germany, it emerged, could no longer plot a course for the whole of the European Union, as they had before 1989. They still aspired to be the 'magnetic core' of the EU but had the reverse effect: magnetically repelling rather than attracting other European states. The neo-Gaullist vision of a unipolar Europe in a multipolar world ended with a multipolar Europe in a still unipolar world. Europe – to be more accurate, the part of Europe France and Germany could rally – was not powerful enough to stop the United States doing what it wanted. America can win the hot wars on its own. This does not mean it can win the subsequent peace, as it has discovered in Iraq. For that, it will always need the help of others, but whether those others have to include the reluctant powers of 'old Europe' is an open question. One of the secondary political resources available to Washington is its ability to play European countries off against each other, as offshore imperial Britain did in the nineteenth century.

This critical verdict on the failure of the Chiracian version of Euro-Gaullism does not mean that the Blairite version of Euroatlanticism was a success, or any more likely to succeed in future. Blair failed quite as much as Chirac to rally Europe around his position. A policy aimed at uniting the West ended up helping to split it more sharply. This in turn strengthened the popular support for Euro-Gaullism in much of Europe, including Britain, thus making the prospect of Europe-wide consensus on a Euroatlanticist position more remote than before. A Euroatlanticist strategy is necessarily based on the hope that Washington will want the European Union to be a single coherent partner for the United States. But why should Washington want that, when it can choose its partners, mission by mission, from among the disunited states of Europe? Perhaps American leaders will be quite content, now the Soviet Union no longer threatens us all, to see Europe carry on in mild disarray? Why take the risk of the old world uniting against the new, as a rival superpower? If European nationalists can think more than they say in public, so can American nationalists. They can be 'polite' too.

Any serious judgement on the right way forward for Europe therefore depends on an assessment of the trajectory, motives and interests of the United States of America. To this I now turn.

# 3

# America, the Powerful

## INSIDE THE GIANT

Sometimes one remark says it all. President George W. Bush is talking to a small group of visitors in the oval drawing room on the first
floor of the White House. From its windows, they have a fine view of
planes taking off from Ronald Reagan National Airport. This is one
of the last months of the innocent time when planes in the skies over
Washington are just that – planes – and not potential weapons of
mass destruction. The meeting is to prepare the president, still new in
office, for his first official trip to Europe, but just now he's recalling,
in his clipped, tautly smiling way, a Summit of the Americas the previous month. At one point during the summit, feeling that he had
already talked too much, he had indicated to the chairman that he
would 'pass' on this topic. 'But Mr President,' the chairman expostu-
lated, 'you are the most powerful man on earth.' As President Bush
reflects on this, he comments wryly, 'It takes a little time to grow into
this job.'[1]

   That could also be said of the whole country, in its new job. After
the fall of the Berlin Wall on 9 November 1989 (9/11, European-style),
America gradually woke up to the realization that it was no longer just
one of two competing superpowers. 'Hyperpower', 'superduper-
power', 'American empire', 'new Rome', 'unipolar world' – all these
terms attempt to capture the new reality of a global predominance that
arguably has no precedent in the history of the world. After the fall of
the twin towers on 11 September 2001 (9/11, American-style), the
United States has been wrestling with the revelation that all this plenitude of power could not protect its own innocent civilians from

foreign attack in the heart of the American homeland, a trauma Americans had not experienced since British troops sacked the White House in 1814. Incomparable power, unprecedented vulnerability.

Something else is new too: the world can not merely observe the actions but actually sees inside the brain of this giant called America, as it wrestles with its paradoxical pre-eminence. Like a bank of electronic monitors on a hospital ward, CNN, the BBC and the World Wide Web register every heart-beat, every spasm. Like anxious relatives, hundreds of millions of people, from London to Sydney, watch through the glass. Washington 'players', known across the globe simply as 'Bush', 'Condi' and 'Kerry' become characters in a worldwide soap opera, a kind of political *ER*. On Thursday, you watch the fictionalized *West Wing*; the rest of the week, you have the real thing. Europeans, like Latin Americans, Asians and Africans, often know better what is going on in Washington than they do what is happening in other capital cities on their own continent.

Monitoring America seems so much easier than monitoring Europe. Europe is more than forty countries, governments and national foreign policies; the United States is just one of each – or so, at least, it claims. Beside the plethora of information about the inner workings of American domestic and foreign policy there is a wealth of analysis. The European stereotype used to be – and for some still is – that experienced old Europeans have the sophisticated, detailed understanding of the world ('*l'intelligence européenne*') while Americans are like the hapless Pyle in Graham Greene's *The Quiet American*, well meaning but brash and ignorant, blundering into complex foreign crises without knowing a *stupa* from a beehive. The truth is that Washington has at its fingertips a range and depth of foreign policy analysis, in government, think tanks, universities and the media, which London has not matched for fifty years and no other European capital, least of all the EU 'capital' of Brussels, can begin to approach. This analysis probes every corner of the world; even more, it probes Washington's own policies.

The commendation of that large advantage must be hedged about with a few warning notes. This sophisticated self-analysis of the Washington body politic has two characteristic shortcomings which are the products, respectively, of the commercial and the political marketplace. As analysts jostle for attention in the crowded market of ideas they have to shout loudly, like traders on the floor of a stock exchange. Shouting loudly, to clinch an intellectual 'trade', requires overstatement. It means taking a grand, simplifying idea and, egged on by your magazine editor or book publisher, hyping it still further: The End of History! The Clash of Civilizations! Europeans are from Venus! The Coming Anarchy! The End of the American Era! Here are the *terribles simplificateurs* of whom the great nineteenth-century Swiss historian Jacob Burckhardt once warned, but now they are driven less by ideological fervour or philosophical hubris than by the commercial pressures of, so to speak, intellectual capitalism.

Then there's the political marketplace. In Washington, some three to five thousand jobs in government are filled by political appointees every time a new administration comes to power. Many people, in think tanks, academe and journalism, covet these jobs. You, too, could be a Kissinger, a Brzezinski, an Albright or a Rice! So they cast and trim their analyses to increase their chances of getting the job – or, at least, of continued access to and influence upon those who hold the top jobs. 'Thanks for e-mailing me your entry in the Kennan stakes; here's mine,' wrote one such aspirant to another, at a time when American journals were full of attempts to do for post-9/11 American foreign policy what George Kennan's 'Mr X' article in *Foreign Affairs* did for its Cold War policy. The waters of American self-analysis are therefore deep but far from pure. Description and prescription, the personal and the political, are always mixed. In each case you have to ask 'where's he or she coming from?', which often means 'to what office would he or she like to go?' Many's the book or article whose unwritten sub-title is 'A Job Application'.

I just suggested that, unlike Europe, America is one country with one government and one foreign policy, but anyone who knows Washington will tell you that this is a most dangerous oversimplification. Not only does American foreign policy change rapidly over time, in the course of as well as between administrations, but on any given day there are usually two or three American foreign policies: one from the State Department, another from the Pentagon, perhaps a third from the National Security Adviser. And a fourth will be inserted, episodically, by Congress, which plays a role as part of 'the government' unlike that of any parliament in any major European state. As for 'one country', that is, in some obvious sense, true – the United States is a single federal nation-state. But in another sense it is less true, since the country has become increasingly divided and polarized on cultural-political lines, so the voters of 'red' (Republican) and 'blue' (Democrat) America disagree sharply on fundamental issues. Controversies about foreign policy, especially on national security policy, are less clearly polarized on party lines, but they are still quite sharp. At any given moment, you therefore have to ask 'which foreign policy?', 'which government?' and 'which America?'. 'The US', writes the British Euro-Gaullist Will Hutton, 'is hostile to all forms of international cooperation and multilateralist endeavour.'[2] *The* US? Which US?

One illuminating analysis, by Walter Russell Mead, identifies four American ways of looking at foreign policy which, he argues, have competed and coexisted through two centuries. 'Hamiltonians', he suggests, look to increase domestic prosperity by securing a favourable external environment for trade and business; 'Wilsonians' believe in spreading democracy, self-government and the rule of law; 'Jeffersonians' think it matters more to safeguard democracy at home, leading the world mainly by example; 'Jacksonians' make fierce, warlike defence of the physical security and economic well-being of the American people.[3] In practice, these approaches ebb and flow between and within groups, and even within individuals. For example, someone might be more 'Jacksonian' after the 9/11 attacks than he or she was before.

Others emphasize the importance of 'where you're coming from' being understood quite literally. A background on the East or West coast, in the Midwest, the deep South or, not least, in the great state of Texas, shapes how a particular policymaker views the world. 'I sit before you an unvarnished Texan,' said President George W. Bush, introducing that White House discussion of Europe with polished, not to say varnished self-deprecation. Yet for all his Yaley varnish, George W. Bush was the first Southern conservative to occupy the White House since before the American Civil War.[4] At critical moments the decision would come down, as it always does, to a set of individual biographies interacting with a set of unforeseen events.

My purpose in this chapter is obviously not to treat the whole of American foreign policy. It's to seek an answer to this question: how likely is it that we will (again) see a United States that treats Europeans, and other free people, as full and serious partners in a common enterprise? For one major cause of this crisis of the West is that many Europeans, and other free people, have not felt they are being so treated.

## A TALE OF TWO NEW EUROPES

In the beginning, the United States was the new Europe. It defined itself against what Alexander Hamilton called 'the pernicious labyrinths of European politics'.[5] Bad old Europe was, in this sense, America's founding 'Other'. The temporal adjective – old – was as important as the spatial noun – Europe. European nations might forge their identities from an imagined past, American identity would flow from an imagined future. The nineteenth-century novelist Herman Melville summed up this quintessentially American belief. 'The Past', he wrote, 'is the Textbook of Tyrants; the Future the Bible of the Free.'[6] In a New England, free men and women would build a new Jerusalem, Governor John Winthrop's 'City upon a Hill', and in a New Orleans they would make a better France. In the New Amsterdam that became the multinational city of New York, genera-tions of European immigrants to the United States relived this history in their own personal biographies. Summarizing the background of a Californian billionaire of Hungarian origin, the money magazine *Forbes* said simply: 'family fled Europe'.[7] Europe was the place you fled.

But America was not simply the Not-Europe; it was the Would-Be-Better-Europe. 'America,' wrote Irving Howe, 'began as an idea of Europe. Whatever may be reformative in European culture, and a modest part of whatever is revolutionary, finds a locus of desire in the idea of America.'[8] Many of the Founding Fathers were Englishmen with a deep admiration for France. Thomas Jefferson wrote that if he could not live in America, he would choose to live in France.[9] Alexis de Tocqueville repaid the compliment, with his admiring account of

*Democracy in America.* In the nineteenth century, the English in Massachusetts and Virginia, the French in Louisiana, the Spanish in California, the Poles in Chicago, the Germans in Wisconsin and the Scandinavians in Minnesota created what Jacob Burckhardt called 'a large-scale laboratory experiment of Europe's future'.[10] America was the first European Union.*

This ambivalence about Europe, this mixture of fascination and repulsion, runs through American history. In every period, one can find examples of anti-Europeanism and Europhilia, just as in every period of European history one can find anti-Americanism and Americanophilia ('*Amerika, Du hast es besser!*' wrote Goethe. 'America, you're better off!'[11]). What matters, on both sides, is the way the mixture changes and how it translates into policy. At the turn of the nineteenth to the twentieth century, there was a clear rapprochement between the United States and the two European nations which had done most to define it at birth: England and France. Winston Churchill, with his British father and American mother, was quite literally the child of this coming-closer. The Statue of Liberty, a present to the United States from the people of France, was its enduring monument.[12] Henry James's *The Europeans* portrays the intricate dance of attraction and repulsion between the transatlantic cousins at this quivering moment.

In the First World War, a sense of cultural and political solidarity with the Anglo-French West became military commitment. One of the leading American historians of 'Western Civ', William H. McNeill, tells us that the first course in Western Civilization at Columbia University in New York was 'designed to teach soldiers what it was they would be fighting for in Flanders Fields'.[13] While America soon withdrew militarily from Europe, the teaching of Western Civilization continued at Columbia, Chicago and other American universities. It was, as McNeill recalled from his own student days, a 'liberating message . . . it conveyed membership in the great cultivated, sophisticated world of "us" . . .'[14]

---

* Of course this first European Union was also built on the labour of slaves, thus storing up generations of shame and trouble for itself; but then, today's European Union has been partly built on the labour of darker-skinned immigrant workers – poorly treated by the higher standards of our time – thus storing up future trouble for itself.

That American self-image of a common transatlantic 'us' was reinforced by the experience of fighting together in the Second World War and then standing together in the Cold War. The author of *Life's Picture History of Western Man* expressed this naively but also quite eloquently in 1951:

On his lonely pinnacle, the American can survey more history than he has seen before. During the past generation, he rediscovered his personal links with Western Man and his membership in Western civilization. Somewhere in these turbulent years America's acceptance of responsibility for its parents' lands, for the mother and father of its own past, quietly placed itself beyond question. When Franklin Roosevelt in 1939 said, 'Our American frontier is on the Rhine,' he felt obliged to deny that he had said it. That frontier has subsequently been placed on the Elbe without objection.[15]

Well, almost without objection. Actually, a proposal for American 'Disengagement' from Europe emerged soon thereafter from one of the leading architects of America's Cold War policy, George Kennan, and the temptation of disengagement recurred throughout the Cold War. Indeed, the temptation of disengagement – sometimes more pejoratively called 'isolationism' – must be considered an enduring feature of such a vast, self-defining and in many ways still inward-looking country. We are told that roughly four out of every five Americans don't even have a passport.

While working on this book, I travelled to the heartland Bible-belt states of Kansas and Missouri. Wherever I went, I asked the people I met – farmers, shop assistants, high school students – a simple question: 'If I say "Europe", what do you think of?' Many reacted with a long, baffled silence, sometimes punctuated by giggles. They really, visibly, could not think of anything. Vernon Masqua, a carpenter in McLouth, said: 'Well, I guess they don't have much huntin' down there.' Richard Souza, whose parents came from France and Portugal, reflected: 'Well, it's a long way from home.' And after a very long pause for thought, Jack Weishaar, an elderly farmer of German descent, weightily concluded: 'Well, it's quite a ways across the pond.' If you said 'America' to a farmer or carpenter in Europe, even in the remotest mountain village of transcarpathian Ruthenia, he would, you may be sure, have a whole lot more to say on the subject. And many of those I talked to in Kansas and Missouri thought America should concentrate on putting its own house in order. James Kimmel, a farmer on the road to McLouth, told me: 'I think we're trying to run the business of the world too much . . . like the Romans used to . . .'[16]

However, I also met, in chance encounters, local people who had served in the American armed forces in Europe or had otherwise lived, worked or travelled there. The human bonds developed over more than sixty years of large-scale American presence in Europe, from the 1940s to the 1990s, are not just confined to some 'East coast elite'. The 'us' of the West is much wider than that. Many millions of former US service people, and their families, have vivid memories of life in Europe. Folk memories also live on among those who have never been to Europe. Jack Weishaar, the Kansas farmer, had never travelled to the East or West coasts of the US, let alone abroad, but when I asked him for his view of the Germans he said, 'Well, I'd better not have anything against them because that's where my ancestors came from.' Even historical ignorance can foster transatlantic warmth. More than half of those asked in a national test of high school seniors were unable say who the US fought against in the Second World War. Nearly one in five believed that the Germans had been America's allies.[17]

The United States, that first European Union across the sea, also encouraged on the old continent the creation of a new European Union. The US supported early European federalist movements, both overtly and covertly. It made Marshall Aid conditional on closer economic cooperation between European states. Praising the project of European union in 1962, President John F. Kennedy said: 'The United States looks on this valiant enterprise with hope and admiration. We don't regard a strong, united Europe as a rival but as a partner. To aid its progress has been the basic objective of our foreign policy for the past seventeen years.'[18] Making generous allowance for the gilded hyperbole of Camelot ('*the* basic objective'?) that was a fair statement of the broad strategic direction of American policy. Speaking in Philadelphia on America's Independence Day, Kennedy went on to call for a 'Declaration of Interdependence' between the 'new union now emerging in Europe and the old American Union founded here 175 years ago'.

With many hesitations, and perhaps growing ambivalence, the United States continued to encourage the 'valiant enterprise' of European integration for another thirty years, until that enterprise formally became, shortly after the end of the Cold War, the European Union. This support was partly the product of sympathy and idealism: after all, one of the first proposals for a 'United Europe' was made in 1693 by William Penn, the founder of Pennsylvania.[19] However, post-1945 American policy was far more the product of enlightened self-interest. By increasing the attraction of the free western half of Europe to the unfree eastern half, European integration strengthened America's hand in a global duel with the Soviet Union whose main geopolitical arena was Europe and whose centre was Berlin. The magnetic dynamism of the European Community in the 1970s and 1980s, with its visionary goal of a single market to be 'completed' in 1992, did then contribute directly to the end of communism in the Soviet bloc. Western Europe's '1992' was a cause of Eastern Europe's 1989.

The fall of the Berlin Wall signalled that the Soviet Union had lost this Cold War with the United States. The administration of President George H. W. Bush sealed the victory, using quiet, skilful multilateral diplomacy to help the Germans – America's new 'partners in leadership' – to win Gorbachev's assent to their unification. President Bush (Senior) also summarized Europe's own larger purpose better than any European in a single phrase: 'Europe whole and free'. On Christmas Day 1991, Mikhail Gorbachev gave the West his final gift, sealing the end of the Soviet Union by his resignation.* Just a fortnight earlier, the leaders of the European Community had resolved at the Dutch town of Maastricht to make an economic and monetary union. This was designed to ensure, among other things, that the new, united, sovereign Germany would be firmly held within a warm European embrace. In anticipation, the Community renamed itself the European Union. Then the two halves of the old Cold War West had to consider what the relationship between the new EU and the new US would be.

---

* Perhaps fittingly, this was Christmas Day in the Western Christian but not the Eastern (Orthodox) Calendar.

As I have stressed already, this geopolitical shift on the continent of Europe was fundamental, but there were also two longer-term cultural-historical shifts on the American continent. First, the ethnic character and cultural self-identification of the United States changed as a result of the long-overdue recognition of the equal civil rights of African-Americans in the 1960s and the growth of immigration from countries outside Europe following the 1965 Immigration and Nationality Act. In the next quarter-century, more than fifteen million people entered the United States legally under the provisions of that Act.[20] The Asian-American population rose from 1.5 million in 1970 to nearly 12 million in 2000.[21] More than 20 million Mexicans have come across the Rio Grande. Together with another 15 million people from other parts of Latin America, they constitute a large and growing group of Hispanic-Americans.

Generally, these non-European Americans have a higher birth rate than European Americans.[22] The population has also grown more on the Pacific coast, looking to Asia, and in the South, looking to Latin America, than on the Atlantic seaboard of the country, looking to Europe. The proportion of US citizens who are of European origin is projected to decline from 80 per cent in 1980 to 64 per cent in 2020, while that of Hispanic-Americans is expected to rise from 6 to 15 per cent and of Asian-Americans from 2 to 7 per cent.[23] Even on these projections, European Americans will remain a clear majority. Hispanic-Americans come from Latin America but they speak a European language, Spanish – a fact which Spain very reasonably hopes to capitalize on, strengthening its own special relationship across the Atlantic. Most Hispanic-Americans are also members of a Christian church that still has its headquarters in Rome, Europe.[24] Nevertheless, the change is fraught with consequence.

African-Americans, Hispanic-Americans and Asian-Americans can hardly think of Europe as 'parents' lands' or 'mother and father', to recall the language of *Life*'s 1951 picture history, in the way that Jack Weishaar somehow still does. Nor can they readily identify with Western Man ('fair of skin, hardy of limb'). Instead, their cultural representatives have recalled the 'Black Atlantic' of the slave trade, demanded that less attention be paid to authors who are Dead White European Males, and chanted 'Heigh ho, heigh ho, Western Civ has got to go!' Which it has, in most American universities, at least in name. A country that is increasingly multi-ethnic in practice has become self-consciously multicultural in theory. At the beginning of the twentieth century, few Americans doubted that America was in some sense a child of Europe – a better version of an older self. At the beginning of the twenty-first, many no longer think of it as umbilically linked to Europe.

A second underlying change has occurred among European Americans, especially those of a younger generation. Crudely put, this is the fading of the Henry Jamesian cultural fascination with Europe and the disappearance of any lingering sense of cultural inferiority. No longer does the celebration of a shared Western Civilization give American students the thrill of belonging, in William McNeill's perhaps unintentionally revealing words, to a 'great, *cultivated, sophisticated* world of "us"' (my italics). Gone are the days when a young American would sit star-struck in a corner of the Deux Magots café in Paris, while intellectual demi-gods called Sartre or Merleau-Ponty swanned by, and remain long in awe of Oxford's honey-stoned medieval quadrangles. A retired American diplomat of long European experience expressed this subtle change vividly in an e-mail to me. 'When I first went to Europe in the 1940s and 1950s,' he wrote, 'Europe was superior to us. The superiority was not personal – I never felt demeaned even by condescending people – but civilizational.' Not any more. America, he concluded, 'is no longer abashed'.[25]

Europeans, especially British Europeans, sometimes still like to think they can be, as Harold Macmillan put it, Greeks to America's Rome.[26] But the new Rome has absorbed what the Greeks have to offer. Its best universities, journals and think tanks are, on the whole, better than Europe's. The traffic in ideas now generally flows from New York to Paris and Harvard to Oxford, not the other way round. And if there are still a few clever Greeks left, well, they can usually be hired to augment those American universities, journals and think tanks.

The end of the Cold War made a difference in this respect, too. During the Cold War, Americans might not have liked the ideas coming out of Paris or Rome or Berlin, but they clearly mattered since the

United States was engaged in a political conflict, centred on Europe, that was also an ideological one – a battle of ideas. Today, who cares what Paris is thinking? Yet five minutes in any Parisian bookshop shows you how passionately Paris still cares what Washington is thinking. The connection between the balance of power and what we might call the balance of fascination is complex and two-sided. Power is fascinating. (Americans were a lot more interested in what Russian novelists wrote when Russia was a superpower.) But being fascinating is also power. The charms of both 'high' and popular culture are part of what Joseph Nye has called 'soft power',[27] the power to attract, and this is by no means simply a by-product of military or economic power. Like the balance of hard power, the balance of fascination has shifted from Europe to America.

The gradual metamorphosis in European–American relations can be illuminated by pursuing the family metaphors so often invoked to characterize those relations. For the growing number of non-European Americans, Europe never was 'mother' or 'father'. For many European Americans, *Life*'s 'mother and father' have become somewhat troublesome adolescent children. This is an image I heard repeatedly in the 1990s, not least from members of the Clinton administration. But for many Europeans the 'daughter of Europe' – as de Gaulle called the United States – has turned into a large and bossy uncle. Europeans don't like to think of themselves as America's nephew, let alone its son – are they not, after all, its parents? – but some such dependent relationship is implicit when they talk of 'emancipation'. Parents do not usually seek 'emancipation' from their children. Putting this all together, we find that Europe is an adolescent son rebelling against an American uncle who was himself originally Europe's daughter. These hopelessly mixed metaphors of age, sex and family relationship are not simply the product of confusion. Rather, they perfectly reflect the tangled historical and emotional crossovers between the old new Europe on the western side of the Atlantic and the new old Europe on its eastern side.

Let's stay for a moment with the American picture of Europe as 'petulant sixteen-year-old'.[28] Anyone who has had teenage sons knows how uneven they can be: very mature in one way, still childish in another. Today's EU is a clear case of uneven development: already middle-aged as an economic power; a young adult in civilian aspects of foreign policy; pre-pubescent in its (in)capacity for coordinated military action. Yet the US also exhibits symptoms of parental ambivalence. Its usual complaint is that 'the Europeans' cannot 'get their act together', but it's equally worried when they do – in trade disputes, for example, or on environmental policy. It was easy for John F. Kennedy to say in 1962 that the United States did not regard a strong, united Europe as a rival, since the then European Economic Community of just six countries, with Germany divided and wholly dependent on American protection, could not possibly be a rival to the United States. Viewing the European Union of 1992 and after, that is less immediately clear – to Europeans, especially Euro-Gaullists, but also to Americans. So America's problem with Europe is partly that it will not 'grow up' and partly that it has.

## EUROPEAN AMERICANS AT WORK

Iraq was not the first post-Cold War crisis of the West. Bosnia was. When Yugoslavia began to be torn apart by post-communist nation-alists in 1991, the administration of President George H. W. Bush decided to leave this one to 'the Europeans', as the United States' European allies are habitually known in Washington. 'We have no dog in that fight,' Secretary of State James Baker is often quoted as saying.[29] Some European leaders, levitating with the euphoria of the time, were delighted to take up the challenge. The Luxembourgeois foreign minister Jacques Poos, on a mission to disintegrating Yugoslavia, declared that the hour of Europe had come.[30] 'If one problem can be solved by the Europeans,' said the ineffable Poos, 'it is the Yugoslav problem. It is not up to the Americans or anyone else.'[31]

A year later James Baker seriously considered military intervention against the Bosnian Serbs, but his right-hand man and successor Lawrence Eagleburger was adamant: the US should not intervene. This would be a test for the Europeans. If they managed to pass it, that would lighten an American foreign policy agenda already heavy with the disintegration of the Soviet Union and the Gulf War against the occupier of Kuwait, Saddam Hussein. If they failed, as Eagle-burger suspected they would, that could usefully curb their Euro-Gaullist pride. 'They will screw it up,' Eagleburger said, according to a note-taker present at one State Department meeting, 'and this will teach them a lesson.'[32]

Europe 'screwed it up' all right. While EU representatives made endless diplomatic efforts to halt the bloodshed, and while EU national governments argued among themselves, more than 200,000 Europeans, among them many unarmed civilians, women and chil-dren, were brutally murdered by other Europeans. At least 3 million people were driven out of their homes. This was bad old Europe, as it had not been seen since 1945. If Milošević was the new Hitler, then for some politically engaged Americans the British prime minister, John Major, was the new Neville Chamberlain, closely followed by the perfidious French. The point here is not to argue the justice or injustice of these American charges.* The point is about the impact on American attitudes to Europe.

Bosnia made many in Washington feel – or feel once more – that you could not trust 'the Europeans'. The Europeans were appeasers: weak, divided, duplicitous and even downright treacherous. (Three French officers were found to have been spying for the Serbs.) The sentiment could be heard not just among right-wing Republicans traditionally suspicious of Europe but among lifelong liberal Euro-peanists, in the State Department and elsewhere. On this occasion, the British were definitely among 'the Europeans'. In stark contrast to the Iraq crisis, Britain stood shoulder-to-shoulder with France in blocking American policy over Bosnia. Indeed, for some Americans involved, John Major and his foreign secretary, Douglas Hurd, rep-resented the worst of cynical old European *Realpolitik*. By the autumn of 1994, when transatlantic tensions came to a head over the issue of whether to launch air strikes to save the so-called 'safe area' of Bihać, sober observers suggested that relations between Washington and London were as bad as they had been during the Suez Crisis of 1956 – when Britain had also stood with France.

* In truth, every major Western state, including the United States, deserved a share of the blame, but it would require another book – an important book, and one that still needs to be written – to establish in what proportions.

Yet what was most instructive was the outcome of this first post-Cold War crisis of the West. The Clinton administration, which had agonized and vacillated about Bosnia ever since it had come to power in January 1993, decided that mending the rifts in the transatlantic alliance took priority over air strikes to drive back the Serbs around Bihać. As one senior official explained at the time, American leaders 'agreed that Nato is more important than Bosnia . . .'[33]

By 1995, the Clinton administration had finally resolved to end the Bosnian war, an engagement personified by the rumbunctious figure of Richard Holbrooke. However, it would do so multilaterally, not unilaterally. It would work with its traditional European allies, forcefully, even overbearingly in private, but still work with them and not around them. If military force was needed to stop the Bosnian Serbs, and Slobodan Milošević, it would wherever possible apply that force through its long-established transatlantic alliance. What's more, the Clinton administration would make the renewal and enlargement of Nato, to include the new democracies of post-communist Europe, the strategic centrepiece of its European policy. Beside the new EU there should be a new Nato. Together, these should constitute the 'Euro-atlantic structures' to sustain a Europe whole and free, as Václav Havel and other central European leaders put it repeatedly, to some effect in Washington. The West could be reborn, even without a Soviet devil to fight.

This was the strategy the Clinton administration pursued for the next six years. Its climax came in the spring of 1999 when Nato was enlarged to include Poland, the Czech Republic and Hungary, and then, within a fortnight, went to war for the first time in its history to prevent Milošević perpetrating 'another Bosnia' in Kosovo. Americans were also influential behind the scenes in supporting the Serbs who finally overthrew Milošević in a largely peaceful revolution in the autumn of 2000. The European Union carried the main burden of civil reconstruction after conflict, in Bosnia and elsewhere, but wherever I went in the Balkans at this time, people said 'the international community . . . I mean, the Americans'. Poles, Czechs and Hungarians felt that, of the two great Brussels-based institutions of the Cold War West, the American-led Nato had embraced them sooner and more warmly than the European Union. They had thought the EU was their family but found it behaved towards them like a rich man's club; they had thought Nato was an exclusive Western club, but received a family welcome.

There were good as well as bad reasons for this asymmetry. The EU was a qualitatively different and far more complicated organization than Nato. It asked more of new members but would also, in time, give them more. None the less, the contrast reinforced an already very positive image of America in most of central and eastern Europe. When Donald Rumsfeld noted with satisfaction the positive stance taken by 'new Europe' towards America's policy of toppling Saddam Hussein, he was benefiting from the aversion to dictators of people who had until recently lived under dictators; he was also bringing in Clinton's harvest.

This policy reflected a rational calculation of enlightened self-interest by the United States. It was the work of European Americans and American Europeanists, moved by memories and sentiments as well as calculations. Clinton's second Secretary of State, Madeleine Albright, was Czech. She had been born in Prague and her family driven into exile by the communist takeover in 1948. She was steeped in the lessons of European history. At one fractious meeting about Kosovo in London, she dismissed a compromise proposal with the words 'do you think we're in Munich?'.[34] You had only to see Madeleine Albright in the company of Václav Havel and other Czech friends to understand how much it meant to her that her native land should join Nato. Richard Holbrooke had worked in the trans-atlantic foreign policy community for years, and been ambassador to Germany. A concluding section of his book on Bosnia was entitled 'America, Still a European Power'.[35] Another of Clinton's key foreign policy advisers, Strobe Talbott, was a leading specialist on Russia. He had started translating Khrushchev's memoirs while at Oxford University, and much of his life had been spent charting Soviet–American relations. Clinton himself had studied at Oxford. He had written essays on European politics, demonstrated in London against the Vietnam War and travelled to Scandinavia, the Soviet Union, Czechoslovakia and Spain.

These biographies matter. Clinton's elective affinities with Europe were also ideological. In what he called a 'floating opera'[36] of meetings to discuss a political 'third way' he sought broad, internationalist left-liberal answers to the common problems facing developed capitalist democracies in an age of globalization. This dialogue was wider than just Europe and America – it included Australia, Canada and Latin American countries such as Brazil – but at its heart was a transatlantic conversation with fellow left-liberal politicians of the same generation, especially Tony Blair and Gerhard Schröder. Instead of confronting a common military enemy, the Soviet Union, they would now tackle common economic and social challenges. For example, Clinton argued that a free market society like the United States had a regrettably high level of income inequality but 'in countries that have chosen to make sure that did not happen, very often there have been quite high levels of unemployment . . . which is another form of social inequality'. However, he went on, 'I think virtually every European country has done a better job than the United States in providing adequate family leave policies, adequate child care policies, adequate supports.'[37]

Unsurprisingly, this kind of discourse went down well in Europe. When Clinton then talked of 'shared values' between Europe and America, Europeans were more likely to believe him. Except for his Baptist religiosity, the internationalist, welfare-oriented, socially and sexually liberal old '68er Bill Clinton spoke like a European – which is precisely what the Republican right hated about him. America's cultural revolution of the 1960s had provoked a cultural counter-revolution. During the 1990s, the divide between these two Americas widened. In her book *One Nation, Two Cultures*, the conservative historian Gertrude Himmelfarb wrote 'Europeans used to complain of the Americanization (the "coca-colaization") of European culture. They may be getting their revenge by witnessing the Europeanization (or de-moralization) of American culture.'[38] So for Himmelfarb, Europeanization meant de-moralization.

Polemicists of the right attacked both Clintonites and liberal Europeans with equal acerbity. One of the most outspoken of them, Jonah Goldberg, popularized the label 'cheese-eating surrender monkeys', originally drawn from an episode of *The Simpsons*, to describe the French, and charged Europeans with 'thinking they achieved lasting peace through endless conversations in Swiss hotels with bottles of bubbly water and plates of runny cheese scattered around the table'.[39] In attacking 'Europeans', Goldberg explained to me in a conversation in Washington, he and his fellow conservatives were also attacking self-hating American liberals who assumed that abroad, especially Europe, must be better. Conversely, 'Europeans' were also stalking-horses for American liberals. So, in effect, Clinton was a European? 'Yes,' said Goldberg, 'or at least, he *thinks* like a European.'[40]

This was not intended as a compliment. But it could be taken as such, especially if the president happened to be in Europe. At the end of his second term, Clinton was awarded the Charlemagne Prize in Aachen – the first American president ever to receive this most prestigious European political honour. In his acceptance speech, a summing-up of his European policy, he said '[the] shining light of European Union is a matter of the utmost importance, not just to Europeans, but to everyone on this planet'.[41] The EU could be a model for other parts of the earth. Europe was 'a unifying idea as much as a particular place'. Europe and the United States had repeated differences, but 'the simple fact is that, since Europe is an idea as much as a place, America also is a part of Europe, bound by ties of family, history and values'. Emphasizing the scale of transatlantic economic interdependence, he concluded: 'Lord Palmerston's rule that countries have no permanent alliances, only permanent interests, simply does not apply to our relationship. For America has a permanent interest in a permanent alliance with Europe.' You must, of course, discount for the speaker's desire to please his European audience of the day, but this still remains an amazing statement of commitment. Ten years after the end of the Cold War, and 224 years after the Declaration of Independence, an American president said: 'America also is a part of Europe.'

As Clinton's presidency came to an end, the transatlantic alliance had therefore in some respects been renewed. Conducting a bombing campaign with eighteen allies – some of them demanding a veto on individual targets – had not endeared the idea of coalition warfare to the Pentagon. The failure to reach a peace settlement between Israel and the Palestinians, despite all Clinton's strenuous efforts, left a time-bomb still ticking for transatlantic relations. There were nagging concerns about differing responses to international terrorism, Iran and Saddam Hussein's Iraq. But the Democrats' candidate to succeed Clinton, Al Gore, could look forward to addressing these problems with, for the most part, like-minded Europeans, and Europeans could look forward to working with a man they already knew quite well.

In the presidential election of 2000, Al Gore won roughly half a million more votes than George W. Bush. It is, of course, impossible to know what would have happened if the American electoral system had translated those votes into victory or if the Supreme Court had not stopped the Florida recount. It would be absurd to imagine that any president could simply have continued with 'business as usual' after the 9/11 attacks, but Gore's track record as vice president in the Clinton administration would suggest an approach to the world in general, and Europe in particular, very different from that of George W. Bush.

If so, a President Gore would have had some support from his voters. In December 2002, the Ipsos-Reid polling group included in their regular survey of American public opinion a few questions formulated for the purposes of this book.[42] Asked to choose one of four statements about American versus European approaches to diplomacy and war, 30 per cent of Democratic voters but only 6 per cent of Republican voters chose 'The Europeans seem to prefer diplomatic solutions over war and that is a positive value Americans could learn from.' By contrast, only 13 per cent of Democrats but 35 per cent of Republicans chose 'The Europeans are too willing to seek compromise rather than to stand up for freedom even if it means war, and that is a negative thing.' The divide was even clearer when respondents were asked to pick between two statements about 'the way in which the war on Iraq should be conducted'. Fifty-nine per cent of Republicans as opposed to just 33 per cent of Democrats chose 'The US must remain in control of all operations and prevent its European allies from limiting the States' room to maneuver.' By contrast, 55 per cent of Democrats and just 34 per cent of Republicans chose 'It is imperative that the United States allies itself with European countries, even if it limits its ability to make its own decisions.'

So was it, as Robert Kagan would argue, that Europeans were

from Mars and Americans were from Venus? Or was it simply that Republicans were from Mars and Democrats from Venus?

## UNILATERALISM

'Do we want the European Union to succeed?' asked President Bush, at the White House meeting to prepare him for his first official visit to Europe in the summer of 2001.[43] When two British visitors insisted that they certainly did, and the United States should too, the president quickly said, with a tight smile, 'that was a provocation!'. But he was not alone in posing this question. Many American policymakers, especially but not exclusively Republicans, were asking whether it was in the American national interest to have a strong, united Europe. The answer was less evident to them than it had been to American presidents from Truman to Clinton.

At the same time, Europe was simply less important to them than it had been to Americans for at least sixty years, since the United States entered the Second World War in 1941. From the lofty vantage point of Washington's new global pre-eminence, politicians who had no special ties to Europe could view the old continent as just one among many. Europe was no longer the central theatre of world politics. With Milošević gone, it was not the source of any urgent foreign policy problem for the United States. Given the European Union's underdeveloped foreign policy coordination and military capability, it was a complicated, troublesome, endlessly time-consuming partner – and one that seemed inclined to define itself, in Gaullist fashion, against the United States. Perhaps, in the new strategic situation of the United States, it might be simpler and more rewarding to build alliances with a few major individual European powers?

We should always beware the danger of attributing to an American administration a coherence that it does not possess. The Bush administration was torn between strong personalities in key departments with differing approaches: Colin Powell at the State Department, Donald Rumsfeld at the Pentagon, Dick Cheney as vice president. Each can only be properly understood through an individual biography. But in this administration there were at least three distinct strands. One was a traditional moderate Republicanism, pursuing American national goals through what Colin Powell called 'a strategy of partnerships'.[44] Another, endlessly discussed by Europeans, was the 'neoconservatives': highly focused, ideological, committed to building up American military strength but also to a policy of actively transforming the Middle East around Israel, in the name of American values as well as interests. The third strand was an American nationalism which looked to make the United States a dominant, even invulnerable power, both militarily and economically, but did not have an ideological agenda for the domestic transformation of other parts of the world. Although this strand was often hard to separate from the 'neoconservative' one, and practically allied to it in many cases, the starting-point was different. Cheney, Rumsfeld and probably Bush himself started closer to this position.

Nationalism is such a chameleon word, and nowadays usually a pejorative one, that I should say briefly what I mean here. European nationalists, in the particular sense in which I have used the term, aspire to make Europe a nation, and preferably a second 'world nation' to rival the United States. Like nineteenth-century German, Italian or Polish nationalists, their aim is to create a political entity that does not yet exist. American nationalists, in the sense in which I'm using the term here, are different. Their sovereign nation-state already exists. But for them, the pursuit of its military, economic and political interests, including its thirst for oil, will almost always override those of other nations or a wider international community, let alone the long-term future of humankind on this planet. Where exactly someone crosses the line between patriotism, in the sober defence of your country's legitimate interests, and this kind of nationalism is often hard to say. It would be foolish to pretend this is a sharp, clear-cut distinction. But I have no hesitation in asserting that this administration contained American nationalists. The one thing they had in common with European nationalists was the mental habit, so sharply identified by George Orwell, of assuming that whole blocks of tens of millions of human beings can be lumped together and confidently labelled 'good' or 'bad'.

In the end, the president's voice would be decisive, but in the summer of 2001 the president was still finding his way. He started, as he told his European visitors, with 'a certain feeling' that 'our great country' was too much tied into multilateral alliances and inter-national organizations. He also felt that the Clinton administration had intervened too indiscriminately in countries around the world, using soldiers for inappropriate humanitarian tasks, such as escorting children to school – 'cross-walk soldiers', as he put it – and for so-called nation-building.

With little personal knowledge of Europe, he set a lot of store by his personal impressions of individual European leaders. He liked Blair and, funnily enough in the light of subsequent developments, he liked Jacques Chirac. He 'had some problems' with Gerhard Schröder and Joschka Fischer. Part of his problem, I suspect, was that both were '68ers, of the kind he thoroughly distrusted. He was himself the flip side of that '68er generation: the conservative un-Clinton. Schröder was a German Clinton and Joschka Fischer, worse still, was a Green. If there was one thing Bush definitely did not like, it was Greens. (A former speechwriter, David Frum, reports that he pri-vately referred to them as 'green-green-lima-beans'.[45]) So he had no regrets about withdrawing from the Kyoto Treaty on global warm-ing. 'Kyoto is mush,' he said. It would have been bad for the US and, frankly, he thought that in the Kyoto negotiation the Europeans 'were trying to screw us'. The US needed more energy, not less. Other, tech-nologically smart ways should be found to conserve energy and save the environment – and he had some people looking into them.[46]

The environment was one of two foreign policy areas on which the new president had firm, well-developed views. The other was defence. He made a sharp and passionate case for a space-based national missile defence. In his inaugural address, he had said plainly: 'we will build our defenses beyond challenge'.[47] A detailed report from an important conservative pressure group, the Project for a New American Century, had already spelled out in September 2000 how this should be done and what extra defence spending would be needed. Several of its signatories – including Paul Wolfowitz, I. Lewis ('Scooter') Libby and Dov Zakheim – were now on the job, in the Pentagon and the vice president's office. In the summer of 2001, they had already requested a $32 billion increase in defence spending.[48]

This administration's neo-Reaganite determination to seize a historic opportunity to make the United States militarily invincible predated the 9/11 attacks.

In these two areas, to the horror of most Europeans, the Bush administration started life by walking away from a whole series of proposed or existing international agreements, not only the Kyoto accord but a treaty to control the worldwide traffic in small arms, a treaty to eliminate landmines, and the Biological and Toxic Weapons Convention. It clearly signalled its intention to terminate the Anti-Ballistic Missile (ABM) Treaty with Russia and to oppose the creation of an International Criminal Court. This approach was celebrated by one of its most vigorous journalistic supporters, Charles Krauthammer, as 'the new unilateralism'. 'After a decade of Prometheus playing pygmy,' he wrote, here at last was 'an administration willing to assert American freedom of action and the primacy of American national interests'.[49] Prometheus unbound.

Assertive unilateralism was thus a hallmark of the second Bush presidency from the outset. But in many areas of policy its position was still unclear – and internally disputed. The first presidential trip to Europe, in June 2001, was conciliatory in tone. It included a strong endorsement for the further eastward enlargement of America's favourite multilateral organization, Nato, a more perfunctory expression of support for the EU, and a clear statement that there was no conflict between the two. His choice of destinations was interesting: not France or Germany, not even Britain, but, apart from Brussels for a Nato summit, Sweden, Spain and Poland. Was this already Rumsfeld's 'new Europe' in the making? Or was it the crablike beginning of a return to a more multilateral approach? What would have happened if Osama bin Laden had not attacked the United States? We will never know. George W. Bush himself cannot know what George W. Bush would have done in less traumatic circumstances.

## WAR

'The Pearl Harbor of the 21st century took place today,' Bush dictated into his diary on the night of 11 September 2001.[50] That comparison with Pearl Harbor was repeatedly made by Condoleeza Rice, his National Security Adviser. The media agreed with the president that America was now 'at war'. The country was bedecked with flags and joined in a great outpouring of patriotic solidarity, from sea to shining sea. Only the most hard-bitten European anti-American could remain unmoved by the suffering of the victims' relatives and the spontaneous singing of 'America, the Beautiful'. There was also a harsher tune, which sounded through already in the rescue workers' persistent chants of 'USA! USA!' as President Bush visited Ground Zero for the first time – a note of belligerent defiance, hissing, like the rattlesnake on the old Revolutionary flag, 'Don't Tread on Me'. Bush would catch that Jacksonian note very clearly.

In Washington, more clearly than anywhere else, you saw the clash of power and vulnerability; and the closer you were to the centre of power, the stronger your sense of both. The 'most powerful man on earth' was told after the 9/11 attacks that any one of those planes he could watch through the windows of the oval drawing room, taking off from Ronald Reagan National Airport and flying up the River Potomac, could alter course and hit the White House in about forty seconds.[51] A senior military aide to the vice president told me that the more they learned about possible ways for terrorists to use atomic, biological or chemical weapons, the more alarming it became. However, the people at the top also knew better than anyone what extraordinary, no longer just metaphorically 'space-age', military power lay at their disposal. The so-called 'revolution in military affairs' had already taken them another technological generation beyond the satellite-controlled precision bombing of Kosovo. Like the Martians in H. G. Wells's *War of the Worlds*, they possessed the technology to find and destroy almost anything or anyone, anywhere in the world, with the target never knowing what had hit him.[52] Yet it was they, the Martians, who had been hit. They must fight back, and win. But how, and against whom?

If Americans outside Washington gradually lost this sense of being actively 'at war', most Europeans never had it. Tony Blair, who flew to New York and Washington immediately after the attacks, was an exception to prove the rule. During the Cold War, Atlanticists had constantly worried whether America would really put its life on the line against a threat which only directly affected Europe. Few had anticipated that it would happen the other way round: an attack on America which did not directly threaten Europe. Yet initially, Europeans rallied to America as if the Red Army had just attacked Berlin. A black drape on the Brandenburg Gate declared 'we mourn with you'. For the first time in its history, Nato invoked Article 5 of the 1949 North Atlantic Treaty, declaring this attack on one Nato member to be an attack on them all, and offering every possible assistance.

The offer was politely acknowledged, but not taken up. A revealing account of a meeting between Bush's top officials on 30 September 2001, based on official records, notes 'after a brief discussion of the Nato resolution invoking Article 5 . . . Rumsfeld turned to the idea of a white paper'.[53] Pressed by Condoleeza Rice to say what the French, Germans, Canadians or 'Aussies' could do to help, Rumsfeld stalled. As the veteran reporter Bob Woodward summarizes Rumsfeld's argument: 'The coalition had to fit the conflict and not the other way round . . . Maybe they didn't need a French frigate.'[54]

It's interesting to speculate what would have happened if the Bush administration had taken a conscious political decision to make the war of self-defence against al-Qaeda in Afghanistan a Nato war, however little that helped – indeed, however much that complicated – the actual military operation. That was what the more instinctively multilateralist administration of George H. W. Bush probably would have done, but the ways of the son were not those of the father. Nato might still be the centrepiece of America's political strategy for Europe; it would be marginal to America's military strategy for a global 'war on terror'.

Over the next eighteen months, America acted and Europe reacted. Although the bombing of civilians in Afghanistan was fiercely criticized by anti-war protesters in Europe, the Afghan war against al-Qaeda generally carried mainstream European opinion with it. However, a first wave of wider criticism followed the detention without trial or customary rights of suspected terrorists at Guantanamo Bay, including some who were citizens of European states. Bush's State of the Union address in January 2002 then identified an 'axis of evil' linking Iraq, Iran and North Korea. Europeans were unsettled by the religious moralism of the word 'evil', but even more by the word 'axis'. For unlike the Second World War 'Axis' of Nazi Germany, fascist Italy and imperial Japan, Iraq, Iran and North Korea were not allied in any way. European policymakers saw their policy of constructive engagement with 'reformers' inside the Iranian regime threatened by this rhetoric, rather as they had seen their policy of détente with Eastern Europe in the 1980s imperilled by Ronald Reagan's description of the Soviet Union as an 'evil empire'.

In early 2002, the conflict between a renewed Palestinian intifada and the militant, right-wing Sharon government in Israel reached new heights of brutality, with Palestinian suicide bombers killing Israeli civilians and Sharon's forces killing Palestinian civilians and besieging Yasser Arafat in his headquarters. That time-bomb for transatlantic relations, which Clinton had tried so hard to defuse, now exploded. Few Europeans noticed that Clinton himself had blamed Arafat for failing to accept the best offer of a Palestinian state that Israel had ever been persuaded to make. (When Arafat congratulated Clinton on being 'a great man', the outgoing president reportedly replied: 'The hell I am. I'm a colossal failure, and you made me one.'[55]) But for months the Bush administration's policy was one-sided: effectively demanding that the Palestinians replace Arafat with another leader while endorsing Sharon's brutal campaign as part of the global 'war on terror'. It was no accident that the largest banner at an anti-Bush demonstration in Trafalgar Square, on the president's visit to London in 2003, read simply 'Free Palestine'.

However, European support for the Palestinian cause was often as one-eyed as the Bush administration's endorsement of the Sharon government. European pro-Palestinianism, in turn, fed accusations on the Republican right that the old vampire of anti-Semitism was again abroad in Europe. 'In Europe, it is not very safe to be a Jew,' wrote Charles Krauthammer in the *Washington Post*. 'What we are seeing is pent-up anti-Semitism, the release – with Israel as the trigger – of a millennium-old urge that powerfully infected and shaped European history.'[56] In making these sweeping charges, American commentators conflated three different things: European sympathy with the Palestinians and criticism of Washington's one-sided support of Sharon's Israel; residual or revived anti-Semitism among Europe's native populist right; and violent attacks on Jews by Muslims living in Europe. The first was disqualified by conflating it with the second and third. Such swingeing accusations, in turn, encouraged some Europeans to mutter about the influence of a 'Jewish lobby' or 'Zionist neoconservatives' in the US, which, in turn, spawned more accusations of European anti-Semitism, and so on and down.

Innocuous by comparison, but none the less contributing to the deterioration, was President Bush's imposition in March 2002 of tariffs on imports of European steel. This undermined the Hamiltonian high ground he had consistently taken on free trade. It was seen for what it was: a piece of political opportunism, wooing steel-producing swing states before the mid-term Congressional elections. Above all, it reinforced his pre-9/11 reputation for unilateralism.

In September, the president unveiled his new national security strategy.[57] Europeans fastened, with alarm, on two points: his aspiration to put American military power 'beyond challenge' and his endorsement of 'pre-emptive actions' against threats from terrorists and rogue states, such as had materialized on 9/11 a year before. In fact, the aspiration to make America militarily invincible had been expressed in identical words in his inaugural address, well before 9/11. The doctrine of pre-emption, however, was new. To be sure, President Clinton had already ordered, in a 1995 directive on US counter-terrorism policy, that the US should 'deter *and pre-empt*, apprehend and prosecute . . . individuals who perpetrate *or plan to perpetrate* [terrorist] attacks' (my italics).[58] There was 'no higher priority', Clinton's directive concluded, than preventing terrorist groups acquiring weapons of mass destruction. But it took the combination of the 9/11 shock and this particular administration to make pre-emption a central plank of national security strategy.

Europeans rightly argued – as did many Americans – that this doctrine could set a dangerous precedent. Any state could strike at any other, claiming that it was thereby 'pre-empting' a potential terrorist threat. (When Israel had bombed an Iraqi nuclear reactor in 1981, the United States had condemned the attack.) Moreover, any state might claim that, in order to protect its sources of secret intelligence, it could not even fully divulge the nature of the threat. You'd just have to take it on trust. On the other hand, Europeans, not feeling themselves to be at war, were slow to acknowledge that the combination of secret terrorist cells, rogue or failed states and weapons of mass destruction posed a qualitatively new kind of threat. Did Europeans have any security strategy of their own to meet this challenge? They did not. The EU's High Representative for Foreign and Security Policy, Javier Solana, only produced a draft European security strategy nine months later, trailing behind the American one.

Europeans also fixed on a blank restatement, in the national security strategy, of America's refusal to submit its citizens, and especially its soldiers, to the International Criminal Court. Yet they often ignored the rest of the document, which emphasized the need for international cooperation, the importance of free markets and free trade (give or take the odd steel tariff), the imperative of development aid for the half of humankind living on less than $2 a day, and, above all, the need to spread human rights, the rule of law and democracy. 'Banalities', you might say, 'like motherhood and apple pie.' But you would be wrong. This was seriously meant, and it was a significant departure for a president who had started with an instinctive preference for preserving America as a Jeffersonian beacon rather than making it a Wilsonian crusader for democracy. 'Wilsonianism' is not a quality I'm arbitrarily attributing to this document. Lamenting European reaction to the national security strategy, one senior administration official told me 'the Wilsonian is getting buried'. What they aimed to do, said this very senior official, was 'to merge Wilsonianism with power'.[59]

The test case, both for pre-emption and for offensive Wilsonianism, was to be Iraq. Pre-emptive actions, said the national security strategy, would always be 'to eliminate a specific threat to the United States or our allies and friends. The reasons for our action will be clear, the force measured, and the cause just.' What was the 'specific threat' in Iraq? What were 'the reasons for our action'? Plainly, no one believed that Saddam was behind al-Qaeda. Did American leaders really conclude from their own intelligence sources that there was a clear and present danger from Saddam's weapons of mass destruction? Tony Blair convinced himself of that, but did George W. Bush?

Iraq had been unfinished business for some Republicans ever since President George H. W. Bush had refrained from going all the way to Baghdad at the end of the first Gulf War. When Saddam Hussein expelled UN weapon inspectors in 1998, the Project for a New American Century had written to President Clinton urging that American policy should now aim 'at the removal of Saddam Hussein's regime from power'.[60] An impressive number of signatories to that letter were now in key positions in the second Bush administration. They included Donald Rumsfeld, Paul Wolfowitz and Richard Perle, all now at the Pentagon; John Bolton and Richard Armitage, both now at the State Department; and Robert F. Zoellick, the country's main trade negotiator.

At the very first meeting of the new National Security Council, in January 2001, Bush asked of his National Security Adviser, Condoleeza Rice, 'what's on the agenda?' and she replied 'How Iraq is destabilizing the region, Mr President'. They then pored over a 'tablecloth-size' grainy photograph of what the director of the CIA, George Tenet, said might be a factory producing materials for chemical or biological weapons.[61] We also know that Rumsfeld and Wolfowitz forcefully raised the possibility of going after Iraq at top-level meetings with the president immediately following the 9/11 attacks. But a decision was taken: not now, not yet.[62]

Seen from the Oval Office, the escalation to war with Iraq was therefore slow and measured. It had been on the conservative agenda long before George W. Bush came to power. It had been considered and put aside, for the time being, in September 2001. Washington was at war, and this 'war on terror' was not going to stop with Afghanistan – especially as the United States had been denied the crowning symbolic victory of capturing Osama bin Laden, dead or alive. Militarily, Iraq was a conventional war which the United States' armed forces could undoubtedly win, unlike the shadowy war against al-Qaeda. It was the obvious next step. Should the United States do it unilaterally? The president's position was much as it had been over Afghanistan: 'if we have to go it alone, we'll go it alone; but I'd rather not'.[63] Blair's was only one voice among many that took him down 'the UN route'. Bush gave the UN route six months and Colin Powell's best shot, but he would not wait any longer for two second-rank old European powers, France and Britain, to sort out their obstinate diplomatic differences. So far as he was concerned, it was not for the US to prove its case to the UN; it was for the UN to prove its relevance in a global war against evil.

Our subject here is not America's long and winding road to war with Iraq; it's what that road revealed about America's changing attitude to multilateralism, to working with 'the Europeans' and other free people around the world, including Canadians, 'Aussies' and many more. As regards Europe specifically, three elements were both highlighted and exacerbated. First, there was Europe's lost centrality. In the index to Bob Woodward's blow-by-blow account of Washington's policy from 9/11 to the end of the war in Afghanistan, the names Chirac and Schröder do not appear at all, and Nato only gets six mentions.[64] If President Bush did not phone Chancellor Schröder for months at the height of the Iraq crisis, thus encouraging Schröder to line up with Chirac against Blair, this was partly because Bush felt he had been double-crossed by that German Clinton. But it was also because an American president no longer felt he needed to phone the German chancellor on the central issue of the day.

Second, there was an undercurrent of anti-Europeanism. The Bush administration had European Americans and American Europeanists of its own. Donald Rumsfeld himself was of German ancestry and had served as ambassador to Nato in Brussels. Richard Perle and Paul Wolfowitz knew Europe well. But precisely those who knew Europe best were most suspicious of it. 'The Europeans', in their view, had been weak, divided, duplicitous appeasers of Hitler in the 1930s, of Moscow in the Reaganite 1980s, of Milošević over Bosnia in the early 1990s; now they would again be weak, divided, duplicitous appeasers of Saddam. In the tradition of cynical European *Realpolitik*, 'the Europeans' cared in each case more for 'stability' than for human rights and democracy. Europe, said Richard Perle in November 2002, had lost its 'moral compass' and France its 'moral fibre'.[65] To the extent that Britain was an exception, it was not European.

In addition, Europeans were smothered by outsize welfare states, rampant relativism, and lifestyle liberalism: they were, so to speak, congenitally Clintonian. Also, the old European demon of anti-Semitism was raising its head again over the issue of Israel and

Palestine, while European countries with large Muslim populations (such as France) were appeasing their own minorities. Taken all in all, this amounted to a settled, negative view of 'the Europeans' which can fairly be described as anti-Europeanism, although anti-Europeans would naturally deny that charge, just as anti-Americans usually deny being anti-American. Anti-Europeanism and anti-Americanism are, however, deeply asymmetrical. The emotional leit-motif of European anti-Americanism is resentment mingled with envy; that of American anti-Europeanism is irritation mixed with contempt.[66]

Finally, there was the temptation to divide and rule. During the Bush administration, the United States' growing ambivalence about the European Union for the first time resulted in the formulation of an American policy of 'disaggregation'.[67] That term came from Richard Haass, a moderate Republican Europeanist at the State Department. Haass himself explained this as a pragmatic reaction to the difficulty of getting a coherent position out of a divided and enlarging Europe. He would subsequently praise Europe as America's 'best pool of partners' in the world.[68] But the image of a 'pool of part-ners' itself implies something very different from the old Nato alliance. If all the little and medium-sized European fish want to swim along with the big American carp, as one European shoal, that's fine; if not, America will find enough individual fish for any given purpose.

One conservative commentator went further, arguing that the United States should have a conscious strategy of 'cherry-picking' its allies in Europe.[69] Given the presence of pro-American governments in Britain, Spain and Italy, and what the Bush administration tended to see as a solidly pro-American bloc in central and eastern Europe, why not call upon this 'new Europe' to redress the balance of the old? In summer 2003, the *Wall Street Journal Europe* spelled out the logi-cal conclusion. If French hostility to the US persisted, it threatened, 'the US will have no choice but to treat the Atlantic alliance itself as a coalition of the willing'.[70]

This notion of 'coalitions of the willing' did not apply only to Europe. As early as 1992, a draft Defense Planning Guidance pre-pared by Paul Wolfowitz in the Pentagon had observed 'we should expect future coalitions to be ad hoc assemblies, often not lasting beyond the crisis being confronted, and in many cases carrying only general agreement over the objectives to be accomplished'.[71] Donald Rumsfeld repeated almost as a mantra the view that he had articulated soon after 9/11, responding to the Nato offer of support: 'the mission determines the coalition; the coalition must not determine the mission'.[72] When Britain's participation in the war looked politically uncertain, he said that America didn't even need the help of British forces to defeat Saddam Hussein.

At the height of the Iraq crisis I talked to another very senior administration official. In the course of our conversation, he several times referred to 'the Europeans' as 'a pain in the butt'. When I asked him 'Do you need the Europeans?' his answer was, 'no, militarily not at all'. What if Europe continued to be weak, self-obsessed and carping, as he had characterized it? 'Well,' he said, 'the first question is: does it matter?' To some modest extent yes, he answered himself, mainly because America needed the cooperation of European intelligence agencies and police forces to track down the Islamist terrorists, many of whom came through Europe.

And how would this 'war on terror' end? 'With the elimination of the terrorists.'[73] Although he did go on to say that the United States would have to do 'nation-building' after occupying Iraq – and he acknowledged that the administration had changed its mind on nation-building since 9/11 – the implication was that the United States could unilaterally, or with some limited help from a 'coalition of the willing', win the 'war on terror' by military and police means. Power seemed to be equated in his mind almost exclusively with military power. Savour his phrase: 'The *elimination* of the terrorists.' The ancient Greeks had a word for such an attitude. They called it hubris. This was the hubris of men and women who knew, like no one else, the full extent of America's military power, but who had also felt the shock of America's vulnerability after 9/11. It was the hubris of the wounded.

## RETURN TO A NEW STARTING-POINT

After the predictable military victory and the symbolic toppling of the statue of Saddam in Baghdad on 9 April 2003, two things changed.

First, the chorus of American and European voices calling for the transatlantic relationship to be 'repaired', 'renewed' or 'reborn' rose to the fortissimi of the last movement of Beethoven's Ninth Symphony. Not a day passed without at least one op-ed commentary, open letter, speech, conference, workshop, think tank meeting, high-level group or task force devoted to putting the West together again. Often these meetings or initiatives were financed by a German-owned American company, or an American-owned British company, or one of the hundreds of other businesses with a direct stake in the transatlantic economy. The Atlantic community which had grown over sixty years – and, in a larger but weaker sense, over four hundred years – defended itself like a human body fighting off a virus.

Secondly, hubris was punished, as it always is. In this case, it was punished on the streets of Iraq, where the American military found themselves experiencing the very same mixture of power and vulnerability that Washington had felt after 9/11. The euphoric flowering of Iraqi democracy, promised by Iraqi exiles to Pentagon civilians such as Paul Wolfowitz and Richard Perle, and by them to the president and the American people, was, to say the least, slow to materialize. Against the advice of its professional military commanders, the United States did not have enough troops on the ground to cope with initial anarchy and then guerrilla war. In the six months after President Bush announced the end of 'major combat operations', on 1 May 2003, more American soldiers were killed in Iraq than during the war itself.[74] Most of these killings were calculated for maximum media effect, and the American media were happy to oblige: 'if it bleeds, it leads'.

Had the United States been the oil-thirsty bully of anti-American caricature, none of this would have mattered so much. After 'pre-emptively' removing the alleged Saddamite threat, it could have handed over to some new but friendly despot, brought most of its troops home, and let the oil flow to the United States under the protection of an autocratic local regime, as it had for decades in Saudi Arabia. Now no one could accuse this administration, headed by a former oilman, of being indifferent to the interests of the oil industry. As early as February 2001, the Defense Intelligence Agency had prepared a document on 'Foreign Suitors for Iraqi Oilfield Contracts'.[75]

But the United States was not that simple caricature. Nor were the dreaded neoconservatives. They might be the people most ready to use America's military power unilaterally for the advancement of American interests, but they were also those most committed to an ambitious plan to spread democracy in the Middle East, starting with a beacon of post-Saddamite democracy in Iraq.

It was precisely through democratic modernization that they hoped to 'drain the swamp' in which the terrorists that threatened the US multiplied like mosquitoes, and, at the same time, to produce a more favourable neighbourhood for embattled Israel. In fact, their Iraq policy started from a critique of old-fashioned conservative 'realism', such as had characterized the first Bush administration, with its readiness to prefer 'stability' in places like Saudi Arabia to the spread of democracy and human rights in the Middle East. So they were fiercely Jacksonian but also boldly Wilsonian. They plotted nothing less than a revolution from above. Trotsky, an inspiration to some of them in their youth, would have applauded the means though not the end. Recalling a famous description of Napoleon as 'the French Revolution in boots', Pierre Hassner described this approach as 'Wilsonianism in boots'.[76]

Faced with the chorus for transatlantic renewal, and the quagmire in Iraq, the Bush administration moved – somewhat. In Afghanistan, it had long since accepted a European lead in the post-war occupation and, in the summer of 2003, handed overall control to Nato. Now it started looking beyond its 'coalition of the willing' for assistance in policing post-war Iraq, and sought a role for Nato there, as well as proposing a faster handover of power to Iraqis. America had spurned Nato in winning those wars; now it was calling on Nato to help it not lose the peace.

In November 2003, President Bush gave a speech in London strikingly different in tone and content from those of two or three years before. The peace and security of 'free nations', he argued, rested on three pillars.[77] First, 'international organizations must be equal to the challenges facing our world'. 'Like eleven Presidents before me,' he said, 'I believe in the international institutions and alliances that America helped to form and helps to lead.' In case you're wondering, 'eleven Presidents' takes you back to Franklin Delano Roosevelt. He even uttered the M-word, with a brief, tight-lipped prayer for 'the success of multilateralism'. His second pillar was the readiness of free nations 'when the last resort arrives, to restrain aggression and evil by force'.*

The third pillar was 'the global expansion of democracy'. The cause of freedom required more development aid, the fight against AIDS and 'working for justice' in Burma, the Sudan and Zimbabwe. But central to it now was the hope of 'the greater Middle East' joining 'the democratic revolution'. 'In an arc of reform from Morocco to Jordan to Qatar, we are seeing elections and new protections for women and the stirring of political pluralism.' Islam was entirely compatible with democracy. And then he made a remarkable confession: 'We must shake off decades of failed policy in the Middle East. Your nation and mine, in the past, have been willing to make a bargain, to tolerate oppression for the sake of stability. Longstanding ties often led us to overlook the faults of local elites.' Listen and tremble, the house of Saud. 'Yet this bargain did not bring stability or make us safe. It merely bought time, while problems festered and ideologies of violence took hold.' Instead, his administration was now 'pursuing a different course, a forward strategy of freedom in the Middle East'.

Obviously Bush was seeking to please a particular audience, and these fine words might not be matched by deeds. In the Middle East, unlike in central Europe, the United States had given repeated cause to doubt its staying power. But they still marked an extraordinary change from the offensive unilateralism of Bush's early months and the hubris of the wounded at the height of Washington's war of 9/11. The president who had started out so sceptical about foreign entanglements, 'cross-walk soldiers' and nation-building now publicly endorsed both Wilsonianism and multilateralism. This was in some sense a return to the great continuity of those eleven Presidents since Roosevelt, but it was a return to a new starting-point.

* What he actually said was '*retain* aggression and evil' but a footnote to the transcript on the White House website reassuringly indicates that 'restrain' is what he was meant to say.

# PARTNER?

What, then, can Europeans and other free people expect from this new old United States in the first decades of the twenty-first century? When Harold Macmillan was asked to identify his biggest problem as prime minister he is said to have replied 'events, dear boy, events'.[78] So also for the political writer. If the event is a big one, the outdating effect is more extreme. A political book finished on 10 September 2001 would have been seriously outdated on 11 September 2001. But that's a risk you always have to take, if you want to draw lessons for the future from the recent past. Accepting that we will always be surprised by what Donald Rumsfeld once called, in an unfairly derided distinction, 'the unknown unknowns', we can still say something about what he called the 'known knowns' and the 'known unknowns'.[79] The word 'probably' is to be understood next to most of the statements that follow.

First among the 'known knowns' is American hyperpower. This is three-dimensional. In 2002 the United States spent more on defence than did the next eighteen military powers combined.[80] The imbalance can be seen clearly on the proportional map on page 255. For 2004, its defence spending was lifted yet again, to around $400 billion. Its cumulative military advantage is multiplied by its space-age technological edge. In large-scale wars, the American military can defeat anyone anywhere. Its regional commands cover the whole of the earth's surface and their commanders-in-chief are, as one of them himself observes, the new proconsuls.[81] America has no military rival in sight.

Another proportional map of the world, on page 254, gives a vivid impression of America's economic strength. If you replace the names of the federal states on a more conventional map of the US with those of national economies of equal size, Texas is Canada, California is France and the whole of Russia fits into New Jersey. This is, to be sure, the dimension of American power over which there hangs the largest question mark. How long can a country with, as I write, a $500 billion budget deficit, and a trade deficit of about the same size, sustain a $400 billion annual defence budget, and still meet a growing demand for social spending? The historian Paul Kennedy has suggested that the United States, like most previous great powers, may eventually succumb to the tension between military superstructure and economic base.

None the less, according to current projections the United States is still set fair to remain the world's largest economy for three decades to come.[82] The European Union can grow larger geographically, in a way the United States would find difficult. (Canada and Mexico are not applying for US membership.) However, America will, on current trends, grow faster demographically. That demographic growth, in which successfully absorbed immigration plays a large part, will probably help increase the gross domestic product of the United States beyond that of even a further enlarged European Union.[83] Last but not least, America's soft power, its worldwide power to attract, through everything from Hollywood, McDonald's and Levi's to Stanford, Toni Morrison and the Metropolitan Opera, will remain intensely fascinating for as far ahead as the eye can see.

This power, especially the military power, will continue to bring with it the temptation of unilateralism: go it alone, just because you can. The argument made by many mainstream American policymakers, including John Kerry, that patient multilateralism is in the United States' long-term self-interest, will constantly rub up against this short-term temptation. Moreover, America will continue to defend an unbridled national sovereignty which most European states have long since abandoned. Thomas Jefferson wrote in 1791: 'No court can have jurisdiction over a sovereign nation.'[84] That remains his country's position. The United States is now, in effect, the last truly sovereign European nation-state. This respect for sovereignty does not, however, apply equally to foreign states, especially those from which the United States sees threats to its own security. The asymmetry between America's calculus of sovereignty for itself and that for other states will not always be as extreme as it was during the post-9/11 wars of Afghanistan and Iraq, but it will still be there. We can expect it to be sustained by a fierce and sometimes bellicose patriotism, spilling over into nationalism, of a kind rarely to be found in contemporary Europe.

Uniquely, America will continue to define its national purpose in idealistic terms originally drafted by a group of often Francophile

Englishmen more than two centuries ago. Of course the content of this 'American creed' has developed with time, but its central commandments remain remarkably constant. Contemporary Europe has nothing to compare.[85] The American creed has two gods: one is called Freedom, the other is called God. In the scattersheet of early twenty-first-century capitalist democracies, religion is more than ever at the heart of American exceptionalism. America's muscular Christianity feeds into a moralistic rhetoric of freedom which many Europeans dismiss as humbug.

'They say Christ and mean Cotton,' the great nineteenth-century German novelist Theodor Fontane has one of his characters say of the imperial Englishmen of his time.[86] 'They say Democracy and mean Oil,' is the modern German version, applied to today's imperial Americans. As with the rhetoric of all great powers in history, there is certainly some humbug, although the boundaries between outright lies, semi-conscious hypocrisy and genuine belief are always unclear. The late nineteenth-century President McKinley gave a wonderful account of pacing the floor of the White House night after night, praying to 'Almighty God' for guidance, until his divine national security adviser persuaded him that he had no alternative but to occupy the Philippines 'and educate the Filipinos, and uplift and civilize and Christianize them, and by God's grace do the very best we could by them as our fellow-men for whom Christ also died'.[87] One day we may read an account of the advice that the Almighty gave George W. Bush. Bush clearly saw the war on terror as part of a Christian's 'good fight' against evil. 'I think,' a friend told a *New York Times* reporter, 'in his frame, this is what God has asked him to do.'[88]

It's a great mistake, made by many Europeans, to assume that America's moralistic rhetoric of freedom is merely a cloak for self-interest. Rather, belief in the twin gods of the American creed is a genuine, autonomous motivating force. Americans were Wilsonian long before Woodrow Wilson, and it seems a safe guess that some version of 'Wilsonianism in boots' or the 'marriage of Wilsonianism with power' will remain a recurring feature of American policy for years to come. The fact that American foreign policy perennially defines itself by values as well as interests is a challenge that Europeans will, if they are wise, prepare to take up. The core of American foreign

policy, writes the neoconservative Richard Perle, is 'the universalization of American principles'.[89] But most of these 'American principles' are actually new versions of old European ones, or, in some
cases, old American versions of principles now being newly defined in
the European Union.

America, at the beginning of the twenty-first century, is deeply
engaged in the world, and most Americans support this in principle.
Seventy-seven per cent of those asked in one poll in summer 2003 said
it was best for the future of the US to take an active part in world
affairs, the highest figure since 1947.[90] Another polling organization
found that 50 per cent completely and 40 per cent mostly agreed with
an almost identical proposition. What is more, the combined figure
for those who agreed had remained around 90 per cent since the late
1980s.[91] However, they also found 76 per cent agreeing with the suggestion that less attention should be paid to problems overseas and
more to those at home.

The temptation of disengagement will remain for a country which,
unlike imperial Britain, is itself a huge continental empire – Jefferson's
'empire for liberty'. There will always be an inclination, when the
going gets rough abroad or when times get hard at home, for America
to withdraw into its own 'vast carelessness' – to adapt a telling phrase
from Scott Fitzgerald's *Great Gatsby* – leaving the job half done in
Somalia, or Bosnia, or Kosovo, or Afghanistan, or Iraq, or wherever.
This will be exacerbated by the media's short attention span, the
seemingly congenital difficulty of getting Washington to concentrate
on more than one major foreign policy issue at a time, and the
pressure of the electoral cycle.

So far as American policy towards Europe is concerned, first
among the 'known knowns' is the old continent's loss of centrality in
world affairs. This was bound to happen sooner or later. Europe
hastened its own toppling, with a sustained period of European barbarism and self-destruction in what has been called the 'European
civil war' or 'second Thirty Years War' from 1914 to 1945. However,
the Cold War then artificially restored Europe's centrality, since the
western end of Eurasia became the main theatre of confrontation
between two half-European superpowers. With the benefit of hindsight, the Clinton administration looks like a long afterglow of

habitual American Europeanism. If the West is now to be renewed, it will be in a different shape and on different terms.

As Europe has lost its geopolitical centrality to the United States, it has also lost much of its centuries-old Jamesian cultural fascination. The balance of fascination has shifted, like the balance of hard power. And militarily, Europe is a dwarf beside the American giant. In 2003, the non-American members of Nato (including that almost-European country, Canada) had some 1.25 million men and women under arms, and a further 1 million in reserve, but only 55,000 troops that could be deployed at any one time.[92] These troops would usually be airlifted in somebody else's transport planes and guided by American satellites. Even if Europe's national armed forces are prepared to combine (which they will do only very slowly and reluctantly), even if they can agree on standardized equipment (ditto), even if they buy their own transport planes and send up their own satellites (ditto), even if Americans share some of their secret space-age weapons technology (ditto), even if European publics are ready to pay to make Europe a military superpower (which all polls suggest they are not), even then, Europe will still only be a sluggish five footer to America's six foot six inch military Michael Jordan. A European rapid reaction capability will make Europe militarily more relevant to the US, but still very far from an equal. Seen from the Pentagon, it will have roughly the importance of the reformed alcoholic deputy sheriff in the film *Rio Bravo*.

Economics is a different matter. Even if the American economy will again pull ahead of the combined European economy in absolute size, while China and India are rising fast, Europe will still be the United States' nearest competitor for the foreseeable future. And the two are now so deeply intertwined. In case we get numbed by shorthand billions and trillions, it's worth spelling out the zeros in full: in 2000 American firms had some $3,000,000,000,000 worth of assets in Europe, and European firms had some $3,300,000,000,000 worth of assets in America.[93] There is more European investment in Texas than there is American investment in all of Japan. The US also partly depends on Europeans continuing to buy American bonds, to sustain those huge deficits. In trade negotiations, the EU talks to the US as giant to giant. The Euro has the potential to became a rival reserve currency to the dollar, especially if oil sales begin to be denominated in Euros. American notions of unbridled sovereignty will be qualified by these economic realities. Yet the fact that America has to take Europe seriously economically does not mean it will do so politically. As in pre-1914 Europe, there is no automatic 'read-across' from economics to politics. All that European investment in Texas did not stop George W. Bush behaving as he did.

As Bill Clinton might have said: 'It's the politics, stupid.' The politics of the American approach to Europe is the most difficult part to guess. So much will depend on the 'known unknowns'. European policy is unpredictable because it is made by twenty-five going on forty different nations; American policy, because of the competition between different institutional parts of the government. Washington's motto comes from Walt Whitman:

> Do I contradict myself?
> Very well then I contradict myself,
> (I am large, I contain multitudes.)[94]

While foreign policy approaches do not correlate neatly with party affiliation, Democrats tend to be more like Europeans in cultural attitudes and somewhat more pro-European, whereas Republicans are more susceptible to anti-Europeanism. These differences have deepened with the growing divide between the 'two nations', or at least, two cultures, in America. For Europe, the oscillation between Democrat and Republican administrations may therefore be even more unsettling than it was during the Cold War.

In a system where the making of foreign policy depends so much on the decisions of a few men and women at the apex of a highly politicized upper bureaucracy, personalities and biographies will continue to matter enormously. If Europeans are canny, they will redouble their efforts to seduce young, bright, politically minded Americans with the fading charms of the old continent. (Reversing the Greek myth, Europa starts nuzzling the bull.) It will make a difference if a future American president has known, as a young man or woman, the glories of Rome and the beauties of Kraków.

American policy will continue to be its own prime mover. We will be sure to see again that familiar pattern: America acts, Europe reacts.

None the less, the transatlantic interaction is an important input to this policy. American anti-Europeanism, for example, is much stirred by European anti-Americanism, and real or imputed European anti-Semitism. Anti-Europeanism in turn stokes that anti-Americanism. The crucial interaction, however, will be between two strategic arguments, one on each side of the Atlantic. The European argument, as we saw in the last chapter, is about America: Euro-Gaullism versus Euroatlanticism. The American argument is about America's own role in the world. To simplify, it is the debate between unilateralism and multilateralism.

How might these two great debates influence each other? Let's play through the transatlantic variations. A solidly Gaullist Europe will certainly encourage American unilateralism. (You cooperate with a would-be partner but try to beat a would-be rival.) Equally, a unilateralist America will strengthen Euro-Gaullism, as we saw plainly during the Iraq crisis. A solidly Atlanticist European Union will encourage a multilateralist United States; indeed, it will have the economic and soft power to exert some pressure on the United States to be more multilateralist. Equally, a multilateralist US will encourage European Atlanticism. But none of these pure variants is likely. So far as we can foresee, Europe will continue to be torn between powerful constituencies for Euro-Gaullism and Euroatlanticism, while America will continue to be torn between the temptations of unilateralism and the sober councils of multilateralism.

So the question then becomes: what effect might a divided Europe have on a divided America, and vice versa? A Europe divided between Gaullist and Atlanticist national governments will, as we saw during the Iraq War, encourage the United States to steer a course somewhere in between unilateralism and multilateralism. This is the politics of à la carte multilateralism and 'coalitions of the willing', also known as 'cherry-picking', 'disaggregation' or divide-and-rule. Conversely, an America oscillating between unilateralism and multilateralism will encourage European mood-swings between Euro-Gaullism and Euroatlanticism.

Will the United States want a more united Europe? As we emerge from the most acute period of this crisis of the West, we find a strategic stand-off. In effect, America says to Europe: 'we'll again support

European unity if you assure us it won't be directed against us'. Europe says to America: 'our efforts to unite won't be directed against you, so long as you can assure us that you'll take more notice of what we say'. The main heirs of the old West are like the two proverbial Polish noblemen standing in the pouring rain outside a restaurant door, saying 'after you!', 'no, after you!', 'but I insist, after you!', 'but no, it's *I* who insist', and so on for half an hour, while both get soaked. In this joke, told by Poles at their own expense, one of the noblemen does finally go first and the other says, 'shameful – he argues with me for half an hour and then he goes first anyway!' Can Europe and America be more sensible?

Before turning to that question, we need to spend a little time looking at the rain in which both are standing. What are the new threats and global challenges of the early twenty-first century that will shape the future of both Europe and America? Will they impact differently on the two continents, creating a further divergence of attitudes? Or do Europe and America really have a common interest in confronting these problems and, so to speak, getting out of the rain?

# 4

## The New Red Armies

### TERROR AGAINST HOPE

History books record that from 1939 to 1945 the world was engaged in the Second World War and, from about 1946 to 1989, in the Cold War. What will historians call the chapter of world history that began on 11 September 2001? 'The War on Terror' suggested the Bush administration. But what does that mean? Nazi Germany and the Soviet Union were states; terror is a state of mind. Even if we understand 'terror' to be just a snappier word for terrorism, it's still quite unclear what the aims of this war are and in what circumstances it can reasonably be said to be won.

A senior State Department official responsible for counterterrorism has described the goal of American policy as being 'to assure final victory in the global war against terrorism'.[1] Terrorism is defined by the US government as 'premeditated, politically motivated violence perpetrated against noncombatant targets by subnational groups or clandestine agents, usually intended to influence an audience'.[2] The State Department's annual reports on *Patterns of Global Terrorism* judge that what they call 'domestic' terrorism is probably more widespread than 'international' terrorism, but concentrate on the latter because it has a 'direct impact on US interests'. People getting killed in Chechnya, Rwanda or Sri Lanka are, by this criterion, of less concern. Defining international terrorism as 'involving citizens or the territory of more than one country', these reports chart a history of international terrorist attacks which reached a numerical high point in the late 1980s but then generally declined.[3] Because of the scale of the 11 September atrocity, 2001 bucked the trend, but the report for 2002 noted a 45 per cent drop on the previous year, with 196 attacks by 'international terrorists' rather than the previous year's 355, and 717 people killed.[4]

These 'frozen tears',[5] as one statistician called such cold numbers, only tell a small part of the story, but they do raise some interesting questions. Will the agenda of world politics really continue to be dominated for decades to come by a few hundred international terrorist attacks, especially if their number is generally diminishing? Each individual attack, with its televised horror and unquantifiable human tragedy, can be linked, by politicians and the media, in a meta-story of 'War on Terror' – especially if the victims are Westerners. But how long will such television images retain the interest and maintain the political support of an already horror-jaded public? If there is no second major attack on the American homeland, might not the day come when an American president will be tempted to declare the end of, so to speak, 'major combat operations' in the War on Terror? To say, as I did at the beginning of this book, that America's 9/11 of fear began the twenty-first century does not mean that the United States will spend the next hundred years fighting a few thousand terrorists. Even a big war need not be a long one: the Second World War lasted less than six years. And in international relations, as in life, problems are often not solved, just overtaken by other problems. The world has plenty of those to offer.

If, however, we consider these 'frozen tears' to be just the tip of an iceberg; if, to change the metaphor, international terrorist attacks are like boils on the skin of the body politic, merely the symptoms of more serious diseases below; then the agenda is a huge one, stretching decades ahead. It will involve tackling not just the terrorist groups but the rogue or failed states which support or shelter them and the proliferation of weapons of mass destruction. In the wrong hands, these weapons can be instruments of terror a thousand times worse than a hijacked airliner flown into a tower block.

The War on Terror will end, that senior Bush administration official told me, 'with the elimination of the terrorists'. But there is no finite stock of terrorists to be 'eliminated'. People are not born terrorists, as they are born English, Chinese or Creek Indians. They become terrorists in specific political and personal circumstances, and might cease to be terrorists when those circumstances change. At one point in his career, Nelson Mandela was arguably, by the State Department's definition, a terrorist. If you kill ten terrorists, without changing the political circumstances, and they become martyrs for their own community, you can give birth to a hundred more. Terror is a means not an end – except for a few psychopaths. To be sure, even for non-psychopaths, terrorism can, with time, become a way of life, and of supposedly honourable death. It is often deeply entangled with organized crime and profiteering. None the less, for most terrorist leaders, most of the time, terror is like war in Clausewitz's famous definition: the continuation of politics by other means.

If you look more closely at the politics of early twenty-first-century terrorism, the distinction between 'domestic' and 'international' soon becomes blurred. 'Domestic' in this context means 'inside one country'. But what most terrorists in the world want is precisely that one country should become two, or that two parts of different countries should become one new country, or, in any case, that a state should be fundamentally re-made. The point about those 'subnational groups' is usually that they wish not to be *sub*national any more. This is true, for example, of the Irish Republican Army, the Basque ETA, Kurdish terrrorist organizations, the Kosovo Liberation Army (which the United States first characterized as terrorists and then worked closely with), the Tamil Tigers, the Palestine Liberation Organization and Hamas. As the last two cases indicate, a national grievance – that of the Palestinians – can also be a cause of international terrorism. On one interpretation, Osama bin Laden's first concern was the Islamic 'purification' of the politics of his own country, Saudi Arabia. So to eliminate the causes that might turn people into 'international terrorists' the West (in so far as it still exists) will have to address a baffling range of national political grievances across the globe.

And not just national grievances. The suicide terrorists of 11 September 2001 were not poor, but surroundings of poverty and hopelessness can feed the desperation that leads men and women to kill civilians, and themselves, for a cause. The suicide bombers who claimed the life of the British consul in Istanbul in November 2003 came from one of the poorest Kurdish areas of Turkey. In any case, President Bush made this connection. Announcing a 50 per cent increase in the United States' official development aid, previously the lowest of any country in the developed world, he said: 'We fight against poverty because hope is an answer to terror.'[6]

The section of America's 2002 national security strategy devoted to combating 'Global Terrorism' made another very large connection, between the lack of political freedom and terrorism. 'Freedom and fear', it said, 'are at war.'[7] The epigraph to that section quoted President Bush's still more ambitious claim, in his address in Washington's National Cathedral three days after the 9/11 attacks, that America's 'responsibility to history' was 'to answer these attacks and *rid the world of evil*' (my italics). Following more conventional Christian theology, the only way to rid the world of evil would be to rid the world of human beings, but even if one takes a secular, Enlightenment view of human nature this would be no small task.

I don't mean to be snide at the expense of political and moral hyperbole in a moment of national extremity. I merely want to show how the agenda of an American-led 'War on Terror' could begin as a focused military, intelligence and police operation, to prevent a few thousand existing terrorists from taking another American life, and end up as a plan to change the whole world by lifting more than two billion people out of poverty and unfreedom in a way not attempted by any power in history. For against their own narrative of fear, starting from the trauma of 9/11, Americans have unrolled an even more dramatic narrative of hope. This is the story, told by both Republicans and Democrats, of the global spread of freedom and democracy. In telling it, they reach back to the Founding Fathers and the Wilsonian tradition. They also stand in a great continuity of American policy, from Roosevelt's 1941 proclamation of the 'four freedoms'[8] – of speech and of religion, from want and from fear – through the whole of the Cold War and the generous American response to Europe's 9/11 of hope in 1989.

'The human race has witnessed,' writes Condoleeza Rice, 'in little more than a generation, the swiftest advance of freedom in the 2,500-year story of democracy.'[9] American scholars, of both left and right, have gathered evidence to support this bold claim. At the turn of the nineteenth to the twentieth century, there were some ten to twenty countries in the world which could make some plausible claim to having their governments changed by popular vote, although none of them met today's requirements for being full liberal democracies.[10] Five, including the largest, were the children of England: the United States, Britain, Canada, Australia and New Zealand. The second largest group comprised continental European countries, of which the most important was France. Ancient European republics like Switzerland were joined by constitutional monarchies with varying degrees of limited parliamentary democracy, including Denmark, Holland, Belgium, Portugal, Sweden, Norway, Greece and, to some extent, Italy and Germany. They all had their own native traditions of freedom, but were also influenced by the signal examples of France and England. A third group was in Latin America. A half-century later, in 1950, some 22 of the then 80 sovereign states in the world were democracies, by a much more exacting standard.[11] Most of these democracies were in what was then called the West. By 1973, there were 39, but since the number of sovereign states had grown as a result of decolonization, the proportion was still about the same – just over a quarter.

In the spring of 1974, with the 'revolution of the carnations' in Portugal, there began what can be seen, with hindsight, as an extraordinary rolling wave of democratization around the world. Greece followed, and Spain, and much of Latin America, and the Philippines, and then, after the velvet revolutions of 1989, most of the post-communist world. It didn't stop there. Thirty years on, Freedom House counts 117 democracies out of 192 sovereign states in the world – that is, nearly two thirds of them.[12] One can argue about the inclusion of this or that state as a democracy. There is also a very important distinction, made by these scholars themselves, between 'electoral democracies' and full 'liberal democracies'. Beside regular elections, liberal democracies have an effective rule of law, an independent judiciary, well-protected individual freedoms, human rights and minority rights, free, pluralist media, civilian control of the military and a strong civil society.[13] Only these countries truly enjoy the liberty which, as John Locke insisted, is inseparable from law.

Freedom House has developed a rough and ready way of measuring political rights and civil liberties. It finds that only 88 of those 117 electoral democracies are, by these criteria, 'free'.[14] Another 55 states are, it finds, 'partly free'. (Note that a country can be 'partly free' even if it is not a democracy, as was the case of many European countries with constitutionally limited government in the nineteenth century.) Only 49 countries are simply 'unfree'. By this reckoning, some 2.8 billion people, nearly half the world's population, live in countries that are free, some 1.3 billion in those classified as partly free, and some 2.2 billion are unfree. Of the unfree, more than half are accounted for by just one state – China. So in these thirty years, the realm of freedom has extended far beyond the West, by all but the most generous definition of that term.

This is, obviously, to paint with a very broad brush. There is a real question how many of those 2.8 billion men, women and children living in states classed as free are in any meaningful sense themselves, individually, free. The great twentieth-century liberal philosopher Isaiah Berlin always insisted, against the Marxists of his time, that we keep two things distinct: freedom is freedom, poverty is poverty. Everything is what it is and not another thing. But plainly the unemployed Moroccan illegal immigrant I met one sultry evening in the Lavapiés neighbourhood of Madrid – 'I live', he told me, 'like a wolf' – is not free in the sense that I and you, if you have the money, education and leisure to read this book, are free. 'Are the poor free?' is one of the most pressing questions facing us, the free, at the beginning of the twenty-first century.

It applies most painfully to the nearly half of humankind living on less than $2 a day.[15] The economist Amartya Sen argues compellingly that freedom and development are inextricable.[16] Only above a certain level of development can we seriously talk of people being free, but equally, a certain level of political freedom, good government and the rule of law is indispensable for development. You have to be free to develop and develop to be free. Sen famously observes that no democracy has ever known a famine. Other writers spell out the connection between democracy and development. It is plainly wrong to maintain that no poor country can be a democracy: Sen's own mother country, India, is a billion-strong counter-example. And it is wrong to suggest that people in poor countries, whether Islamic, Confucian or African, do not want freedom and democracy: opinion surveys consistently show that they do. But it does seem to be empirically, historically true that the higher a country's per capita GDP, the better its chance of becoming and *remaining* a democracy. Above about $6,500 dollars a head, it is rare for a country not to be a democracy – although there are, as always, exceptions, notably the oil-rich Arab states. Below $2,000 dollars a head, it is rare for a country to remain a democracy for long.[17] The tasks of freedom and development are therefore inseparable.

Now Americans, with their characteristic historical optimism, have laid out a breathtaking proposition to the world: that we – we, the free – can, by our own endeavours, so foster this unprecedented advance of freedom that it will, in time, embrace the whole of humankind. Then there will be no cause for terror. Underlying the starkest version of this vision is an equally breathtaking analytical premiss: that there is now 'a single sustainable model for national success: freedom, democracy and free enterprise'.[18] This recalls Francis Fukuyama's argument for a 'worldwide liberal revolution' in his hugely influential article of 1989 and subsequent book on *The End of History*,[19] and the so-called 'Washington Consensus' of the IMF and World Bank in the 1990s.

The bald simplicity of this claim for a 'single sustainable model', with its implicit image of America as a model for the future of all humankind, has offended many Europeans, Africans, Asians and others who have themselves long been committed to such a post-Enlightenment, global meliorist aspiration. Kofi Annan, for example, in accepting the 2000 Nobel Peace Prize for his work as secretary-general of the United Nations, quietly observed: 'The idea that there is one people in possession of the truth, one answer to the world's ills, or one solution to humanity's needs, has done untold harm throughout history – especially in the last century.'[20]

The claim is also contested inside America. Samuel Huntington's *Clash of Civilizations*, a political essay even more influential than Fukuyama's, is underpinned by profound, almost old-European intellectual pessimism. Huntington argues, like Oswald Spengler, that the West is in decline.[21] The decline of the West, he suggests, might take as long as the rise of the West – about four hundred years – which may be some consolation. Yet the West is already being challenged by two competing 'civilizations' in particular, those of Islam and China.

These civilizations are incompatible with the West, and its model of democracy, and likely to clash with it. 'Some Westerners,' Huntington wrote in 1997, 'including President Bill Clinton, have argued that the West does not have problems with Islam but only with violent Islamist extremists. Fourteen hundred years of history demonstrate otherwise.'[22] And he concluded by imagining a war between the United States and China in 2010. The United States should leave other 'core states' to look after their cultural neighbourhoods, and defend its own – the declining West.

Of course these are not the only narratives or paradigms by which political writers are attempting at once to interpret and to change the world at the century's beginning. Another popular paradigm is 'globalization', carefully defined by Joseph Stiglitz as 'the closer integration of the countries and peoples of the world which has been brought about by the enormous reduction of costs of transportation and communication, and the breaking down of artificial barriers to the flows of goods, services, capital, knowledge, and (to a lesser extent) people across borders'.[23] People 'living on opposite sides of the world [are now] linked in ways previously unimaginable', writes Peter Singer, in his marvellous book on the ethics of globalization, One World.[24] Sitting at home in Paris, you can play chess on the internet with someone in China. When you go to a remote African village, you find the locals watching Basic Instinct on video.[25]

The rapid, worldwide spread of this notion of 'globalization' is both a product and a catalyst of the process it describes. To some extent, it's a self-fulfilling prophecy. The more reports we have on World Population, World Development, World Trade, World Drugs, World Crime, World Cinema, Global Public Goods, World Sport, World Health, Global Civil Society, and the more international organizations, both official and non-govermental, monitor violations of human rights and minority rights, elections, war, genocide or AIDS worldwide, the more we think of it as one world. The more we think of it as one world, the more it is one world. For many free people under the age of thirty, the nation is no longer the main political locus of 'imagined community'. At one level, globalization is a hard, economic and technical process, driven by satellites, microchips and the latest technologies of information, transport and communications. At another, it's what the poet W. H. Auden called a 'mind-event'.

Globalization, this Microsoft among concepts, none the less faces major competitors. One is the revival of the term 'empire' – now used to describe not the old colonial powers, such as Britain or France, but the former champion of anti-colonialism, America. The United States' role in the world is today almost routinely characterized as that of an empire. The European Union is also described by some analysts as an empire, although they add the tags 'post-modern' or 'neo-medieval' – the two apparently meaning very similar things.[26] Then there's the stark thesis of the *New York Times*' foreign affairs columnist Thomas Friedman that 9/11 began 'World War III' between the 'World of Order' (built on 'five pillars', the US, the EU, Russia, India and China) and the 'World of Disorder' (comprised of rogue states, failed states, messy states, terrorists and organized crime).[27] Or Philip Bobbitt's argument that nation-states are increasingly becoming 'market states'.[28]

Any serious attempt to analyse – that is, to simplify the better to understand – this new world is welcome. Such ideas matter, not least because they sometimes influence, directly or indirectly, what our leaders do. For example, the mistaken idea that the wars of the Yugoslav succession were the inevitable product of centuries-old 'ancestral hatreds' reinforced the reluctance of Western governments to become involved there. That meant people got killed who might otherwise still be alive.

In this chapter, I will look briefly at four important global challenges to the West as it begins to emerge from its turn-of-the-century crisis. I will ask: What is the basic character of each challenge? How big an issue is it, compared with those that preoccupy Americans and Europeans elsewhere in their mutual relations? Do Americans, Europeans and other free people have convergent or divergent interests in this field? What potential is there for them to disagree even if their interests largely coincide? What difference can it make if Europeans, Americans and other free people cooperate rather than compete in their response?

## NEAR EAST

In the beginning, none of the places we call the East thought of themselves as the East. All versions of the East – whether European, Communist, Near, Middle or Far – were originally coined by people living in the West. The label was sometimes then accepted by some of the people living in these places, but often not. From the late 1940s until 1989, we talked of 'Eastern Europe', 'the East bloc' and 'East–West relations'. At the beginning of the twenty-first century, that East has gone; older ones have re-emerged. Young men and women who in the 1950s would have learned Russian now queue up to study Arabic, in courses still quaintly called Oriental Studies. But what is the unity or bloc they should study?

One popular answer is 'Islam'. This term is confusing, since it refers both to a religion and to the history and culture of the peoples who profess that religion – as if we had only one word for both 'Christianity' and 'Christendom'. Yet the claim of the Huntingtonian 'clash of civilizations' school is precisely that political effects can be predicted from the fact that a group of people, whether in a state, a nation or a 'subnational group', profess the Islamic faith. In fact, Huntington took the very phrase 'clash of civilizations' from a discussion of 'Muslim Rage' by one of the West's most influential orientalists, Bernard Lewis.[29]

Two contrasting interpretations have received wide currency since the 9/11 attacks. One, favoured by secular Europeans as well as Huntingtonians, sees the heart of the problem in the Islamic religion itself. Islam, it is said, needs to have 'its Reformation', by which secular Europeans often really mean its Enlightenment – and preferably its outright European-style secularization. The other interpretation is that these attacks are the result of a specific history of particular people, many of whom had been radicalized and battle-hardened while fighting against the Russians in Afghanistan, with American support. The holy men of Islam should no more be held responsible for the fact that Osama bin Laden attacked the twin towers in the name of Allah than the Pope or the Archbishop of Canterbury should be blamed if a madman murders in the name of Christ.

For obvious reasons, Western leaders like Tony Blair and, after one unfortunate early use of the word 'crusade', George W. Bush have publicly given Islam the benefit of the doubt. Both Western and Islamic analysts support this in two ways. First, they show how the Koran, and its acknowledged interpreters, condemn the killing of innocent civilians and, in important passages, call for tolerance, pluralism, justice and good government. To be sure, these passages and interpretations are contradicted by others; like all religions, Islam is 'multi-vocal'. Second, they point out that roughly half the world's Muslims live in electoral democracies. However, many of them do so as minorities in states of another majority culture. The second largest Muslim population in the world is in India.

Among countries with a Muslim majority, the record of democracy is thinner. None the less, at this writing, Turkey is an electoral democracy, with an Islamist government behaving moderately in power; the world's largest Muslim country, Indonesia, is trying to be a democracy, though with very serious flaws, as is Bangladesh; small, impoverished Mali and Senegal are not just electoral democracies but ranked by Freedom House as free countries; and Europeans should not forget their own chaotic, semi-democratic Albania, and the EU protectorate of Bosnia, with its culturally Muslim plurality. Anyway, perhaps Muslim majority countries have a thinner record of democracy because they are poor rather than because they are Muslim? Two scholars have shown that, in sustaining electoral democracies, *non-Arab* states with a Muslim majority have done as well as, if not better than, countries of comparable poverty.[30]

So perhaps the real problem is not 'Islam' but the particular history of the Arabs? Here, the record is most depressing. Of the twenty-two members of the Arab League – twenty-one sovereign states and the Palestinian Authority – none is a democracy, unless you are now prepared to count Iraq. The landmark *Arab Human Development Report* of 2002, compiled by Arab scholars, dwelt at length on the region's 'freedom deficit'.[31] It produced a chart of 'freedom scores', aggregating civil and political liberties, on which Arab countries emerged as by far the worst in the world, achieving less than half the 'freedom score' of the next-worst region – Sub-Saharan Africa.

Having advanced this tough self-criticism, the authors nevertheless argued that the problem of Israel and Palestine – what they called

'Israel's illegal occupation of Arab lands'[32] – was one of the largest obstacles to progress across the Arab world. The Palestinian issue, they said, was used by Arab rulers as an 'excuse' for 'retarding political development'.[33] The successor report, in 2003, began with a wail of pain about the suffering of the Palestinians under Israeli occupation, with more than 2,400 dead and more than 40,000 wounded in twenty months after September 2001. They also made a more cautious complaint about how the American occupation of Iraq had inflamed Arab opinion and delayed reform in other Arab countries.[34]

Without minimizing the threats of non-Arab Islamist terrorism, as seen also in Indonesia and Afghanistan, it therefore seems clear that the major challenge to the West lies in the region that is now usually called, in English, the Middle East. I prefer the older English term 'near East', which is still used in many other European languages. If we say 'the Middle East', people generally think of Israel and Palestine, and the Arab countries around them, whereas in fact we need to look at the whole arc of Arab countries from Morocco to Iraq, as well as Iran and Turkey. Moreover, the term 'near East' usefully reminds us Europeans just how near this region is: nine miles at its closest point to Spain. You can cross the Straits of Gibraltar in a small boat, and many thousands of Moroccans already have.

This very near East presents three main challenges: the economic, political and social development of the Arab countries and the Islamic Republic of Iran; the creation of a viable state for the Palestinians in a peace settlement that should also enhance the future security of Israel; and the possible future of a Turkish liberal democracy in a further enlarged European Union, with knock-on effects for its neighbours on all sides, from the Balkans to the Caucasus to Iraq. Each challenge is daunting in a different way.

Despite the immense oil revenues of some Arab states, the combined gross domestic product of the 280 million citizens of the Arab League is less than that of Spain.[35] Of twenty-two countries across the world identified by the World Bank as being below the 'water poverty line' of a thousand cubic metres of water per person per year, fifteen are Arab.[36] Illiteracy rates are the highest of any region in the world.[37] Less than half the women in the Arab countries can read or write. Women are routinely deprived of what in the West are considered basic, universal human rights. The media are largely unfree. Education is often heavily influenced by Islamist sects, such as the Wahhabis in Saudi Arabia. Under the guise of semi-Western constitutional forms, distended 'royal families', clans and tribes rule through the old virtue of 'asabiyya, defined by a great historian of the Arab peoples, Albert Hourani, as 'solidarity directed towards acquiring and keeping power'.[38]

They have been encouraged or at least tolerated in these ways by the West for much of the twentieth century. European colonial powers originally drew the arbitrary frontiers of their states, installed some of their ancestors as rulers, and sought to preserve cosy 'client' relationships even after decolonization: the British with the King of Jordan, the French with the King of Morocco, and so on. The anti-colonial United States has for decades been prepared to treat the oil-producing Arab countries as 'a big dumb gas station', in Thomas Friedman's striking phrase.[39] If an Arab country does hold an election there is now always a danger that a radical Islamist party will come to power – and then it might be 'one man, one vote, once'. Where there has been a revolution, in Iran, it was an Islamic revolution. The Iranian experience suggests there might be no better cure for radical Islamism than a good long dose of Islamist rule, but such countries may be even more uncomfortable company for the West during the years or decades that the patient is taking that cure.

If dealing with the communist East kept the Cold War West together, dealing with this near East has been the source of some of the most bitter arguments between Europe and America. Even during the Second World War, Britain and America quarrelled over Arabia. The Suez Crisis was all about differing approaches to the near East, and the 'oil price shock' of the early 1970s also generated transatlantic tensions. The early twenty-first-century crisis of the West began in the near East (the leaders of al-Qaeda were a Saudi and an Egyptian), was exacerbated by events in the near East (the alienating impact on European opinion of America's support for the military and police campaign against the Palestinians by Israeli Prime Minister Ariel Sharon – a 'man of peace', according to George W. Bush), and culminated in the near East (the storm over Iraq). As we have seen, it has revived the worst mutual stereotypes. Conservative American polemicists denounce

Europeans as anti-Semites and appeasers. Appeasers, that is, of both near Eastern dictators and their own growing Muslim populations. Liberal Europeans mutter about the influence of 'the Jewish lobby' in the United States, and complain that America is behaving like a cowboy in a mosque. They insist that the negative consequences will be felt in Europe, not across the Atlantic. Contemplating the large Muslim minority in France, one senior French official said: 'US policy in the Middle East could be seen as a security risk by my government.'[40]

Of all the difficult regions in the world, the near East seems the one most likely to keep dividing the West. Yet transatlantic arguments are more about means than about ends. To be sure, the European Union's 2003 strategy paper on relations with 'the Arab world' is less explicit and missionary about the goal of spreading Freedom and Democracy, with a capital F and D. It prefers more cautious, eirenic formulations such as 'prosperity, peace and stability', with 'political pluralism and democracy' consigned to a second paragraph.[41] But the main transatlantic differences are those about means that we've already rehearsed, with Europeans preferring quiet diplomacy, 'constructive engagement' and UN-led multilateralism to an American policy of kick-starting regional democratization through the unilateral invasion of Iraq, accompanied by a megaphone diplomacy of eradicating 'evil'.

The fundamental interests of Europe and America in the near East are, if anything, more convergent in the early twenty-first century than before. For a start, both Europe and America are painfully dependent on imported energy. America is the great gas-guzzler, the SUV among nations, but the EU's security strategy soberly notes that Europe is the world's largest importer of oil and gas. These energy imports account for 50 per cent of Europe's energy consumption, projected to rise to 70 per cent by 2030, and most of it comes from the Gulf, North Africa and Russia.[42] We can imagine competition between Europe and America for scarce energy, and there are active rivalries between oil companies and governments for particular souces of supply. However, oil companies like the merged BP-Arco-Amoco are themselves part of an increasingly integrated transatlantic economy. The national or corporate special interest in a particular deal is dwarfed by the common interest of these two vast, interdependent economies in securing their overall sources of supply.

Politically, the 9/11 attacks have revealed a deeper common interest in a new way. The near East is near to Europe but far from America. In classic geopolitics, such a geographical difference would suggest a political difference. But Osama bin Laden and his associates have shown that the Atlantic can be narrower than the Mediterranean. In an age of 'globalization', terrorism, too, is global. Several of the 9/11 terrorists came through Europe. The United States, the 'Great Satan', will probably continue to be their first target, but, as the Madrid bombings of 11 March 2004 showed, European countries come a close second in what al-Qaeda calls 'the Crusader-Zionist alliance'.

If the fabric of American democracy is threatened by terrorist attacks, and by the curtailment of civil liberties in response to those attacks, that of European democracy is threatened by the difficulties most European countries experience in making millions of mainly Muslim immigrants from the near East feel at home. 'Our suburbs, after all, pray to Allah,' writes the French socialist Régis Debray.[43] Not just our suburbs and not just in France. I shall never forget standing in Trafalgar Square one cold November afternoon in 2003. Just down the road, Tony Blair and George W. Bush were discussing the future of Iraq. As darkness fell, I stood amidst a large protesting crowd ('Stop Bush!') and listened to a voice from loudspeakers at the foot of Nelson's column booming out across the square: '*Allahu akbar*! Allah is great!' (What would Nelson have made of it?)

The alienation and radicalization of the second generation of often unemployed Arab and Turkish youth in Spain, France, Italy and Germany is already far advanced. Meanwhile, nativist resentment of immigration has spawned a poisonous populist politics, from Jean-Marie Le Pen in France, through Pim Fortuyn in the Netherlands, to Jörg Haider in Austria. These populists have come close to destabilizing the traditional party system in long-established European democracies.* What these quite disparate populist parties have in common is one theme: hostility to immigration. Anti-Muslimism is now more widespread among post-Christian Europeans than anti-Semitism,

---

* Jacques Chirac owed his re-election in 2002 only to the fact that his opponent in the second round run-off was Le Pen. 'Better a crook than a fascist,' said French leftists, voting unhappily for Chirac.

while the worst anti-Semitic outrages are sometimes the work of Muslims rather than post-Christian Europeans.

Coping with this immigration from the near East, and the ugly native European reactions to it, is the biggest single challenge for European domestic politics at the century's beginning. But the once-sharp distinction between domestic and foreign policy is impossible to maintain. With Europe's population of working age in sharp decline, Europeans will have to accept many more of these immigrants, in their own interest. Yet Europe must simultaneously address the reasons why these people flee the near East, concealed in packing cases, hidden under lorries, risking their lives in tiny, leaking boats, to make a new life here.

The population of the Arab countries is expected to rise from 280 million to somewhere between 410 and 460 million in 2020 – roughly equal to the projected population of the EU of twenty-five member states in the same year.[44] The majority of this population will be under thirty years of age. Roughly half the teenage Arabs interviewed in a recent survey conducted by Arab scholars say they wish to emigrate from their own countries.[45] Of those who wish to emigrate, somewhere between a third and a half say they would like to come to Europe.* You don't have to be Albert Einstein to do the resulting equation. If nothing changes in their Arab homelands, tens of millions of young people will want to leave the near East for the near West. If Europe does not bring more prosperity and freedom to these young Arabs, these young Arabs will come to Europe. So the peaceful economic and political transformation of the near East is an even more vital interest for Europe than it is for America.

Moreover, it's impossible to see how Europe can achieve that transformation without America, or America without Europe. Their strengths lie in different departments, but the instruments at their disposal are complementary. For example, it is now more than ever a distinct American interest that Turkey should remain a Western-oriented democracy, especially if it has an Islamist party in power. But the key to that lies in Turkey's relations with the EU. When the US Deputy Defense Secretary Paul Wolfowitz was trying to secure Turkish

* Another third to a half say they would like to go to America or Canada, but it's harder to take a small boat from Morocco to New York.

support for the invasion of Iraq, he came to Europe and told the EU it must accept Turkey as a member. This was not tactful or clever.* However, it did illustrate the point. The United States has a vital interest in something only Europe can do.

In the case of Israel and Palestine, America will remain the principal outside voice. None the less, Europeans have developed a close working relationship with the Palestinians, funded many of their civil projects and perhaps won their trust. It is naive to imagine that Europe can 'deliver' the Palestinians to a peace settlement while America 'delivers' Israel; but it can certainly help. And the diplomacy of the so-called Middle East Peace Process is carried forward by a 'Quartet' consisting of the US, the EU, Russia and the UN.

There is no way that America can achieve on its own the peaceful transformation of what Americans have taken to calling 'the wider Middle East'. The real question is whether America and Europe, acting together, have the means, commitment and tact to enable the Arabs to do it for themselves. In the aftermath of the Iraq War, we saw how Arab countries might sometimes prefer to be seen to make concessions to European diplomacy rather than to American force. In a rare piece of high-profile coordinated action between Europe's 'big three', the French, German and British foreign ministers jointly visited Teheran, and secured some assurances from the Iranian regime on subjecting its nuclear programme to international supervision. Colonel Gaddafi of Libya went via the British to negotiate secretly with America the dismantling of his weapons of mass destruction. In both cases, it seems reasonable to assume that the threat of American force helped persuade these near Eastern regimes to shift their position, but it certainly did no harm to have the softballing Europeans on hand for the talking. As during the Cold War, the division of labour between a European 'soft cop' and an American 'hard cop' can be effective, even though – or perhaps especially because – it is less a calculated double-act than two cops genuinely disagreeing about the best way to handle a suspect.

In the longer term, the countries of the near East can only be stable

* Imagine a European politician travelling to Washington to tell the United States it must accept Mexico as the fifty-first state, so that Mexico would support a European invasion of Guatemala.

and free if they develop. So long as they only export oil, or other raw materials, they are likely to remain *rentier* states, not democracies. Development means enabling people to make goods or deliver services which others want to buy. Who will buy these goods or services? Next door, in Europe, is one of the largest markets in the world. Inside its borders, millions of people from the near East already live and work. Europe therefore stands to the near East as the United States does to Mexico. Either you allow in more of your poor neighbour's goods or you take more of their people. Without a Mediterranean Free Trade Area, which only the EU can create, an American development strategy for the 'wider Middle East' is unsustainable. It is also mainly up to Europeans to demonstrate that Muslims have a lasting and secure place, as Muslims, in Western societies that once defined themselves against Islam.

Now many Europeans rightly argue that invading and occupying Iraq was not the best way to initiate this peaceful transformation of the Arab world. Quietly supporting the forces for change inside countries such as Iran, Egypt and Saudi Arabia, while advancing a peace settlement between Israel and Palestine, would have been a better way to start. But the occupation of Iraq has happened, for reasons we have explored. Europeans may wish to say, like the man asked for directions at a fork in the road, 'If I were you, I wouldn't start from here', but here is where we are. Now it is in the long-term interest of Europeans even more than Americans that Iraq should become a stable, prosperous, free country. Worse will not be better for anyone except the Islamist enemies of the West.

Even if the West unites to pursue a sustained strategic project for the near East, this will be a very tall order. Yet such a project has one priceless ally: people in the near East themselves. The *New York Times* columnist Thomas Friedman reports that wherever he travels in the region, strangers sidle up to him to express quiet support for his advocacy of democratic change.[46] For the most part, this support can only be articulated in private, since media are under state control and dissidents thrown into prison, but the websites, satellite television and newspapers based in less oppressive places give it public voice. One talkshow on the satellite television channel al-Jazeera debated the question, 'Have the existing Arab regimes become worse than colonialism?' Seventy-six per cent of those who phoned in said 'yes'.[47] A brave Egyptian dissident, Saad Eddine Ibrahim, who was imprisoned for nearly three years by America's protégé, President Hosni Mubarak, finds in the seventh-century Charter of Medina, 'some five to six hundred years before Magna Carta . . . all the elements of pluralism, which is the prerequisite of democracy'.[48] If this is not so much accurate history as the 'invention of tradition', who is the West to complain? We've been at it ourselves for centuries.

Comparative opinion polls show a high level of support for democracy even in Arab and Muslim countries where hostility to the United States is most acute, especially in the wake of the Iraq War.[49] A commentator in the Arabic international newspaper *Al-Hayat* captures this ambivalence in a single sentence: 'We need to reform our educational systems even though the Americans tell us to.'[50] Most remarkably, data from the World Values Survey shows that rejection of authoritarian rule and belief that 'democracy is the best form of government' are higher in the Arab countries than in any other region of the world, including Western Europe, the United States and other English-speaking democracies.[51] Those that have freedom least want it most.

## FAR EAST

Among the heterogeneous half of humankind that Europeans and Americans, following the lead of the ancient Greeks, have arbitrarily lumped together as 'Asia', there is almost every kind of state – except the integrated, 'post-modern' European variety. These 'Asian' states offer almost every kind of difficulty known to international relations. In what Westerners call the far East, North Korea poses the urgent problem of a totalitarian regime acquiring nuclear weapons while starving its own people; Burma that of an Orwellian dictatorship oppressing its own people while some of them grow opium for the world; Indonesia and Malaysia those of possible Yugoslav-style fragmentation in the always explosive transition from multi-ethnic dictatorship to multi-ethnic democracy.

Yet the main challenge that the far East poses to the West is very different from that in the near East. It's not these failed, rogue or messy states, troublesome though they are. It's not even economic backwardness, although more than half the world's poorest people are still to be found in Asia.[52] On a stage many times larger than the near East by any measure – geographic, demographic, economic or military – what the West faces here is the challenge not of failing but of rising powers. As you can see from the proportional map on page 257, China and India have more people in one country than the whole of Europe and America combined. Each of those countries is not just a nation but a whole civilization concentrated in a single state. Both are getting stronger. These huge rising powers have the potential, over the next two to five decades, to shift the global balance of power from the Atlantic to the Pacific.

In the longer perspective of centuries, the shift would be from one end of the Eurasian landmass to the other – or rather, back to the other. For in what Western history books called the Dark and Middle Ages, the places Europeans saw as the East had civilizations that were, by many of the criteria traditionally used to measure civilization, more advanced than those of the West. This was true of the world of Islam in Europe's Dark and early Middle Ages, and of China until what Europeans themselves called Europe's 'rebirth', its 'Renaissance', in the fourteenth and fifteenth centuries according to the Christian calendar – that is, until the middle of the fourth millennium of Chinese civilization. As late as 1800, China alone still had a larger share of world manufacturing output than the whole of the West.[53] The West achieved its unprecedented, capitalist industrial 'take-off' partly by borrowing skills and technologies from the East. China, for example, led the way in developing gunpowder, printing, the compass and a meritocratic state bureaucracy. (The British still call their senior civil servants 'mandarins'.)

Now the East has borrowed back. In what Alice Amsden has called 'The Rise of the Rest', most of the non-Western countries that have achieved economic take-off since 1945 lie in Asia.[54] They have launched into rapid, sustained economic growth not by making their own inventions but by borrowing Western ones and improving on them, or simply by manufacturing them cheaper, witness the Japanese cars on our roads and the Chinese radios, saucepans and tools in our homes. China has become, in the words of one specialist, 'a manu-facturing hub for the rest of the world in low-end labour-intensive goods'.[55] Meanwhile, India shows that services as well as manufac-turing can be lifted from the West. When you ring your building society in Edinburgh or your bank in Boston, you can easily find yourself talking to someone sitting in a call-centre in Bangalore. The oldest symbolic meanings of West and East are now revived to serve in a thousand business-page headlines: the West as the evening coun-try, the *Abendland*, where the setting sun goes in search of Elysium, the East as the realm of the rising sun.

Just how quickly that sun will rise is disputed. Japan was already held to be the world's second largest national economy in the 1990s, but how big are the economies of China and India, how fast are they growing and how fast are they likely to grow? Depending on your level of distrust in official statistics, and whether or not you use 'pur-chasing power parities', you can put China as the sixth or the second largest economy in the world today, India as the eleventh or the fourth.[56] You can have the Chinese economy growing at an average of 9.5 per cent between 1979 and 2001, or much less than that.[57] These varying assessments imply important differences in time-scales; none casts doubt on the basic direction.

Whether fast or slowly, the eastern economic sun is rising. What does this mean for politics? Henry Kissinger has made the interesting suggestion that 'the international order of Asia . . . resembles that of nineteenth-century Europe more than that of the twenty-first-century North Atlantic'.[58] These states use their new wealth to build up armies. Their forces are still no match for American military hyper-power, to be sure, but they are gradually modernizing their arma-ments and, in the case of China, India and Pakistan, they possess the trump card of nuclear weapons. As in nineteenth-century Europe, these states also have disputed borders and contested territories. China and India fought a minor border war in 1962. India and Pakistan have clashed in Kashmir, the Alsace-Lorraine of South Asia.

Meanwhile, China claims Taiwan, in the name of 'the reunification of the motherland'.[59] European visitors to the region find a kind of nationalism that has largely died out in twenty-first-century Europe. These nationalisms are fed by memories of past victories, defeats and occupations – as, for example, between China and Japan. India aspires to a kind of hegemony in the subcontinent, following, in this respect, the strategy of the British Raj. China seemed to be patiently edging towards something similar in East Asia. A Western analyst describes China's diplomatic strategy as 'neo-Bismarckian'.[60] Chinese commentators themselves recommend that their country should move from a 'victim mentality' to a 'great power mentality'.[61] Here, then, are rising great powers jockeying for position in all too familiar fashion. When the historian A. J. P. Taylor wrote a book about nineteenth-century European diplomacy, he called it *The Struggle for Mastery in Europe*. Perhaps one day another historian will write *The Struggle for Mastery in Asia*? Wars between these Asian 'strategic rivals' are not likely, writes Kissinger, 'but neither are they excluded'.[62]

Against this sombre interpretation, several counter-arguments are advanced. First, these Asian states may look like the European nation-states that emerged after the seventeenth-century Peace of Westphalia, but they are informed by different spirits, whether Confucian, Buddhist, Muslim or Hindu. The region is 'dressed in Westphalian clothes but . . . not performing according to a Westphalian script'.[63] Second, their overwhelming imperative is domestic economic modernization. In a globalized economy, dependent on volatile capital markets, this requires states to behave differently from nineteenth-century Germany, Austria or France. In any case, Japan has, under American tutelage, long practised pacific multilateral cooperation, though combined with statist protectionism at home. India has, in the tradition of Gandhi and Nehru, been a pillar of the United Nations and all its works. China is increasingly engaged in all sorts of international institutions, notably the World Trade Organization, and multilateral ties. Having got over Nato's accidental bombing of its embassy in Belgrade, it even approached Nato for a series of 'conversations'. In a unipolar world, Chinese leaders also see 'multipolarity' as a way of constraining a unilateralist hyperpower America.

In their international relations, there is therefore some chance that these rising powers of Asia can, as it were, skip the European twentieth century, jumping from nineteenth-century, European-style great-power rivalry to twenty-first-century, Euroatlantic-style strategic cooperation. (After all, Asia has already had a terrible twentieth century of its own.) Certainly, it is the overwhelming common interest of America, Europe and free people everywhere to encourage that outcome. Few things are more important for the future of the free.

Do American and European interests in the region otherwise diverge? Take two definitions of the American national interest in Asia. According to the conservative realist Henry Kissinger, 'America's national interest in Asia is to prevent domination of the continent by any single power, especially an adversarial one; to enlist the contribution of Asian nations to overall global prosperity; and to mitigate intra-Asian conflicts.'[64] The liberal internationalist Bill Clinton identifies no less than six American national interests in relations with China: global order, with China 'not only playing by the rules of international behaviour but helping to write and enforce them'; 'peace and stability in Asia', including the restraint of North Korea; 'keeping weapons of mass destruction . . . out of unstable regions and away from rogue states and terrorists' (this, *nota bene*, in a speech delivered in 1997); 'fighting drug trafficking and international organized crime', which is often based in China and neighbouring areas; 'making global trade and investment as free, fair and open as possible', especially for American exports to China; and, finally, China will soon overtake the United States as the world's largest emitter of greenhouse gases which, this American president stated categorically, 'lead to climate change'.[65]

Is there a single one of these interests, whether on Kissinger's list or Clinton's, that Europe does not wholly share? Roughly two thirds of America's foreign trade is with Asia. In 2002, China overtook Japan to become the EU's second largest trading partner outside Europe.[66] Both America and Europe run monster trade deficits with China, $105 billion for the US and €47 billion for the EU in 2002.[67] Both are anxious to sell more of their goods in a market potentially bigger than the whole European Union and North American Free Trade Area combined. Both have large and growing stocks of direct investment in Asia.

Not just the economic but the military and diplomatic behaviour of these rising powers will be shaped by the evolution of their domestic politics. Japan is a secure democracy, though of a slightly peculiar kind. India shows that you can already have a democracy in a vast, linguistically diverse and still poor country, but its tolerant pluralism is threatened by drastic inequality, Hindu nationalism and answering fanaticisms. Pakistan is a deeply unstable regime, hovering between flawed democracy, military dictatorship and Islamist extremism.

In China, nobody can predict how the politics of combining a still ostensibly communist regime with a vibrant, corrupt, drastically unequal capitalist economy will work out. 'Leninist capitalism' does not seem a stable condition. If the correlation that we explored earlier between per capita GDP and democracy holds good, then China should be a democracy some time in the 2020s.[68] But nobody knows if the correlation will hold for a vast country with such old and different political traditions. To give just one example: the bedrock of a secure liberal capitalist democracy is what the early nineteenth-century American president John Adams called 'the government of laws, and not of men'. But the Sinologist Simon Leys notes that in the Confucian understanding, 'the government is of men, not of laws'. This, he adds, 'remains one of the most dangerous flaws in the Chinese political tradition'.[69] Yet optimists see the rule of law already beginning to take hold, in response to the requirements of a market economy.[70]

So the long-term interests of America and Europe in the far East largely coincide. This does not, however, result in Americans and Europeans being equally interested, let alone in coordinated long-term policies. Anyone who spends time on both continents can see that America is, as a matter of observable everyday fact, much more interested in the far East than Europe is. For example, you cannot keep reliably informed about the politics of the region from the newspapers and journals of any European country, including Britain.[71] On the West coast of America, by contrast, it is sometimes difficult to keep informed about anywhere but Asia.

The United States entered the Second World War not following Roosevelt's meeting with Churchill in Placentia Bay – despite the Atlantic Charter – but when the Japanese bombed the American fleet at Pearl Harbor, on an island in the Pacific. For many Americans, the war in the Pacific was *the* war. As Kissinger points out, the US then fought two more major foreign wars, in Korea and Vietnam, to prevent a single, hostile power becoming predominant in Asia. The US military's Pacific Command has some 300,000 serving men and women deployed in some forty-three countries and ten US territories across the whole region. It has 37,000 troops stationed in South Korea alone. If mainland China threatens Taiwan, the US has said it will go to Taiwan's aid. (President George W. Bush ended the earlier policy of 'strategic ambiguity'.) This interest in the region is now stoked by 12 million Asian-Americans, whose votes every national politician has to weigh and woo. If anything, Washington's problem has been a surfeit rather than a dearth of Asian policies.

None of this applies to Europe. Following the handover to China of Hong Kong and Macao, no European power has any significant territory or military presence in the region. European investors and businesspeople are deeply engaged in Asia, but political and public interest in the far East is sporadic at best. Britain is the only European country to have a significant Asian population, but even in Britain the level of ignorance is impressive. In one session of the British television quiz show *University Challenge*, eight of the country's brightest, best-informed students were shown a map of India, with the position of several main cities marked by anonymous blobs. No one could name a single one. (Churchill must be harrumphing in his grave.)

Europe as a whole has nothing that can seriously be described as a far Eastern strategy. Instead, individual European countries conduct policies towards individual Asian countries, or groups of them, based on historic ties, national perceptions and commercial self-interest. For China, as for America, this brings the irresistible temptation to divide and rule. In the late 1990s, for example, China consummately picked away country after country from public condemnation of its abysmal human rights record. It punished those European states, such as Denmark, that supported the regular condemnatory motion at the UN Human Rights Commission in Geneva, while rewarding those, such as France and Germany, which refrained. So much for European solidarity.[72] Mindful of this experience, which he had watched at first hand from Hong Kong, the EU's External Relations Commissioner, Chris Patten, subsequently pulled together, on paper at least, an EU policy towards China.[73] But European solidarity is still in short supply, particularly when national economic advantage is involved.

The far East seems less likely than the near East to divide Europe from America, simply because Europe is so relatively uninterested, with no alternative strategy of its own. There will continue to be fierce competition for commercial advantage, although this will be as much between multinational companies as between nations. There will surely be differences of diplomatic emphasis, often along familiar lines, with continental Europeans tending to prefer dialogue and 'quiet diplomacy' to America's more public denunciations of human rights abuses, and Britain, together with Anglosphere countries such as Canada and Australia, standing somewhere in between. If tensions in the far East lead to a military confrontation involving the United States – over North Korea, for example, or over Taiwan – there is the potential for another crisis of the West, with Europeans shying away even from the threat of warlike action, especially in the defence of faraway countries of which they know little.

Yet there is also a real opportunity for a coordinated strategy, involving not just Europe and America but also the free countries in the region itself, including the old-established Anglosphere democracies of Australia and New Zealand. Such a strategy must be based on a sober assessment of the limits of Western power. The truth is that even the most powerful country in the history of the earth, the early twenty-first-century United States, can have only a secondary impact on the internal evolution of a huge, proud and self-referential country like China. If most of the free countries of the world, which for the time being still control most of the world's wealth, adopt a similar basic approach, coordinated in all the international fora where China wishes to be accepted and respected, the positive impact could be slightly greater.

Even if the odds against success are long, the prize is enormous. To have China eventually join Japan and India as a cooperative liberal democracy would be the biggest payout in the history of freedom. Then the great and once great powers of the West might look forward, not with complete equanimity, but certainly with less alarm, to history's slow, glacial shift in the balance of power, from West back to East.

## RICH NORTH, POOR SOUTH

If you think of the world as a city, then the early twenty-first-century West is a gated community of the rich, surrounded by poorer neighbourhoods and terrible slums. In round figures, roughly one billion of the world's six billion inhabitants are rich. They have an average income of approximately $70 a day – which means, of course, that many have less but some have much more.[74] They live mainly in Europe, North America, Japan, and a few other prosperous countries. In the mental geography of development rather than geopolitics, the West of the free is the 'North' of the rich. (Thus Australia, though in the southern hemisphere, is part of the 'North'.) At the other end, in the poor 'South', more than one billion men, women and children live on less than $1 a day. Only slightly better off are another one to two billion people living on less than $2 a day. According to UN figures, between 1999 and 2001, some 840 million people went hungry; one in every seven people in the world.[75] At the same time, nearly one third of Americans suffer from the serious health problem of obesity. Who needs a parable? In the South, men, women and children are dying because they don't have enough to eat; in the North, they are dying because they eat too much.

It has been estimated that in 1999 the assets of the world's three richest people, Bill Gates, Warren Buffett and Paul Allen, exceeded the total annual gross national product of all the world's least developed countries, with a combined population of some 600 million.[76] At the World Economic Forum in Davos in 2001, where companies with combined annual sales of around $5 trillion were represented, the immensely decent-seeming John Thornton, then president of Goldman Sachs, said that when he contemplated the way in which some parts of the world were so much focused on accumulating ever more private wealth he felt 'almost a kind of embarrassment'.[77] Almost a kind of . . .

On 11 September 2001, the day that just over 3,000 people were killed in the al-Qaeda attacks on New York and Washington, some 30,000 children died around the world from preventable disease.[78] And the next day. And the day after that. And every day of the year. Altogether, an estimated 22 million people died from preventable disease in 2001, of whom more than 10 million were children.[79] Ten million is the population of Greater London and its suburbs inside the M25 motorway; of Michigan; of Hungary. Please take a moment to picture to yourself a London peopled entirely with dying children. And the next year, a Michigan of dying children. And the year after that, a Hungary.

A cool head and cold heart might retort: "twas ever thus'. So far back as historians can discern, a large part of humankind has always lived on the edge of extreme poverty, with the accompanying plagues of hunger, disease, unfreedom, illiteracy, violence and early death. But some things have changed. In the past, the world's rich were not able to watch, on their television screens, as the world's poor died. A growing number of the world's poor can also glimpse, on video, film or television, how the other half live. Never before has the world had the resources, derived from economic growth, to tackle worldwide deprivation. And never in recorded history have the world's rich been so much richer than the world's poor. In 1820, the income gap between the five richest and the five poorest countries in the world is estimated to have been about 3 to 1; in 1913, it was 11 to 1; in 1992, 72 to 1.[80] The main reason for this soaring global inequality is the unprecedented economic development that began in the West with the industrial revolution. This is what has made the rich so much richer. Has it also made the poor poorer?

Here is the charge made against 'globalization' by the so-called 'anti-globalizers'. Yet the more thoughtful of them acknowledge that globalization is too complex a phenomenon to be summarily condemned. Some aspects of economic globalization have been good for some of the world's poor, others bad. The biggest reductions in poverty have come in those Asian countries which have begun to 'take off' economically. Economic growth has enabled them to reduce the number of their people living in absolute poverty, even though their populations have also grown. These countries have 'taken off' precisely because they have managed to plug in to the world economy, selling their goods and services abroad. A team of World Bank economists concludes that poor countries with some 3 billion people are among these 'new globalizers', but around 2 billion people are in danger of falling by the wayside, as their countries fail to break into world markets.[81] So the question at century's beginning is not 'whether globalization?' but 'what kind of globalization?'. Even the 'anti-globalizers' have restyled themselves *altermondialistes* or 'alternative globalizers'. Can we achieve globalization with a human face?

To contribute to this end, the governments of the world held a United Nations 'millennium summit' in 2000. They agreed an unprecedented set of Millennium Development Goals for all humankind. The clearest targets are these: to halve, between 1990 and 2015, the proportion of the human race living on less than $1 a day and the proportion suffering from hunger; to ensure that, by 2015, all the world's children can complete a full course of primary schooling; to reduce by two thirds, between 1990 and 2015, the mortality rate among children under five, and, by three quarters, the mortality rate among mothers giving birth; to have begun to reverse, by 2015, the spread of HIV/AIDS, malaria and other major diseases; and to halve, by 2015, the proportion of people without sustainable access to safe drinking water.[82] These audacious goals will be especially difficult to achieve because the world's population is expected to increase to some 7 billion by 2015, while its natural resources will be diminished.

Most of those professionally involved in fostering development agree that the first responsibility lies with the governments of the developing countries themselves. If a government is corrupt, inefficient and exploitative, as so many of them have been, then all the aid in the world will just be good money thrown after bad. As Amartya Sen argues, the causal connections between freedom and development go both ways. Increasingly, development specialists concentrate on what they call 'good governance' in the countries concerned. This is the key to ensuring that aid and the profits from trade do not go straight into the pockets of the local rulers, their families and their cronies; that budget cuts, where they are demanded by the International Monetary Fund, the World Bank or the European Union, fall on wasteful ostentation, bureaucracy and the military, rather than – as happened too often in the 1990s – further penalizing the poor by cutting expenditure on health systems, education and minimal social security for the unemployed and destitute. None the less, the best imaginable government in the whole poor South cannot achieve balanced, sustainable development for its people without help from the rich North – meaning, mainly, the West.

Beside good advice, the two most important things the poorest countries of the world need from the rich North/West are aid, including debt relief, and trade. How are the main pillars of the North/West doing in these respects? In the fiscal year 2002/3, the United States spent a little over $13 billion on official development assistance. That was just 0.13 per cent of its GDP – or 13 cents out of every $100. This was the lowest proportion of GDP spent by any of the twenty-three rich donor countries in the Development Assistance Committee of the Organization for Economic Cooperation and Development. So the richest country gave least. By comparison, America's defence expenditure in that year, including the costs of the Iraq War and the early months of the occupation, was in the order of $430 billion.[83] Its total expenditure on Iraq alone was roughly eight times what it spent on overseas aid. Moreover, the largest part of this official aid budget is devoted, for political reasons, to a number of countries, including Egypt, Russia, Israel and Serbia, which are by no means among the poorest of the poor.

The official US Agency for International Development argues that 'American aid' overall is much larger than this, claiming a further $12 billion for assistance given by other government agencies, although this very questionably includes items such as Pentagon 'foreign military loans', and a sweeping $33.6 billion for 'private assistance', which even more questionably includes $18 billion for 'individual remittances'.[84] There is just half a point here. As we have seen, Americans tend to do less through the state and more through private giving. At the front line, in countries in distress, you will often find charities like George Soros's Open Society Foundation, Human Rights Watch or the Ford Foundation, working closely with European charities such as the Oxford-based Oxfam, the London-based Amnesty International and the French-founded *Médecins sans frontières*. These voices of the other America are clear and strong in the chorus of what has been called 'global civil society'.[85] But such private generosity does not begin to excuse the American government for a miserliness that truly beggars belief. In the spring of 2002, President George W. Bush announced a headline 'fifty per cent' increase in American development aid, channelled through a Millennium Challenge Account.[86] Welcome though this was, the $13 billion that the richest country in the world condescended to spend on the world's poor would only rise to around $15 billion in 2006.[87] Meanwhile, for the years 2002 to 2004, the United States was already committed to spending more than $165 billion on the occupation of Iraq and Afghanistan.[88]

Europeans pride themselves on doing better. And so they do – relative to the United States. In fact, if one adds together the aid given by individual EU member states and that given collectively by the EU, Europe gives nearly three times more than the United States in foreign aid, despite having a slightly smaller total economy.[89] But in absolute terms, and relative to our overall wealth, the aid record of Europeans is merely bad rather than abysmal. In 1969, the former Canadian prime minister, Lester Pearson, proposed that the rich countries of the world should aim to give 0.7 per cent of their GDP in foreign aid.* This target was endorsed by the UN General Assembly in 1970.[90] Thirty years later, the rich countries of the world gave, on average, just 0.22 per cent of their GDP. Shockingly, this figure has actually fallen since 1990. The West has taken its 'peace dividend' after the end of the Cold War by cutting aid.

Yet to achieve the Millennium Development Goals in 2015, the UN Development Programme reckons that rich countries will have to spend a total of at least $100 billion a year, or roughly double what they give at present. Lester Pearson's 0.7 per cent would make it $165 billion. Here is just one indication of what this increased aid could mean: a group of economists and health specialists working for the World Health Organization calculate that $25 billion would provide basic life-saving health services (immunizations against killer diseases, and so forth) for at least two thirds of the population of the poorest countries. Epidemiologists at the London School of Hygiene and Tropical Medicine estimate that this would save eight million lives per year.[91] Do we think these eight million mainly African lives worth an extra $25 from each of us, the rich billion? Apparently not.

* *The New Republic*, a leading Washington weekly, once held a competition to find a headline even more *boring* than 'Worthwhile Canadian Initiative'. But let them jeer down in Washington, this really was a worthwhile Canadian initiative.

The misery of the world's poor is exacerbated by the fact that many of the poorest countries, especially those in Sub-Saharan Africa, are heavily in debt to Western banks, governments, and international financial institutions such as the World Bank and the IMF. In the past, these loans were often irresponsibly thrust upon them by petrodollar-rich Western banks and misused by corrupt, undemocratic rulers. Some of these tyrants simply siphoned the money back into other Western banks as their private wealth. The interest that their subjects now have to pay back is often more than all the aid their countries receive. Spurred on by an international civil society campaign for debt relief called Jubilee 2000, Western/Northern governments have launched an imaginative if complex initiative for heavily indebted poor countries, but the linkage it makes to IMF programmes is controversial and its progress painfully slow. Even in countries that are doing everything the North/West asked, and have been relieved of much of their debt, the remaining burden of interest payments can still overwhelm their meagre earnings from exports.

The biggest single thing the rich North can do for the poor South is not aid or debt relief, but simply to allow those exports in. Yet this is what rich countries have most spectacularly failed to do. They preach free trade to the world, and even impose it to open up the markets of poorer countries to their goods. But they surround their own markets with high protective walls: permanent, overt ones, called tariffs; temporary, semi-overt ones, called 'anti-dumping' measures; and covert ones, through a tangled skein of special regulations. The World Bank calculates that these trade barriers cost developing countries at least $100 billion a year in lost exports – much more than the rich currently give them in aid.[92]

That's not all. What the poorest of the poor are most likely to be able to export to the rich are the basic products of the earth, grown cheaply on their farms and tended with their hands. Yet rich countries pay huge subsidies to their own agricultural producers. As a result of these subsidies, their exports undercut those of farmers in poor countries. In 2001, the rich countries paid $311 billion in domestic agricultural subsidies: approximately six times what they gave in aid, and more than the total combined GDP of Sub-Saharan Africa.[93]

Many Europeans like to think of themselves as morally superior to

Americans in their concern for the 'Third World' – as some still call it, although the Second has disappeared in the meantime. When it comes to giving aid, they generally are; but not in openness for trade. In a darkly amusing parody of the 'indices' now produced for almost every aspect of global development, Oxfam has compiled a Double Standards Index to show the level of protectionist trade policies against exports from developing countries deployed by the richest and most powerful trading nations. The European Union comes a clear first – that is, worst.[94] In 2000, the annual dairy subsidy paid by the European Union was $913 per cow. This was nearly double the average annual income of someone living in Sub-Saharan Africa. In aid, the EU gave $8 per head to Sub-Saharan Africa. So, that is $913 for a European cow and $8 for an African person.[95] European agricultural exports, subsidized by the EU's Common Agricultural Policy (CAP), drive farmers in poor countries out of business – and into destitution.[96] But where are the crowds on the streets of European capitals protesting against the CAP?

European policymakers are aware of the injustice and have tried to address it. In 2001, the EU took an imaginative initiative to remove tariffs on 'Everything But Arms' imported from the poorest countries in the world.[97] They have also made endless, contorted efforts to reform the CAP. But one of the formative moments of the 'old Europe' alliance in the crisis over Iraq was a deal cut between Schröder and Chirac in the autumn of 2002 which effectively saw off radical reform of the CAP. Defenders of the Common Agricultural Policy say it is needed to preserve the rich, variegated European countryside, yet most of the CAP money goes not to the beautiful, traditional small farms of Provence or Tuscany but to those agricultural industrialists who are defacing the European countryside with endless, hedgeless fields of sugar beet or yellow rape.[98] These agricultural subsidies are still much the largest single item of EU expenditure: 46 per cent of its budget in 2003, and seven times what it spent on foreign aid. So at the heart of what the EU actually does, there is a policy irrefutably causing avoidable harm to the poorest of the world's poor. So much for Europe's moral superiority. America is, in aid policy, the world's leading miser, but Europe is, in trade, the world's leading hypocrite.

To be sure, the United States comes not far behind in the Double Standards Index, followed by Canada and Japan. In 2002, President Bush signed into law a farm bill promising another $180 billion in subsidies to American farmers.[99] Many of these are as indefensible as the European ones. For example, the US gives more than $2 billion in annual subsidies to just 25,000 American cotton farmers.[100] These subsidies depress the world cotton price, costing Third World producers an estimated $350 million a year.[101] Consider the impact on Benin, one of the world's poorest countries, but nevertheless a fragile democracy, classified by Freedom House as 'free'.[102] For years, Benin has been struggling to pay off its inherited debts, with its debt service payments exceeding its spending on basic social services.[103] The key to its development is earnings from exports. Three quarters of its exports are in one crop: cotton. It has seen the world price for cotton fall by more than 40 per cent in the five years from 1997 to 2002.[104] American subsidies are punishing poor cotton farmers in Benin as surely as European subsidies are punishing poor tomato farmers in Ghana.[105]

In yet another index, the Center for Global Development in Washington and *Foreign Policy* magazine rank the rich countries by their 'commitment to development'.[106] They use six measures, starting with aid and trade, but going on to look at foreign investment, migration (letting people into rich countries can help their poor relatives back home), contributions to peacekeeping, and environmental policies (on the grounds that poor countries suffer worse from the effects of climate change, such as drought or flooding, and the spread of infectious diseases). In 2003, the Netherlands did best, closely followed by Denmark and New Zealand. Japan just pipped the United States for bottom place.

Everywhere in the West/North, in America as in Europe, there are committed people using such indices, advertising campaigns, the internet and other new forms of political activism to draw our attention to the selfishness and hypocrisy of all the rich countries. However, twenty-first-century democracies give ever more effective power to another group of highly skilled and motivated people: lobbyists. The two world capitals of lobbying are Washington and Brussels. In Washington, at least 20,000 registered lobbyists represent

myriad special interests and fifty federal states.[107] In Brussels, at least
10,000 lobbyists represent special interests, twenty-five nation-states,
and powerful regions (Bavaria, Galicia, Tuscany etc).

In many areas of trade and development policy progress depends
on a structured, multilateral negotiation in which countries say to
each other 'if you do this, I'll do that'. The most important of these is
the so-called 'Doha round' of trade talks, led by the World Trade
Organization. In recognition of a global priority for development,
this has been dubbed the 'development round'. It was meant to be
completed by the end of 2004, but at Cancún in Mexico in September
2003, the rich countries dismally failed to do enough to satisfy the
increasingly demanding poor. Their hands tied by a thousand lobbies
and special interests, the American miser and the European hypocrite
competed in selfishness.

In making their argument for generosity, the Western/Northern
advocates for the poor often appeal to self-interest. If the West/North
does not do more for the world's poor, so the argument goes, we must
face the consequences in instability, organized crime, drugs, illegal
migration, terrorism and even threats of military action with small,
easily portable weapons of mass destruction. This is true. But it is also
true that women and children dying in Sub-Saharan Africa do not
pose a major security threat to rich people living in the gated community of the West. We can, if we want, afford to let Africans go on
dying miserably in large numbers, as we have for most of recorded
history. There are risks, but they are, on a pure calculus of interest,
manageably small. To be sure, where the poor South actually touches
the rich North/West, as in north Africa, Turkey or central America,
poverty is an immediate political problem, which threatens to de-
stabilize the domestic politics as well as the foreign policies of both
Europe and America. But in regions such as Sub-Saharan Africa,
poverty is essentially a moral challenge to the conscience of the
West/North.

Some would make this moral case by arguing from historic,
collective responsibility: it was the bourgeois capitalist industrial
development of the West which produced this soaring global inequality, and Western colonialism that created the states these people
are now in. But that kind of argument is not necessary, nor especially

wise, since the moral balance sheet of both industrialization and col-
onization is disputed within the West. All that is needed is to refer to
the ethical first principles of the West. The most basic shared moral
claim of Europeans, Americans and free people everywhere is that
every human being has an inalienable right to a life of minimal human
dignity. That right is being denied every day to hundreds of millions
of men, women and children in the poor South. Their miserable lot,
even if it was not originally caused by the West/North, is being
demonstrably and substantially exacerbated by policies of the
North/West. Here is today's moral crisis of the West.


## HUMANS THREATEN EARTH

How long can the planet Earth sustain ever more human beings consuming ever more food, water and energy? That is the largest challenge facing us all at the beginning of the twenty-first century. It is
also the most difficult to write about, since our assessment depends
on fiercely disputed scientific predictions.

With consciously spurious precision, the United Nations declared
12 October 1999 as the day on which the world's population passed
6 billion. They even designated Adnan Mević, born in the Kosevo
Hospital in Sarajevo at one minute past midnight, the 6-billionth
baby.[108] World population growth has been accelerating. We needed
millions of years to reach our first billion, in about 1804. According
to UN estimates, it took 123 years to add the next billion by 1927, 33
years to reach 3 billion in 1960, then 14 years to 4 billion, 13 years
to 5 billion and just 12 years to 6 billion.[109] On a United Nations
website, there's a mesmerizing counter showing the estimated world
population today. At exactly 1 p.m. on Thursday 25 March, just
before I sent this book to the typesetters, the figure was
6,353,098,684, but there's one born every two fifths of a second.[110]

Were the world's population to carry on growing at this rate, it
would be close to 13 billion in 2050.[111] But the experts don't think it
will. They think the world is experiencing an outsize version of the
'demographic transition' that many individual countries have gone
through as they developed. First, food supplies, living conditions and

healthcare improve; as a result, life expectancy goes up while birth rates remain high, so population increases rapidly. Then, as people become more affluent, women more emancipated, and parents more confident that their children will survive, the curve flattens off – until eventually we start worrying about having too few children rather than too many. None the less, the UN's median prediction puts the likely world population at nearly 8 billion by 2025 and just under 9 billion by 2050.[112]

Surprisingly, the experts think that, for the foreseeable future, there will be enough food to go round. In 1798, when the world had barely one billion people, Thomas Malthus foresaw terrible disasters flowing from the imbalance in 'the proportion between the natural increase of population and food'.[113] But in a global perspective of two centuries, Malthus has been proved wrong. Thanks largely to the so-called 'Green revolution', food production per head has increased in every region of the world except Africa since the late 1970s, despite the spectacular growth in the number of mouths to feed. In China, it has nearly doubled.[114] The trouble with the world today is not that we can't grow enough food; it's that too much of the food is in the wrong stomachs. As we have seen, hundreds of millions of people in rich countries eat too much, and suffer ill-health as a result, while more than 700 million still go hungry in Africa and the poorer parts of Asia. Obviously, there are still countries with painful shortfalls in domestic food production, but the main problem is one of distribution – or, if you will, redistribution.

In principle that's also true of the other basic necessity of human existence: water. After all, most of the surface of our 'blue planet' is covered by water, in the oceans and ice caps. In practice we mainly depend on the tiny proportion of the world's water that falls or flows on land, or rests under it. Here there is a gathering crisis. As we've seen, one of the Millennium Development Goals is to halve by 2015 the proportion of people without sustainable access to safe drinking water. At the moment, roughly one in three people in rural areas of the developing world does not have such access.[115] The total number is over 1 billion. As population grows, and water usage increases with economic development, that number may actually get larger. Already, some 1.7 billion people live in countries facing 'water stress'.[116] In

Europe, there are four countries which are considered to be water-stressed – Italy, Spain, Cyprus and Malta. But the shortage is most dramatic in the near East and parts of Africa. Competition for scarce water has sharpened conflicts between states; not least between Israel and its Arab neighbours. Water supplies will probably be further disrupted by the effects of global warming. In the future, we may see 'water wars'.[117]

Then there's energy. We humans, like other animals, derive our basic daily energy from the food we eat. Since the discovery of fire, we have augmented our own body-power by burning wood, dung or other natural products. Astonishingly, some 2.4 billion people still depend entirely on these primitive sources of energy for their cooking and heating.[118] The rest of us can barely imagine living without electricity, gas and oil to heat and light our homes and offices, pump our drinking water, power our cars and buses, and manufacture the objects we use every day. When we have a small taste of life without artificial power, as Bosnians did during the siege of Sarajevo, we talk of a return to barbarism. Most of this external energy is derived from burning the decomposed remains of plants and plankton that have accumulated over 400 million years. These so-called fossil fuels – oil, gas and coal – account for more than three quarters of all the energy we use. As countries develop economically, so their demand for such energy soars.

Looking a quarter-century ahead, the experts predict a future in which total world energy consumption will have grown by nearly two thirds, with the increased demand coming mainly from the developing countries of Asia, and especially China.[119] They seem to agree that most of the extra energy will continue to be derived from burning oil, gas and coal, rather than from nuclear power, or so-called 'renewable' sources such as the natural forces of wind, waves and rivers, the heat of the sun and that of the Earth's own core. They also think that in twenty-five years' time there will still be enough conventional energy sources to meet these increased needs, although, like the food, much of it will not be in the places where it is most needed. The developed countries of Europe and North America will produce less oil and gas of their own, and therefore be more dependent than ever on imports from the OPEC oil- and gas-producing states, especially those in the near East, and from Russia and other countries around the Caspian Sea. These experts may be wrong; but if they are right, important consequences follow.

A better distribution of food is primarily a moral challenge to the West/North. It is part of the agenda of development that I discussed in the last section. So is access to safe drinking water, although the politics of water also have the potential to catalyse conflict in unstable regions of the world, such as the near East. The politics of oil and gas have a more direct impact on Western policies. They heavily influence, some would say dictate, the priority given to some regions and countries rather than others. They generate a constant temptation to tolerate or even prop up undemocratic regimes, as Americans and Europeans have long done in the near East, and are now inclining to do in Russia, central Asia and the Caucasus. Since the vital material interests of states and politically influential corporations are involved, there's also the potential for conflict between free countries. It's unlikely that the dividing line will fall sharply between Europe and America, but this will remain a challenge of the first order for Western policymakers.

Yet securing enough fossil fuel to burn, without coming to blows or utterly compromising our own principles, is only half this challenge. The other half is the long-term threat to human life on Earth that will result from burning too much of it. There are, of course, many other global environmental concerns, most of which flow ultimately from the exponential growth in human exploitation of the physical world since a young Scotsman called James Watt harnessed the power of heated water to turn the first modern steam engine in 1769.[120] Development economists talk of 'global commons': things like the extent of the world's forests or the condition of the oceans. They identify an intrinsic difficulty: individual countries rarely have sufficient incentives to act to preserve these 'global commons', since they can themselves only capture a small part of the rewards for doing so and those rewards will only accrue if others do the same.[121] Indeed, the short-term interests of a single nation and the long-term interests of the wider world will often conflict. Brazilians have short-term economic gains from cutting down their rain-forest, while that reduces for all of us the capacity of the Earth to reabsorb carbon dioxide and other greenhouse gases. Japanese whalers have short-term profits from overfishing the high seas, while the depletion of oceanic fish stocks is a long-term worry for us all.

Of the many such threats to 'global commons', including the degradation of land and sea, persistent pollutants and the dwindling number of plant and animal species, I will concentrate on two: depletion of the ozone layer and global warming. Now you may object that depletion of the ozone layer is yesterday's story. But that's exactly the point. It is yesterday's story because a real danger was met, probably just in time, by coordinated multilateral action to reduce worldwide output of ozone-depleting chlorofluorocarbons, or CFCs. The United States was among the leaders here, banning all non-essential CFC aerosol sprays in 1978 and then signing the multilateral Montreal Treaty in 1987. As a result, the atmospheric concentration of ozone-depleting substances began to fall within a decade.[122]

Nothing of the kind has yet happened with global warming. The main generic reasons are that the problem is bigger and more complex, the human causes of global warming still contested and the financial costs of addressing them much larger. However, a very important specific reason is that the United States, instead of being among the leaders, as it was in saving the ozone layer, has dodged and ducked to evade its unique responsibility.

The facts of global warming are disputed, but there seems to be a consensus of mainstream scientific opinion on the following. Over the past million years, the surface of the Earth has gone through an alternating series of glacial periods, when the ice comes down and the weather is distinctly chilly even for an Inuit, and 'interglacial' periods, when it's warmer. The last of these interglacial periods, the Holocene, began some 10,000 years ago and we're still in it. According to evidence from ice cores, this appears to be the longest stable warm stretch for as far back as we can see.[123] The Holocene is the precondition for all known human civilization. The average surface temperature of the Earth has oscillated throughout these millennia, but not, on the available evidence, by very much in the thousand years from 900 to 1900 CE. We can say with more confidence that it rose sharply from 1910 to 1945, declined somewhat for the next quarter-century, and then started skyrocketing again after 1976.[124] The summer of 2003 was the hottest on record for 500 years.[125]

This rise in global temperature has consequences: melting ice, rising sea levels, more unpredictable storms and floods. According to one of the world's leading reinsurance firms, Munich Re, natural disasters, mostly caused by extreme weather, cost some $60 billion in 2003.[126] As Europeans debated the Iraq War in the summer of 2003, they experienced a heatwave which caused some 20,000 deaths and $10 billion in agricultural losses. We cannot say with absolute certainty that this heatwave was a result of long-term global warming, but the hot air generated by debate about Iraq does not seem a sufficient explanation. On the whole, though, the specialists conclude that the poorer countries will be worst affected by the consequences of climate change. Poorer countries don't have the money or technology to deal with natural disasters. If the Indian ocean rises just one metre, Bangladesh will lose half its current rice production.[127] But will the ocean rise? That depends on the global temperature.

The findings of the Intergovernmental Panel on Climate Change – described by Margaret Thatcher as 'an authoritative early-warning system'[128] – are worth quoting in all their scientific caution. 'There is new and stronger evidence', the panel concludes in its latest report, 'that most of the warming observed over the last 50 years is attributable to human activities.'[129] The main human activities responsible are our increased emissions of greenhouse gases, and, to a lesser degree, our cutting down the forests that reabsorb some of these gases. The panel looks at various scenarios for future emissions, and predicts 'an increase in globally averaged surface temperature of 1.4 to 5.8 degrees Centigrade over the period 1990 to 2100. This is about two to ten times larger than the central value of observed warming over the twentieth century and the projected rate of warming is very likely to be without precedent during at least the last 10,000 years.'[130] Within this range of scenarios, average worldwide sea level could rise between 0.09 and 0.88 metres by 2100, but more in some places and less in others.[131]

The scientific evidence seems beyond reasonable doubt: the world is rapidly getting warmer and the main reason is the heat-retaining greenhouse gases we are pumping into the sky. More than half these harmful emissions are accounted for by one gas, carbon dioxide, which is produced mainly by burning oil, gas and coal. The panel points out that the warming effect will continue long after we've reduced our emissions, since the gases will already be up there. So common sense would suggest that we'll soon be reducing carbon dioxide emissions, as we did those ozone-depleting chlorofluorocarbons. But if we turn back to the authoritative study of world energy use, we read that, on current trends, global energy-related emissions of carbon dioxide will increase by 1.8 per cent per year, reaching 38 billion tonnes in 2030 – 70 per cent more than today.[132] Two thirds of the increase is expected to come in developing countries, especially China, but the largest single emitter will still be the United States.

Here we must confront what I've called the *unique* responsibility of the United States. This responsibility does not derive merely from its position of world leadership, as the sole hyperpower. I have thus far explored many fields in which the differences between Europe and America are smaller than most people think and it is unclear which side of the Atlantic is doing better or worse. Not so with carbon dioxide. Having less than 5 per cent of the world's population, America belches out nearly 25 per cent of humankind's annual production of greenhouse gases.[133] The EU, an economy of roughly equal size to the US, emits much less. Every year, the skies must absorb a staggering twenty metric tons of carbon dioxide for every American, compared with less than nine metric tons for every European.[134] And it has been getting worse. In 2000, America's carbon dioxide emissions were 14 per cent higher than in 1990.[135]

In their profligate burning of fossil fuels, Americans really are living as if there's no tomorrow. Some have suggested that this careless attitude to natural resources lies deep in the psyche of a people who settled such a vast, richly endowed country. The great American novelist John Steinbeck observed that the early settlers 'burned the forests and changed the rainfall; they swept the buffalo from the plains, blasted the streams, set fire to the grass, and ran a reckless scythe through the virgin and noble timber. Perhaps they felt it was limitless and could never be exhausted . . .' Writing in the early 1960s, Steinbeck bitterly concluded: 'We would not think of doing to the moon what we do every day to our own dear country.'[136] Well, Americans are not doing it to the moon, but they are now doing it to the Earth.

When asked by representatives of developing countries to put on the agenda of the 1992 Rio Earth Summit the over-consumption of resources by developed countries, and especially the United States, the administration of President George H. W. Bush replied: 'the American lifestyle is not up for negotiation'.[137] Now that expansive lifestyle is actually one of the aspects of America that most appeals to many Europeans: those outsize cars and fridges, open roads, endless shining lights and, for a European, unbelievably cheap petrol. What is it over-excited English visitors always say about New York? 'I love the *energy*.' Yes, exactly. But an American defence of unbridled national sovereignty in this domain is different from that in any other, since what the United States pumps into the skies from inside its own borders threatens the well-being of everyone outside them. In this context, it is worth reflecting for a moment on the comment of an eminent British climate scientist: 'I have no hesitation in describing [climate change] as a weapon of mass destruction.'[138]

When President George W. Bush decided at the beginning of his administration that he would not pursue ratification of the Kyoto Protocol, under which the Clinton administration had committed itself to a 7 per cent reduction in its greenhouse gas emissions by 2012, he cited, among other objections, the fact that no emission limits were specified for developing countries. After all, most of the global growth in emissions is expected to come from them. Moreover, a country like China emits more carbon dioxide per dollar of GDP than the US – in other words, Chinese industry and domestic heating are a bit 'dirtier' than America's.[139] So instead, President Bush introduced his own Global Climate Change Initiative, trumpeting a commitment by the United States to reduce its 'greenhouse gas intensity' – that is, the amount of greenhouse gas per dollar of GDP – by 18 per cent by 2012.[140] However, his government's own International Energy Administration quietly pointed out that, since current trends of 'business as usual' growth would anyway result in a 14 per cent fall, what the president was promising effectively amounted to a 4 per cent cut against 2002 levels, rather than the Clinton administration's post-Kyoto commitment to 7 per cent on 1990 levels – a huge difference.[141] It was said of ancient Rome that the emperor Nero fiddled while the city burned. In the new Rome, the president fiddled while the Earth burned.

The contrast with Bush's closest European ally, Tony Blair, is instructive. As he was preparing to wage war on Iraq, shoulder-to-shoulder with Bush, Blair delivered a speech in which he reaffirmed Britain's Kyoto commitment to a 12.5 per cent cut in its 1990 greenhouse gas emission levels, which were already much lower than those of the US. He went on to say that even if everyone adhered to Kyoto, it would only produce a global reduction of 2 per cent in emissions, whereas the science suggested that what we need is a 60 per cent reduction by 2050. A team of scientists had reported to him that this could be done, by creative investment in renewable sources of energy (sun, wind, waves) and alternative fuels, such as hydrogen. So he and the Swedish prime minister had written a letter to the EU presidency, proposing that the whole EU should sign up to the target of a 60 per cent reduction by 2050.[142] On global warming, this other weapon of mass destruction, Blair has been every centimetre the European.

Any informed citizen, drawing on reliable science, can see what is now needed. There has to be a multilateral agreement which assigns to all relevant countries, including developing ones like China, a timetabled 'quota' for greenhouse gas emissions. There then has to be provision for 'emissions trading' between countries, which is the most cost-effective way of achieving the desired result. For this to happen, America is, in Madeleine Albright's phrase, the indispensable nation. We cannot possibly expect a booming China to sign on to such an agreement if the largest and richest gas-emitter, the United States, does not. Even with America, Europe and free countries such as Canada and Australia working closely together, it will be difficult enough to persuade newly industrializing states to exercise a restraint that we have ourselves so obviously lacked.

Will America step up to this challenge? Perhaps an alarming consultants' report to the Pentagon, envisaging wars sparked by the effects of climate change, might help to change even right-wing Republicans' minds.[143] But once again, it is a great mistake to confuse America with George W. Bush. The man who got more votes than him in 2000, Al Gore, was on to the issue of climate change sooner than most Europeans. As Clinton's vice president, he flew to Kyoto in 1997 to salvage a last-minute compromise on the Protocol, although he was not able to stop it subsequently being voted down in the US

Senate. The conservative Republican senator John McCain, not an obvious 'green-green-lima-bean' (to recall President Bush's tag for environmentalists), reported that when he went on the campaign trail, 'in town-hall meeting after town-hall meeting, young people would stand up and say: "What is your position on global warming?"'[144] American scientists have been in the forefront of raising international consiousness on the issue.

A great deal can be done by the kind of technological innovation at which America excels, moving rapidly to renewable and low-carbon sources of energy. None the less, this is a major test for American democracy. To give a lead, America will have to change its cherished lifestyle more than any other nation. There are few votes in this for any candidate and immensely powerful lobbies against it. It calls for two of the most difficult things in politics: putting the wider international interest before the narrowly conceived national one; and the long term before the short term. On any sober reading of the past record and current state of American politics, such an outcome looks woefully unlikely. What arguments can America's friends, in Europe and elsewhere, offer to encourage it? Only that on America's choice will depend the fate of the Earth.

## TOGETHER?

We have seen, in previous chapters, that a simple dichotomy between a European model and an American model, European values and American values, is impossible to sustain, even if you look only inside the extended family of the West. There are almost as many contrasts within an ever more diverse Europe, and within an increasingly polarized America, as there are between Europe and America. Important Western countries such as Canada and Australia further complicate the picture, turning a dichotomy into a continuum. In this chapter, we have stepped outside the West into what Westerners call, with a mental geography at once arbitrary and loaded, the East and the South.

If you travel just nine miles south from Spain, across the Mediterranean to the nearest East, all the differences within the West fade into insignificance by comparison with those between the conditions of the Arab and the Western worlds. That is equally true of the contrast with the far East. When you look at the miserable condition of more than a third of humankind, in the poor South, the hyperbolic claims of civilizational difference between 'old Europe' and the United States do not merely seem artificial; they seem criminally self-indulgent. From the viewpoint of someone struggling to survive in Sub-Saharan Africa on less than $1 a day, these internal quarrels of the West can only be characterized by a withering phrase of Sigmund Freud's: the 'narcissism of minor differences'.[145] Finally, the challenge of sustaining dignified human life on the Earth over the next decades, with perhaps 8 or 9 billion human beings demanding more and more of its natural resources, makes these transatlantic squabbles look like the dance of lemmings on a clifftop.

The British diplomat-intellectual Robert Cooper suggests as a maxim of twenty-first-century diplomacy a remark that he attributes to Jean Monnet: if you have a problem you cannot solve, enlarge the context.[146] But this wider, global context of the divisions within the West does not have to be artificially enlarged. It merely has to be seen for what it is. Here are huge common challenges for the West, which, indeed, can no longer be clearly distinguished from the Rest, just as foreign policy can no longer be neatly separated from domestic policy. Tens of millions of people from the Rest already live in the West, shaping its politics. Economically dynamic and increasingly free countries among the Rest are beating the West at its own games. For the poor among the Rest, the rich West is setting the terms of life and death.

To be sure, some areas of the Rest have the potential to divide Europe and America – especially the near East, that most persistent source of crises of the West. But this is not because the interests of Europe and America in these regions fundamentally diverge. Everywhere, there will continue to be competition within the West for commercial advantage and scarce sources of energy. Both of these competitions, however, will as likely be between European states or transatlantic multinational corporations as between one trading bloc and the other. Apart from this, it is impossible, on a sober analysis, to discern any major differences of long-term *interest* between Europe,

America and the other rich and free countries of the West, in any of the fields we have discussed, including the near East. The differences are of historic ties, identities, perceptions and approaches.

Altogether, the argument between Europe and America is most often about means rather than ends. Questions about means can still be first-order questions. Much of the sharpest transatlantic conversation at the beginning of the twenty-first century has been focused on the issue of intervention: when, how, under what conditions and with what authority should one state be allowed to intervene in another? 'Intervention' is generally taken to mean military intervention, although Western states actually intervene in the affairs of other states all the time by economic, diplomatic and cultural means, often quite 'forcefully'. But military intervention is the hardest case, as we saw over Iraq, and before that over Afghanistan, East Timor, Kosovo, Rwanda, Bosnia and Somalia.

There is an extreme 'new American' position: that the United States is entitled to intervene unilaterally anywhere, anytime, to pre-empt a potential threat to its national security which only its secret intelligence can detect, and because the president feels this is theologically right. That is unacceptable to most other free countries in the world. There is an extreme 'old-European' position: that nations can only use force in 'self-defence' against an actual 'armed attack', according to a strict interpretation of Article 51 of the 1945 United Nations Charter, or with explicit authorization from the UN Security Council. This is equally untenable. It is inadequate for the new security risks of the early twenty-first century, in which convergences of international terrorism, rogue or failed states and weapons of mass destruction create threats quite unlike those of a conventional *Wehrmacht* massing at the frontiers of the Third Reich or nuclear missiles in Red Army silos. Al-Qaeda, based in the failed state of Afghanistan, demonstrated that.

It is also, so to speak, morally outdated in the face of an emerging Western consensus on the need to prevent regimes or dominant ethnic groups from committing genocide against people living inside the frontiers of the same state. European states intervened in Kosovo, together with the United States, to stop Slobodan Milošević perpetrating 'another Bosnia' against the mainly Muslim Albanian

Kosovars, although they had no explicit authorization from the UN Security Council to do so. They did, however, have the support of most of the democracies in the world, and most of Serbia's neighbours. A great deal will depend on whether Europe and America, working with other free countries in the United Nations, can now agree some broad 'rules of the road' for future interventions. Each new case will be unique and difficult, with even the facts being disputed, especially if those 'facts' are based on secret intelligence, but it will help to start with some agreed principles. An Italian policy intellectual called Thomas Aquinas prepared an excellent first draft in the thirteenth century, but the 'just war' principles of his *Summa Theologiae* are in need of some revision.[147]

At the beginning of the twenty-first century, a pessimistic 'realist' would judge that the combined power of Europeans, Americans and other free people, working all together, is probably insufficient to meet even the smallest of the global challenges that I have identified: the near East. In any case, this pessimistic 'realist' might add, these Western consumer-oriented teledemocracies do not have the capacity for sustained political engagement abroad and they will not agree among themselves. He, or she, might well prove to be right. Certainly, none of these challenges can be met if Europeans, Americans and other free people work against each other. In each case, progress will only be possible if Europeans and Americans seek to win as allies the free countries that now extend far beyond the boundaries of the old, Cold War West. Vital allies are also to be found among those working for freedom in states that are still unfree. Europe alone is not enough. America alone is not enough. The West alone is not enough.

# Crisis as Opportunity

We have now completed our tour around the jagged landscape illuminated by the early twenty-first-century crisis of the West. A red, double-decker mind-bus has taken us from Baker Street to the ozone layer. You might say that was the wrong way around; logically we should start with the biggest problems and work downwards. But in real life, most of us do think outwards from home. The familiar slogan of alternative globalization, 'think global, act local', makes equally good sense when reversed: 'think local, act global'. A shot fired in Kashmir can hit Putney, through the Ahmadi community in Gressenhall Road. Global warming affects Putney High Street too: when did Ye Olde Spotted Horse last see a white Christmas?* Distant events change our everyday lives, so foreign policy is no longer foreign.

What we have discovered, by the light of this electric storm, is an earthscape very different from the one many people imagined at the height of controversy between the Washington of Bush and the Paris of Chirac. Here is no inexorable drifting apart of two solid continental plates, Europe and America. Quite a lot of people believe this, on both sides of the Atlantic, and we have found clever human beings encouraging this belief, with partial reports, aggregate statistics and terrible simplifications. But looking closely and carefully, what we find are overlapping continental shelves and floating islands. There are not two separate sets of values, 'European' and 'American', but

---

\* But it may again. In a fine example of Murphy's Law, the longer term effect of global warming is predicted to be that Britain will get *colder*. An alarmist consultants' report to the Pentagon has even suggested that, by 2020, Britain's weather might begin to resemble Siberia's.[1]

several intersecting sets of values, with the largest area being the intersection. And we find that the personalities and biographies of individual politicians, domestic political imperatives and historical contingencies are often as important as larger forces. In politics, as Machiavelli once observed, chance and luck are usually the half of it.[2]

There are also deeper trends, resulting both from changes in the international system following the end of the Cold War and from longer-term shifts in the balances of power, wealth and fascination between Europe, America and Asia. These have contributed to two great debates. America is divided by a great argument about itself. Europe is divided by a great argument about America, which is, however, also a symptom of Europe trying to make sense of its own transformation. Both meet in Janus Britain, an 'especially clear case of the modern world'.[3]

We find some real, hard conflicts of political and economic interest, but these are multiple and cross-hatched, running not just between but also within continents and countries. Faced with daunting global challenges – the new Red Armies – Europeans, Americans and free people everywhere have an overwhelming common interest. But will they grasp this? The key to progress lies in how we see and what we think, not in any extra-human reality. Transatlantic continental drift is four parts pyschology to one part geology.

Our lightning tour therefore reveals a possibility: that things may be changed for the better because minds are changed for the clearer. The word 'crisis' is so over-used these days that most have forgotten its original meaning. In sixteenth-century English, 'crisis' meant the decisive moment in a sickness, when you started either to get better or to die. So it is with this crisis of the West. The medicine is in our own hands.

If we choose to start recovering, then we face a great opportunity. Over the sixty years since the 1940s, both wealth and freedom have spread further, faster, than in any earlier period. There is still a vast distance to travel, and many a cold mountain to climb, but it's no longer utopian fantasy to set our sights on the goal of a free world.

# PART TWO

# Opportunity

# Twenty Years and a Thousand Million Citizens

We don't know what will happen tomorrow, let alone in twenty years' time, so why try to write about the future? Because if we don't know where we want to go, all paths are equally good. Let us therefore work out together the direction in which we should head, knowing full well that we'll be knocked off course by unexpected events. I propose that we should set a course from '*the* free world' of the Cold War, which no longer exists, towards *a* free world. Never in the history of grammar has a shift from the definite to the indefinite article been more important.

We won't arrive in twenty years, but I nevertheless suggest aiming twenty years ahead. First of all, this lifts our eyes beyond the four or five years of any particular presidency, chancellorship or premiership. Our leaders come and go, but the problems remain. All the global challenges that I've identified require a longer timescale than the one on which our politicians operate, especially in early twenty-first-century teledemocracies, with their chronic short-termism. The Millennium Development Goals are set for 2015, and that's still ambitious. If democracies start to emerge in the near East, some of them are likely to elect Islamist governments and pass through rocky years of transition. A time-frame of twenty years also reminds us that any larger foreign policy strategy, like that of the Cold War West, must be sustained by a minimal consensus between the main political parties competing for power – Republican and Democrat, Conservative and Labour, Gaullist and Socialist, Christian Democrat and Social Democrat – and between the main countries involved, especially those of Europe and America.

More than twenty years is too long. By sketching possible futures, we aim to change them. Orwell wrote *1984* so that it wouldn't happen. Yet there comes a point when the accumulation of the unpredicted, and perhaps even the corrective impact of our own sketches of the future, makes it essential to revise those sketches. Who could have guessed in 1984 what the world would look like in 2004? And with the accelerating speed of technological change, the half-life of sensible prognosis has probably shortened.

Another reason for not going beyond twenty years concerns the likely rise of the far East. Unless China's economic growth falters dramatically, perhaps due to political turmoil, China in 2025 will be such a major power – with Japan still formidable, and India coming up as well – that there will be no point in conceiving a political strategy for Europe and America separately from the intentions and dynamics of Asia. So the old Atlantic-centred West, which has been shaping the world since about 1500, probably has no more than twenty years left in which it will still be the main world-shaper. That's another reason why it's so stupid for Europeans and Americans to waste any more time squabbling with each other. In a longer historical perspective, this may be our last chance to set the agenda of world politics.

But who do I mean when I say 'our'? If you look at the map on page 258, you will see that freedom has already spread far beyond the bounds of the West, by any traditional definition, whether cultural, historical or geopolitical. In a stimulating account of what they call 'Occidentalism', Ian Buruma and Avishai Margalit write: 'the question, then, is how to protect the legitimate idea of the West, that is to say, the world's liberal democracies, against its enemies. And the West, in this sense, includes such fragile Asian democracies as Indonesia and the Philippines.'[1] But can the term really be thus infinitely extended, with every state that becomes a liberal democracy, whatever its geography or history, immediately adopted as part of the West? Precisely if we do believe that the possibility and value of liberal democracy are not confined to one culture or region, isn't it better to accept that the West, in going so far beyond its historic self, also ceases in some important sense to be the West?

Seeing the collapse of the Cold War West, on the one side, and the spread of liberal democracy on the other, it seems wiser to agree that the thing we are trying to reconstruct should have a different name.

To speak already of a worldwide community of democracies, or a global coalition of the free, is to describe an aspiration rather than a reality. So perhaps, for this transitional period, we should talk of the post-West. Today's post-West still has at its core the free countries on both sides of the Atlantic, but it is already very far from being confined to them. Its future evolution is open-ended. The post-West is a pre-something else. Our goal should be to make that 'something else' a free world.

So, to return to the question posed at the very beginning of this book: who, now, are 'we'? Morally, the answer must be all humankind. 'Moral globalization' is not just a pious dream but a spreading reality. More and more individual men and women, especially in the post-West, really do think of themselves as citizens of the world. One reason younger Europeans don't believe as strongly in Europe as their parents did is that they feel Europe is not enough. They are habitual internationalists and, so to speak, one-worlders. Their race is the human race. This is a great step forward in political consciousness. All it needs now is for passive oneworlders to become active freeworlders.

Morally we should regard the poorest Burmese slave labourer in the jade mines of Hpakant as the equal of a Rockefeller. Yet it is clear that he does not have the same opportunities for influencing the world. He can't even secure freedom for himself, let alone help people in other countries to be free. A Rockefeller can. Fortunately, these days you don't need to be a Rockefeller. Any free person in a rich and free country has some such opportunities.

How big is this operational 'we'? Plainly the number is not as large as the 2.8 billion living in countries classified by Freedom House as 'free'. A beggar in Calcutta may live in a free country, but he is not himself free in the sense that an affluent person in Europe or America is free. By voting in an election, he can theoretically influence the policy of the Indian government towards other countries, but in practice his impact will be negligible. In countries like America or France, by contrast, only a small minority, composed of the truly destitute, incarcerated or otherwise incapacitated, do not belong to the operational 'we'.

If we tot up the free Europeans and Americans who have some real possibilities for affecting the world outside the frontiers of their own state, we may arrive at a figure somewhere between 700 million and 800 million. To them, we must add citizens of other developed, free countries, such as Japan and Australia. We should also include a smaller tally of the well-to-do residing in partly free or unfree countries. Russia's super-rich oligarchs, for example, can affect the balance of freedom, for good or ill, more directly than most middle-class Americans or Europeans. So can the rich of Latin America or the near East. And we should not forget those who, while often in prison and certainly not rich, are working for freedom in the most unfree places in the world. They are free in spirit if not in body:

> Stone walls do not a prison make
> Nor iron bars a cage.[2]

Like the dissidents in communist-ruled Eastern Europe, human rights activists in the military dictatorships of Latin America, and freedom fighters in South Africa under apartheid, they can have an influence way beyond their numbers.

Taking all in all, shall we cautiously estimate our operational 'we' at around a thousand million citizens? That's a lot of people with a lot of money, a lot of votes, a lot of voices. There's a poem by G. K. Chesterton called 'The Secret People', which memorably concludes: 'For we are the people of England, that never have spoken yet.' Well, we are the thousand million, that never have spoken yet.

The trouble is that so many citizens of the post-West are now utterly fed up with politics. It's often those who care most about the state of the world, about poverty in Africa, the environment, Burma and Palestine, who are most likely to say that 'They' – our political leaders – are all in the pockets of big corporations like Shell, Bechtel or Halliburton. Many don't even bother to vote: 'If voting changed anything, they'd abolish it.'[3] Apathy is too weak a word for this attitude; it is active, angry disillusionment. At the same time, since we in the post-West live in quite peaceful, prosperous societies, with no Hitler or Stalin massing troops just down the road or across the water, most people feel there's no great urgency about getting involved in debates about foreign policy. Except when there's a dramatic issue, like Bosnia or the Iraq War, the effect is to leave the conduct of foreign policy to a small group of politicians and officials, influenced by lobbyists, journalists and pollsters.

This is dangerous. Men and women who have reached the top in politics often possess an impressive combination of qualities, amongst which being lucky is merely the most important one. But having a well-informed, enlightened, strategic approach to the rest of the world is not necessarily among those qualities. When you get a few glimpses into the way major foreign policy decisions are made, you are left with a sense of mild incredulity that this is how the world is run. It is vital that we all appreciate this simple truth about our rulers: half the time they really don't know what they're doing.

Foreign policy is too important to be left to the politicians. We need to mix in and shape it ourselves. But how? In the second part of this book, I offer a few personal answers to Vladimir Ilyich Lenin's still pertinent question 'What is to be done?' As in the first part, I proceed in an outward spiral – Britain, Europe, America, world – before ending with a couple of thoughts about direct action by citizens of the world. These personal answers are based on the 'history of the present' analysis contained in the first part, but they don't aspire to be comprehensive in any way. They are simply one citizen's suggestions – to advance a conversation among us, and to lift our leaders' sights.

This means finding the right mix of realism and idealism. There's no point in offering a prescription which is so 'realistic' that it's like a diplomat's internal brief to his or her government – trimmed already to all the existing constraints. There's equally little point in writing a Sermon on the Mount. But when the politicians look only one or two weeks ahead, we, the citizens, should compel them to look one or two years ahead. When they raise their sights to one or two years, we should insist on ten to twenty. We should not demand the impossible of them; just the nearly impossible. Demand it of them, and of ourselves. For we are the thousand million, that never have spoken yet.

# 5

# Britain Finds its Role

'Britain Finds its Role.' What a headline that would be. Dean Acheson's famous jibe that 'Great Britain has lost an empire and not yet found a role' is as apt today as it was when he made it in 1962.[1] Forty years on – older but no wiser. Those to the left say 'choose Europe', those to the right say 'choose America', those behind say 'remain a right little, tight little England', and those in front have no one to support them.

Yet the role for Britain is staring us in the face. Or rather, in the four faces of Janus Britain: Island and World, Europe and America. A country's role must reflect its nature. Historically, Britain is a child of Europe and a parent of America. Those ties were attenuated, but never broken, by the experience of Island-Empire. Since 1940, the fulcrum of the twentieth century, they have grown closer than ever before. Economically, politically, culturally, militarily, intellectually, socially, gastronomically, we are now inextricably intertwined with *both* Europe and America. To choose one or the other would require a major amputation.

It follows that our vital national interest is to bring Europe and America as close together as possible. I have argued that this is in the interest of the world as well; the human race has no chance of making a free world without the combined efforts of its two largest conglomerates of the rich and free. That argument stands or falls irrespective of the special British interest. It is neither true nor false because someone who is British advances it. None the less, the British have no reason to hide this special national interest. In fact, we had better not.

There's an old, bad tradition of states advancing their special interests under the flag of a larger community or common good. 'Europe' is the classic example. 'I have always found the word "Europe"', said Bismarck, 'in the mouths of politicians who wanted from other powers something they did not dare to demand in their own name.'[2] France and Germany have both habitually advanced their national interest in Europe's name. This should not be the British way. We should say frankly: 'Here we stand. Britain is Janus. We have this special motive for wishing to shrink the Atlantic. Now listen to our arguments.'

At the height of the fighting between Serbs and Albanians in Kosovo, I met a woman called Violetta. She was against the fighting. I soon understood why: her mother was Serb, her father Albanian. She, like Britain, had a special motive. But she also happened to be right. Violetta's voice could not stop her mother's people and her father's people killing each other. Britain's voice, alone, cannot bring America and Europe together again, although it counts for a lot more, relatively speaking, than Violetta's did. Fortunately, Britain's voice is not alone. I have quoted in the first part of this book just a few of the many voices urging the same strategic imperative, from both sides of the Atlantic. There is nothing ineluctable about America and Europe drifting apart.

Take continental Europe, for a start. Scepticism is one of the greatest intellectual virtues. Scepticism about the integrity, efficiency and accountability of the organs of the European Union is entirely justified and needed at all times. But this thing we in Britain call Euroscepticism is something else. Euroscepticism is, at bottom, defeatism. It takes Churchill as its mascot, but ducks the good fight. It waves the Union Jack, but its real flag is white. For the basic premiss of Euroscepticism is that the continental Europeans are advancing inexorably towards a federal superstate, like a Napoleonic army. Eurosceptics argue that this Bonapartist superstate, shaped by the French and Germans, will inevitably define itself in a Gaullist way, as a rival to the United States. We can't stop them. The only choice we have is whether to fight or flee back to England. And the plain conclusion of the Eurosceptic argument is that, unlike the Duke of Wellington, we should flee.

Yet across the whole continent there is this massive debate going on about what Europe should be and how it should relate to the United States. Euro-Gaullists and Euroatlanticists are quite evenly balanced, especially in the European Union of twenty-five and more. The British could make a real difference to the outcome. But Eurosceptics would have us linger at the edge of the field. Crying 'no surrender!', they propose that we should surrender. As a historian, I must again give the cautionary warning that we can never know what Churchill would have done, had he been alive today. As a citizen, I say Churchill would have been out there in the heart of the battle, fighting to win the day for the Euroatlanticist cause – and using all his execrably pronounced French to urge our valiant French neighbours to join us.

There is an equal and opposite mistake, which we might call Americascepticism. Americasceptics are not necessarily anti-American, just as Eurosceptics are not necessarily anti-European. However, they assume that the United States is advancing inexorably, like a tank, towards a settled, conservative, rich man's, muscular Christian, imperialist, unilateralist posture in the world: the rogue hyperpower. This assumption is also wrong. America, like Europe, is split down the middle, with a national debate raging around exactly such issues. The most withering critiques of American conservative unilateralism have come from Americans themselves. In fact, British Americasceptics subsist on a healthy American diet of Michael Moore, Paul Krugman, Noam Chomsky, Bill Clinton, Al Franken, Peter Singer and Joseph Stiglitz. Americans, not Europeans, will decide this intra-American argument, but of all Europeans, the British have the best chance to influence it at the margins.

So the role that stares us in the face is to be the most vigorous advocate and creative practitioner of the most intensive cooperation between Europe and America, together with other free countries, especially those of the Anglosphere. To be friend and interpreter in both directions. To take the spirit of a twentieth-century West, created, in no small part, by Winston Churchill, and carry it forward into the twenty-first-century post-West: a West that goes far beyond the boundaries of the historic West, and therefore, in an important sense, ceases to be the West, as it works towards a free world.

Tony Blair has grasped and articulated this British national interest, role and chance better than any of his predecessors. In setting the basic strategic direction for Britain in the world, he has been bold, consistent and sometimes politically brave. But his central image of 'the bridge' is not a good one. Bridges are narrow, rigid structures. To say *the* bridge implies that Britain is the only, or at least the main bridge between America and Europe – which also suggests that Britain is not part of Europe. It confuses the broader purpose with the narrower national one of preserving status and 'rank' for this diminished former world power. To mix Blair's favourite image with another stale metaphor of British diplomacy, 'the bridge' is a way of keeping our 'place at the top table'. Or of kidding ourselves that we do.

Why should a German or Polish or Spanish leader walk over London Bridge to reach Washington? Or an American president to talk to Paris or Rome? In practice, European leaders do sometimes privately turn to London to explain something to Washington, and vice versa. This illustrates the part Britain can play, but the goal of our national strategy must be that other European leaders talk as easily and directly to America as British leaders do. Far from nursing the treasured exclusivity of our Special Relationship – so special, the former German chancellor Helmut Schmidt once remarked, that only one side knows it exists – we should want every country in Europe to have a relationship with the United States as close as ours. In fact, politicians and writers in many other European countries have also suggested that their countries are or could be bridges across the Atlantic. I've heard this said in Poland, Italy and Spain. In Germany, there is even an organization called 'Atlantic Bridge'. This is just as it should be. The bridge we need is one between the *whole* of Europe and America. It should be the biggest bridge in the world: 3,000 miles long and as many lanes wide.

In the new, enlarged European Union, Britain, like America, faces a choice. We can cultivate alliances of the willing, as during the Iraq War, or we can seek to win the whole of Europe to what seems to us the right course. The latter approach is more difficult, but offers a much bigger pay-off at the end. It is on the European side that Blair's bridge strategy has fallen down. Partly because he has felt his hands to be tied by Eurosceptic opinion at home, he has not transformed our relationship with our main continental partners as he had hoped. They still view us as semi-detached.

This is where we have to do more. Ultimately, what we need is nothing less than a historic compromise with our ancient enemy, France. For in respect of relations with America, France and Britain are the two magnetic poles of a divided Europe, tearing it apart between a neo-Gaullist and a neo-Churchillian strategy. The competition between England and France is probably the oldest continuous national rivalry in the world. It dates back at least six centuries, to the Hundred Years War. Britain, as it became Britain rather than England, defined itself as the Not-France. Being rude about the French is still a British national sport. A senior backbench Conservative MP, a 'knight of the shires', was once complaining that Margaret Thatcher was very anti-German. I pointed out that she was also very anti-French. 'Oh, *that's* all right!' said the jovial knight, as if this was self-evident to any right-thinking Englishman.

France and Britain are like Walter Matthau and Jack Lemmon in the film *Grumpy Old Men*, two old-timers who have known each other since they were babies and have so much in common, yet go on hurling childish insults and playing silly tricks. In the footsteps of Churchill and de Gaulle, each country still comports itself as a world power, though privately both must acknowledge that their relative power in the world has diminished, is diminishing, and will continue to diminish. Oddly, Britain is more often defensive and resentful in the relationship than France. Yet, calmly considered, Britain has the stronger position. Because of the hegemonic succession from the British Empire to the United States, the world is speaking English, not French, and more often adopting Anglo-Saxon than Gallic ways. The British are winners acting like losers. We should have the confidence to be more generous.

This historic compromise with France would, by definition, be somewhere between the neo-Churchillian and the neo-Gaullist positions. That is also substantively the best position. Britain alone is too small and weak to be a major partner for the United States, especially since American leaders generally feel they can take the British for granted. If even Churchill, with the whole might of the British Empire behind him, found himself compelled to 'beg, like Fala' (Roosevelt's dog), how much more must that be true of a medium-sized European state in relation to the world's only hyperpower. Blair discovered this over Iraq. Speaking to Washington on behalf of 60 million British is one thing; speaking on behalf of 460 million Europeans would be quite another. By contrast, trying to rally 460 million Europeans around a neo-Gaullist alternative 'pole' to the US is a hopeless cause. Half of them won't follow; the American hyperpower will ignore Paris and go it alone, or divide and rule in Europe.

Trying to gather most Europeans around a common position as a consistently Euroatlanticist partner of the United States is the best course for both Britain and France. It is an honourable compromise between the ghosts of Winston Churchill and Charles de Gaulle – who are, I imagine, still quarrelling in heaven. De Gaulle would wholeheartedly approve the achievement of a common European position, Churchill the spirit of transatlantic partnership.

Crucial to this new understanding will be the voice of Germany, the biggest of Europe's 'big three'. In its own enlightened self-interest, Germany should play the role of 'honest broker' between France and Britain. This alone will allow it to continue its own balancing act between Paris and Washington, which has served the Federal Republic so well. The other nations of Europe, small and large, should also gather round, like weary cousins and exasperated sisters, to urge this reconciliation on the two grumpy old men. America, too, should support this in its own enlightened self-interest. It will not be easy and it will take time, but history is full of surprises, and we are thinking in a time-frame of twenty years. If not with Chirac, then with his successor, if not with Blair, then with his successor, this is the way forward.

At some point down this road, Britain will have to decide whether to join the Eurozone. If the economic case for or against joining becomes distinctly stronger, that may be decisive. Assuming that the economic arguments for and against joining remain as uncomfortably balanced as they are at the moment, this will be a political decision. If we are consciously embarked on such a long-term national strategy, it will probably make political sense to go in, since the fuller our engagement in all the counsels of Europe, the greater the chance of steering them in the right direction. If we are not thus embarked, it may not make sense.

In order to implement this national strategy, however, Britain needs a minimal domestic political consensus on foreign policy. A house divided against itself cannot stand; a country divided against itself will never find its role in the world. Britain is a country divided against itself. We therefore need an internal historic compromise to complement, and in fact permit, the external one with France. The essence of this internal compromise is simple: the British right must accept Europe and the British left must accept America. This certainly doesn't mean to accept every stupid directive that comes out of Brussels or every stupid policy that comes out of Washington. It means accepting the basic reality of Janus Britain: that our future depends on attempting to influence the policies of Europe and America so they are compatible with each other and, so far as possible, with our own particular needs. To achieve this requires patient application, over twenty years. We've now seen a pro-American (as well as pro-European) Labour prime minister; then we need a pro-European (as well as pro-American) Conservative or Liberal prime minister; then another pro-American (as well as pro-European) Labour prime minister, and so on.

Looking at current British politics, this may sound fanciful in the extreme. There is, however, one interesting precedent. I earlier compared Britain, the most painfully torn country in today's divided West, to Germany, the central divided country of the Cold War. After 1949, West German politicians argued for two decades about how best to reunite their country. Then Willy Brandt's Ostpolitik proposed that the only way to put Germany together again was to put Europe together again. While making its own 'small steps' across the Berlin Wall, the Federal Republic would do everything in its power to draw the Soviet-led East and the American-led West closer to each other. This policy was bitterly contested by the conservative opposition, but then gradually accepted and largely continued by them while they were in government, under Helmut Kohl. So for two decades the leaders of the Federal Republic pursued a national strategy based on an attempt to bring together two geopolitical blocs even larger than today's Europe and America.[3]

In the end, just when they had almost given up hope, the Germans succeeded in achieving their original goal, although by a different route from the one they had anticipated and thanks to forces beyond their control. But still: they had a national strategy; they knew where they wanted to go; they plugged away at it for twenty years; they got there in the end. Never mind the different route; as Machiavelli said, success is usually half down to luck. Is it quite unthinkable that the British will one day have the common sense to do the same?

Such a strategic foreign policy consensus between the political parties could not exist in a vacuum. It would have to be sustained by published opinion and accepted by public opinion. The very last thing I want to propose is that the old semi-mythical national narrative of 'Our Island Story', from Alfred the Great to India, should be replaced by a new semi-mythical national narrative: 'Our Continental Story', from Hengist and Horsa to the Eurozone. The historian's job is to dismantle myths, not create new ones. History as teleology is always bunk. But at the moment, because of the way history is taught in British schools, few children can locate themselves in any national story at all.

How about every schoolchild learning the story of Britain in terms of the interaction between those four faces, Island and World, Europe and America? There would obviously be more of one face apparent in some periods of British history than in others. Along the way, schoolbooks and teachers would offer alternative interpretations, so children could get used to making their own judgements. None the less, the schoolbooks would show, in a coherent narrative, how Britain came to be this four-faced Janus. That would involve teaching more American as well as more European history. British children get the American version of the English language from television and films, but if you say 'Thomas Jefferson' they'll probably ask which film he was in.

It would also help if British children knew another European language, which less and less of them do. Just one in three British teenagers speaks any foreign language. The government has recognized that language-learning needs to start in primary school, as in Germany and France.[4] Only when we know the language can we really get inside the skin of France or Spain or Italy, places from which our great British football heroes come and to which we regularly travel in large numbers. All British children should also have the chance to spend some time in the country of their choice, if they want to. A different country, with a different culture and spirit embodied in a different language, yet part of the same extended family: that's Europe, not Brussels bureaucracy and asinine EU regulations. It's also the best way to understand this country better: 'What should they know of England who only England know?'[5]

Finally, there's politics. How many people in Britain grasp the relationship between the US Congress, Supreme Court and President? How many know the difference between the president of the European Commission and the presidency of the European Council? A world island needs a 'civics' to match. Most British school-leavers don't even possess the basic facts. 'European studies' or 'American studies' at British universities are, at the moment, the second storey of a house built on sand.

After education, there's information for adults. Britain is remarkably well informed in some respects. BBC Radio 3 and 4, and the BBC's superb website, are alone worth all the support the BBC receives from the public purse. Our biggest weakness is our newspapers. These serve well as entertainment, and offer a wide range of vigorous, interesting commentary. What they don't give us is enough news, especially foreign news. The term *news*paper is by now a misnomer. If we imagine we can be seriously, accurately informed about what is happening in Europe or Asia by reading a British daily paper, we are suffering a dangerous delusion.[6] (British papers are generally better on America.) Most British papers no longer distinguish between fact, which should be sacred, and opinion, which is free. The distinction between broadsheets and tabloids has increasingly broken down: *The Times* is a broadloid, the *Daily Mail*, a tabsheet. On policy towards Europe, the Eurosceptic papers have tied the hands of governments since about 1990.

What we need is two revolts. We need a revolt of the politicians, who should finally summon the courage to face down the media barons. Politicians, not newspaper proprietors, are the elected representatives of the British people. The press tycoons now more than ever enjoy what an earlier British prime minister called 'power without responsibility, the prerogative of the harlot through the ages'.[7] But we also need a revolt of the journalists. After all, journalists, not proprietors, actually write and edit these papers. Some of the cleverest, best educated, most enterprising people in Britain go into journalism.

In weekly journals, books and American magazines they write accurately, seriously, brilliantly. George Orwell, the patron saint of English journalism, would be proud of them there. Why can't we restore our great tradition of accurate, vivid, fair news reporting to British daily newspapers? We might be surprised how many readers such a newspaper could win.

A Britain thus politically focused, educated and informed will have notable strengths. Being so intimate with Europe and America means we have the chance to take the best of both. In many ways, this is what the New Labour government has tried to do. Gordon Brown puts it pithily: the US has enterprise but not fairness, Europe has fairness but not enterprise.[8] So, he argues, we should aim to combine American-style enterprise and European-style fairness, taking examples of innovation, tax credits and 'welfare to work' from America, but best practice in public healthcare or public transport from Europe. Of course, you can't always mix and match, and you have to make sure that you copy the best and not the worst of each. For instance, we're in danger of getting American prisons and German universities rather than American universities and German prisons. But the chance is there.

Then there's language. In the first part of this book I quoted the proposal of Robert Conquest, the Anglo-American poet and scholar, that Britain should join an English-speaking Union rather than the European Union. America, Canada, Australia – you get the idea. But what would an English-speaking Union really mean today? According to one study, there are now about 340 million native speakers of English, but a further 1,350 million who can use the language with 'reasonable competence'.[9] They speak what has been called English as an International Language or EIL. 'There are', the Czech writer and statesman Václav Havel once quipped, 'three kinds of English. There's the English that Czechs talk to Spaniards and Brazilians talk to Hungarians. Of that, you understand 100 per cent. There's American English – you understand 50 per cent. Then there's English English – and you understand nothing.'[10] Still and all, we invented it. Even if English English has become a strange dialect of itself, there are not many medium-sized nations who have this chance of speaking directly to the world.

All these variants of English can be heard on the streets of London. This world island has a world capital. The manner in which people of different nationalities and ethnicities coexist in London, and to a lesser degree in other British cities and regions, is unmatched in Europe. Here is a peculiarly British way of tolerance. It starts, perhaps, with the habits of privacy and mutual indifference ('live and let live', 'an Englishman's home is his castle'). It continues with the baggy, undemanding nature of 'Britishness', a woolly duffle-coat of an identity that from the start had to embrace four national identities, English, Scottish, Welsh and Irish. Only in pragmatic, illogical Britain could a rugby match between England and Scotland be called a 'home international'. But as the world has come back to the post-imperial island, so the duffle-coat of Britishness has stretched to accommodate many other identities.

In future censuses, we are told, we shall be able to categorize ourselves as 'Afro-Caribbean English', 'Chinese Welsh', or 'Asian Scottish'. Gisela Stuart, herself a German-British MP, describes a neighbourhood in her Birmingham constituency that has a large Asian population. Since Asian parents want the best education for their children, and the best school in the neighbourhood is a convent school, they send their daughters there. Never mind the Catholicism; that can be expunged by Islamic instruction after school hours, at the local *madrasah*. So there they sit, row upon row of girls in their Islamic headscarves, being taught maths, British history and, incidentally, the story of baby Jesus, by nuns in their Christian headscarves.[11] A complete muddle, of course, but Europe will need more such muddling through if it is to make its tens of millions of Muslims feel at home. And not just Muslims. Take Neena Gill, for example, a Sikh-British Member of the European Parliament, married to someone who is half Italian, one quarter English and one quarter Scottish. Her son is therefore Indian-Italian-English-Scottish-European. Welcome to the Europe of tomorrow. The British way of pragmatic, muddled tolerance cannot simply be imitated elsewhere in Europe, but it is a real asset both for ourselves and for a continent struggling with the challenge of inevitable, indispensable immigration.

Among the more traditional national constituencies of Britishness, the Welsh and the Scots seem to have less trouble accepting Europe than the English do. Scots, after all, drive around Britain with the name of their nation written on bumper stickers in French: *Écosse*. The Northern Irish are a small, difficult special case. The big problem is the English, and especially the English middle class. It is they – us – who can't work out what they – we – want Britain to be. Conservative, Eurosceptic English friends say: 'All your talk about "role" – that's Foreign Office talk. A country doesn't need to have a "role". All it needs is to be free, rich and at peace.' This, they suggest, can be achieved by a kind of geopolitical neutrality, semi-detaching ourselves from both Europe and America. Britain should be an off-shore Greater Switzerland.

I respect the clarity of this position, but question its feasibility. Would continental Europeans really give us all the benefits of free trade if we were not in the EU? Would Americans and Asians continue to invest so heavily here? Could we stand aside as an anti-American Europe clashed with an anti-European America? If Britain was unable to remain indifferent to the balance of power on the European continent in the nineteenth century, or to the continental clashes of fascism and communism in the twentieth, how could it in the twenty-first? And the illegal immigrants, terrorists and economic shocks coming from an unreformed near East will not stop at the white cliffs of Dover.

Yet even if this strategy for an offshore Greater Switzerland were sustainable, a further question would remain: is this who we want to be? It's one thing – and a fine thing – for the Swiss to be Swiss. It's quite another for the English to try to be Swiss. The last Archbishop of Canterbury once remarked that Britain is now quite an ordinary little island. Of all the silly remarks made by Archbishops of Canterbury, in the long history of that see, this is one of the silliest. These islands are anything but ordinary: for five centuries, until the American and French Revolutions, we were pioneers of freedom in the West; the British Empire meant oppression, exploitation and racism, but at the end of the day, the great democracies of the twenty-first-century world do include America, Canada, Australia, India and South Africa. Today there is a handful of Western nationalities that you meet around the world, trying to change things for the better, whether in national diplomacy, international organizations, charities, the media or culture. The British are always to be found among these world-shapers.

Of course it is always possible for someone who has the talent and track-record of a great violinist to make his living as a barman. Perhaps he could even be happy as a barman, though you would always doubt his professions of contentment. Yet even if he was happy, you would still feel it was a dreadful waste of his abilities. So also with Britain. This is not just a matter of

> We must be free or die, who speak the tongue
> That Shakespeare spake.[12]

It's a question of whether we could and should be indifferent to the unfreedom of others. I think we probably could not and certainly should not. If so, then we must have a national strategy that engages fully, on all fronts, with the world. The task is daunting but, given luck and the right allies, not impossible – like Churchill's promise of eventual victory in 1940. Writing that same year, Orwell concluded *The Lion and the Unicorn* with these words: 'I believe in England, and I believe that we shall go forward.'[13] We still can. The only obstacle is ourselves.

# 6

# What Europe Can Be

If I go to Warsaw, Berlin, Paris or Madrid I am abroad. If I go to Warsaw, Berlin, Paris or Madrid I am at home. This 'being at home abroad' is the essence and wonder of Europe.[1] So much that makes life rich – the beauty of women and the styles of men, the theatre of politics, language, architecture, newspapers, cuisine – is intriguingly, gloriously different from country to country. Yet still, you are a European at home in Europe, and there's a special thrill that comes from thinking how odd and bold it is that the inhabitants of this tower of Babel have somehow got together in a single commune or condominium.

Some people don't like it. There's an amusing essay by the American comic writer P. J. O'Rourke entitled 'Among the Euro-Weenies'. A founding charter of American satirical anti-Europeanism, this describes a gloomy month he spent in Europe. 'I've had it with these dopey little countries and all their pokey borders,' he writes. 'Even the languages are itty-bitty. Sometimes you need two or three just to get you through till lunch.'[2] But that's exactly the delight. Each of the two or three languages you can talk before lunch reveals a subtly different way of life and thought, accreted over centuries. '*Awantura*' in Polish means a big, loud, yet secretly rather enjoyable row. '*Bella figura*' in Italian is an untranslatable notion of how a woman or man should really wish to be in the company of other men and women. The British say 'what on earth does that mean?' The Germans say 'what in heaven should that mean?' ('*was im Himmel soll das bedeuten?*'). A canyon of profound philosophical difference – empiricist against idealist – is revealed through that tiny semantic crack. As we say in English: *Vive la différence*. Europe is an intricate, multicoloured patchwork, unmatched anywhere else on the globe.

This Europe has an extraordinary story to tell. It's a story of the enlargement of freedom. At the height of the Second World War, in 1942, there were just four perilously free countries in Europe: Britain, Switzerland, Sweden and Ireland. By 1962, most of Western Europe was free, except for Spain and Portugal. By 1982, the Iberian peninsular had joined the free, and Greece had rejoined after an interval of dictatorship, but the whole of what we called Eastern Europe was still unfree. By 2002, there was only one country in Europe that Freedom House classified as 'not free' – Belarus – and just a handful, in the new eastern and south-eastern Europe, that it judged 'partly' rather than wholly free. With the enlargement of the European Union to twenty-five members, and of Nato to twenty-six, most of the countries of Europe belong to the same political, economic and security communities, with equal rights and obligations. That has never been true before. Never in its history has Europe come this close to being 'whole and free'. If that's not a story to be proud of, what is?

Being free is not a direct result of belonging to the European Union; in fact, you have to be free before you can join the EU. But the European Union certainly helps. It helps through the politics of induction.[3] First, there's magnetic induction. The magnetic attractions of West European freedom and prosperity induced in Spaniards, Poles, Czechs and Portuguese a desire to emulate and come closer to them. Then there's formal induction – into membership of the club. Because Europeans not in the club have been so strongly attracted to joining it, they have been prepared to accept its quite intrusive demands as they strive for membership. Those demands, now formalized in the EU's 'Copenhagen Criteria', include the refined essentials of freedom, from free elections, the rule of law and free markets to respect for individual and minority rights. For Poles, as for Spaniards, the return to freedom and the return to Europe have gone hand in hand. These politics of induction are unique to Europe. Southern neighbours of the United States don't imagine they will become states of the Union.

This enlargement of freedom is the great success story of Europe over the sixty years since the Second World War. It also provides a central purpose for the next twenty years. Enlargement is not complete when countries like Slovakia and Estonia are formally members of an EU of twenty-five. It has merely begun. To make the European Union work with so many member states, most of which are much poorer than the average of the EU of fifteen, is already a huge task – and yet it is only half the task. Who seriously imagines that the European Union can stop there for the next twenty years? Firm promises have already been made to Romania and Bulgaria. What earthly justification would there be for refusing the progressive rites of induction to the other hard-tried peoples of the Balkans, as and when they meet the Copenhagen Criteria, especially since the EU is massively present already in Bosnia and Kosovo, as part of an international occupying power? Depending how many new states we end up with in the Balkans – and we should reckon with the emergence of an independent Montenegro and an independent Kosovo – this brings you to an EU of between thirty-two and thirty-four. Then, who could turn away Norway, Switzerland or Iceland if they decided to apply? That makes thirty-seven. And this is on the risky assumption that we have no constitutional dissolution of existing member states: an independent Scotland, for example, or Basque Country, or Flanders and Wallonia.

The time has come for us to say clearly which countries we hold eligible for full membership of the European Union over the next twenty years. This doesn't mean they are any better or worse than others; just that these are the historically European or partly European countries which we believe the European Union can absorb over twenty years without ceasing to be a functioning political community. It is less a value judgement on them than a political judgement on ourselves. Such clarity can be helpful not only to those for whom the answer is 'yes' but also to those for whom the answer is 'no'. In fact, this clarity is a precondition for working out what we can do for the others, short of full membership.

In addition to all the Balkan states mentioned above, we should offer this twenty-year 'yes' to Turkey but not to the rest of the near East, including even very close countries of north Africa such as Morocco. We should offer it to Ukraine, Belarus and Moldova but not to Russia, nor to the states of the Caucasus. This painful choice is justified by current politics and recent history, not by older history, culture or religion. Thus far, Morocco is the only country to have been refused permission even to apply to join the EU, on the grounds that it is not a European country. But with what historical justification? I would hate to plead the case in any historians' court that Morocco is not a European country but Turkey is; even less, that Turkey is a European country but Russia is not. No, for all the historical claims of pre-1453 Constantinople and Byzantium, the plain fact is that by taking in Turkey, the European Union would be crossing one of the oldest borderlines of Europe, first drawn by the geographers of antiquity and central to Europe's self-definition from the fifteenth to the seventeenth centuries.

If we were starting from scratch, we would probably build special partnerships, not based on induction to full membership, with both Russia and Turkey. In these two countries, Europe does not exactly end but, so to speak, fades away into what Europeans have named Asia. However, we are not starting from scratch. We have promises to keep; promises that go back forty years, into the Cold War, and were made explicit at the Nice summit of the EU in 2000. If we break them, this will send a disastrous message to Muslims everywhere that they are not welcome in Europe, however secular their state and moderate their government. Europe will still appear to be what it was for Pope Pius II, a Christian club. If we keep our promises to Turkey, while insisting on the full rigour of the Copenhagen Criteria of freedom, then we may demonstrate that a largely Muslim country can take an honoured place as perhaps the most populous state in the European Union. That political prize is worth the historical inconsistency.

In 2025, the next most populous EU member state might be Ukraine. By bringing in Ukraine and Belarus, after Greece, Bulgaria, Romania and Serbia, the European Union would have crossed another Huntingtonian fault-line between 'civilizations'. For according to Huntington, the Orthodox Christian world is another separate 'civilization', like Islam. So one small thing Europe can do over the next twenty years is to prove Samuel Huntington wrong. By inducting Ukraine, the European Union would enhance the political stability of its own eastern borderlands and influence, for the better, the political formation of a genuinely post-imperial Russia.

The reason Russia itself should not be offered the hope of membership in these two decades has to do not with any civilizational fault-line (truly hard to discern between eastern Ukraine and western Russia) but with its sheer size – a land area larger than the rest of Europe put together and more than 140 million people. Russia's elites are themselves ambivalent about whether they want to be a 'merely' European or a world-straddling Eurasian power. Although formally an electoral democracy, the Russian Federation currently has strong authoritarian tendencies, and is attempting to recreate a sphere of influence in eastern Europe and the Caucasus. The European Union has been feeble in relations with Russia, both because major European states want to deal directly, on their own terms, with the energy-rich former superpower, and because the EU's politics of induction depend on offering a credible prospect of membership. In this case, Europe's other security community can help. Even a fully democratic and committed Russia would be too big for the European Union. It would not be too big for Nato, which already contains one outsize, half-European military power, the United States, and which is fast becoming a transcontinental security and peacekeeping organization. If the European Union should embrace a democratic Turkey, Nato should embrace a democratic Russia.

I've dwelt on these boundaries of enlargement to bring home the scale of the European project over the next two decades. It's daunting enough to make workable arrangements for a European Union of twenty-five states and twenty languages in 2005, but we should already be thinking ahead to an EU of some forty states and at least thirty-three languages in 2025. In the Council of Ministers building, on the Rue de la Loi in Brussels, there's a smart new conference table for fifty people – two representatives from each of the twenty-five states – and no one knows quite how decisions will be reached around it. Imagine the table of eighty.

Constitutionally, the EU is like no other polity. As Giuliano Amato once put it, this is an Unidentified Flying Object. Trying to characterize its existing political system, political scientists have come up with neologisms like 'intensive transgovernmentalism'.[4] Trying to improve it, the Constitutional Convention produced a draft constitutional treaty which somewhat strengthened the parts controlled by member states, through the Council of Ministers, rather than the supposedly supranational parts, especially the European Commission and

Parliament. At the moment, that seems to be the institutional trend of enlargement.

If in ten years' time there is more of a European 'public sphere', if there are more genuinely pan-European political parties, newspapers, television channels, debates and personalities, there might be a renewed strengthening of the supranational. This is unlikely, because of the glorious diversity of Europe's languages and cultures, but if it emerges by mutual consent then it will help the Union to keep going.*
Similarly, it would help if we had more effective means of emotional identification with European institutions – flags, symbols, a European anthem we can sing – to counter the centrifugal effects of enlargement. Ultimately, what matters is not the exact constitutional form, which will inevitably be hybrid. What matters is that the Unidentified Object continues to fly, with a reasonable air cushion of support from a majority of its people.

For this to happen, political pilots in a sufficient number of member states need to agree on a strategic direction for the Union, suggest the way forward to their colleagues in the EU, and secure the assent of their own peoples. But what is a sufficient number? From the early 1950s until the early 1990s, leadership was given by France and Germany. Many episodes in the years since the end of the Cold War, culminating in the Iraq crisis, have shown that a leadership group comprising just France and Germany is no longer sufficient, especially in an enlarged EU. Unless they extend the couple to make a threesome, Britain will form alternative ad hoc alliances, together with states such as Spain, Poland or Italy. Europe will then be torn between two magnetic poles, rather than gathering around one magnetic core. If France and Germany were to go ahead unilaterally in a 'pioneer group' as some, especially in France, like to envisage, they would look behind them and find half their fellow Europeans marching in a different direction. This is a sure formula for the continuation of a multipolar Europe in a unipolar world.

* At the moment, Europe cannot even have its own '9/11', in the sense of a symbolic date associated with an emergency telephone number, because we all think of different national emergency numbers. How many Europeans would know what you meant if you said '112', the standardized, EU-wide emergency number? So instead, Europeans have started referring to the 11 March 2004 Madrid bombings as '3/11', taking an American-style date to make an American allusion.

No, the political question for the European Union at the beginning of the twenty-first century is not 'should France and Germany open their marriage to Britain?'. Obviously they should. It is not even 'can a *ménage à trois* work?' – although most human experience would counsel caution on that score. It is: 'will even those "big three" be enough to provide the strategic leadership and "critical mass" in a European Union of twenty-five, going on forty?'. The answer seems to me self-evidently 'no'. They will need to be joined by at least two or three other medium-weight states, such as Spain, Italy, Poland or the Netherlands. Yet even that constellation would sharpen the divide between so-called 'big' and 'small' countries in the Union, which emerged so clearly in the debates of the Constitutional Convention. It will therefore be essential for some smaller states also to be involved in giving a lead within the existing institutions of the EU.

Such a strategic coalition is very difficult to achieve, given that European politics are still mainly national, and national priorities and governments keep changing. We are more likely to end up with different groups of states working more closely together in different areas of policy. That will not be enough to provide an overall sense of where Europe is heading. We need to keep reminding ourselves that this attempt to bring together the states and peoples of Europe can also fail, as all previous attempts have done. A spectacular crash seems unlikely, but there is a real danger that the institutions of the European Union could gradually weaken into irrelevance, like the Holy Roman Empire, while real politics take place elsewhere.

Over the sixty years since the end of the Second World War, many of the existing member states of the European Union have achieved an enviable combination of economic growth and social solidarity. There is no single 'European model' but a diverse family of socio-economic models. One thing, however, all these diverse European models now have in common: they are all under threat. The EU has solemnly declared its intention to make the European economy the most competitive in the world by 2010. If it succeeds, I will eat my hat – and my shoes for dessert. As more of our manufacturing industries go to China, our service industries to India and our scientists to America, the question for the welfare capitalisms of Europe will be: how much are we prepared to fall behind the growth rates of other economies in order to preserve our social models? Or, how much are we prepared to trim down our social models for economic growth? There is a choice.

Even Jürgen Habermas, in making his case for social Europe as Not-America, would claim only that 'European welfare states were for a long time exemplary'.[5] Note the past tense. There is, to be sure, no reason at all why everyone should adopt the so-called American business model. Sweden has done as well as America. But it will require singular ingenuity for Europeans to continue to work shorter hours, take longer holidays, have a smaller proportion of our population in employment, and still produce as much. Over-regulation and high social costs for employers also lead to more unemployment, which is, as Bill Clinton sharply observed, 'another form of social inequality'.[6]

This challenge to the post-1945 West European way of life comes at a time when our populations are ageing fast. If we carry on as we are at the moment, then in 2025 our welfare states won't be able to pay our retired people a life-supporting pension. If we think that's unacceptable in 'social' Europe, then we need to reform our pension systems, have more children ourselves, and allow in more young and child-bearing immigrants to help fund those pensions. The trouble is that Europe has not been good at making large numbers of immigrants, especially Muslim immigrants, feel at home. Anglophone immigrant countries such as Canada, Australia and America are much better at it – with Britain, as usual, somewhere in between. For a fifteenth-century European, to say 'a Muslim European' or 'a European Muslim' would have been a contradiction in terms, like saying 'a she-man' or 'a he-woman'. In the twenty-first century, it's simply vital that this is possible to say. So far, we're not doing very well. It's quite an achievement for the main political organization of the most secular continent on earth to have come so close to convincing the Muslim world that it's a Christian club.

Being 'European' should be the overarching, multi-ethnic and non-religious identity that enables the Muslim immigrant to feel himself or herself to be a citizen and not a mere denizen – rather as being 'Canadian', 'American' or even 'British' is for citizens of those multi-ethnic polities. Unfortunately, Europeanness doesn't yet work this way. So the test will be whether second-generation immigrants can find secure, civic identities as Asian-British, Moroccan-Spanish, Turkish-German, Tunisian-French and so on. Each national path will be different, but we can learn from each other. As so often, the two extremes will probably be the Cartesian, republican secularism of France (school classes with no Muslim headscarves or yarmulkes) and the pragmatic, muddle-headed pluralism of Britain (schoolgirls in Muslim headscarves being taught by nuns in wimples).

If some or all of us fail, then we face a downward spiral which will be the curse of the national politics of Europe for years ahead. Populist, anti-immigrant parties will regularly break through the 15 per cent mark in regional and national elections, winning the votes of less affluent native-born voters who resent rapid change in their traditional ways of life, and blame immigrants for rising crime and job losses – even if those jobs actually went to Asia. Disaffected immigrant youths, themselves often among the long-term unemployed, will in fact be heavily involved in crime, while a minority will turn to Islamist extremism, anti-Semitic acts and terrorism. That in turn will feed the fires of anti-immigrant populism. To halt this downward spiral is the single most urgent task of European domestic politics in the next decade. We may already be too late.

This domestic imperative also dictates the top foreign policy priority for Europe: supporting change for the better in our 'near abroad'. I have argued in the first part of this book that unless we bring more prosperity and freedom to young Arabs, even more young Arabs will come to us. This formula applies also to Turkey, the Balkans, the new eastern Europe (Ukraine, Belarus and Moldova), the Caucasus and Russia, all of them being, in different degrees, sources of legal and illegal immigration, political radicalism and organized crime. I've suggested that we should pursue the EU's classic 'politics of induction' towards Turkey, the Balkans and the new eastern Europe, in a time-frame of twenty years. For the rest of our 'near abroad', stretching 10,000 kilometres along our southern and eastern borders, we need to craft a new kind of partnership which does not involve the promise – or even the flirted ankle – of full membership.

To create this arc of partnership, we have to combine all the various kinds of instruments that are at present wielded by many different hands, both in the institutions of the EU itself and in national governments. Europe has a hundred left hands and none of them know what the right hand is doing. Trade, development aid, immigration policy, education, cultural exchanges, classic diplomacy, arms sales and anti-proliferation measures, counter-terrorism, the fight against drugs and organized crime: each European policy has an impact, but the effects are fragmented and often self-contradictory. One left hand sells chemical or nuclear technology to a country in our near abroad, a right hand tries to prevent it developing weapons of mass destruction. Another right hand offers generous development aid, a left hand subverts this by trade protectionism.

Trade is our most effective single instrument. Our strategic objective must be to create an open trade area that includes the whole of our near abroad. Either we take more of their goods or we take more of their people. Opening up our markets is also much the biggest thing we can do for the poorest of the world's poor, especially those in Sub-Saharan Africa. Without it, we are giving with one hand and taking with the other. Trade is also Europe's strongest lever for affecting, at the margins, developments in Asia.

Our least effective instrument is military force. Europe can easily afford a well-armed and well-trained rapid reaction force, 60,000 to 100,000 strong. This can and should be used to prevent another Bosnia, whether in our own backyard or further afield. Where rulers or dominant ethnic groups are attempting to commit genocide, Europeans should always be ready to intervene. That is what our own history of European barbarism in the twentieth century cries out for us to do. Europe should also anticipate a lesson of the twenty-first century: that tyrants and terrorists must be prevented from gaining possession of weapons of mass destruction before it's too late. If we don't like the Bush Doctrine of unilateral pre-emption we had better develop a new practice of multilateral prevention. But in the larger scheme of what Europe does in the world beyond its borders, military force almost certainly will, and probably should, take a subordinate place.

At the Congress of Europe in The Hague in May 1948, one of the earliest and most passionate twentieth-century advocates of European union, Count Coudenhove-Kalergi, delivered a memorable warning. 'Let us never forget, my friends,' cried the old count, 'that European Union is a means and no end.'[7] I have now suggested a few answers to the question that a young European might very reasonably pose at the beginning of the twenty-first century: Why Europe? Why, that is, do we need a European Union at all? What is Europe for? The answers are not simple, but they are, I believe, compelling.

We need this Europe to prevent us falling back into the bad old ways of war and European barbarism, which stalked the Balkans into the very last year of the last century. As Bertolt Brecht wrote after 1945, 'The womb is fertile still, from which that crawled.'[8] However, the womb in question is not capitalism, as Brecht claimed to believe, but rather human nature, additionally misshaped by some distinctively European forms of stupidity. To be sure, we can never prove that a continent-wide collection of independent, fully sovereign European democracies would not behave in the same broadly pacific way, without the existence of any European Union. Maybe they would. But would you care to risk it? It makes sense to suppose that an organization, one of whose main original purposes was to prevent the recurrence of war, whose perennial occupation is endless rounds of negotiation to resolve conflicts of national and special interests, whose default setting is compromise and whose biggest product is fudge, should have contributed something to the fact that conflicts between its member states never result in the use of force. To adapt Churchill's famous remark about democracy: this is the worst possible Europe, apart from all the other Europes that have been tried from time to time.

We need this Europe to help us preserve the unprecedented prosperity and social security that West Europeans have acquired over the last sixty years, as we try to share them with the rest of the continent while being challenged by economic competition from Asia and America. If, in some ways, the present, over-regulated EU hinders us in that double task, we should change those ways, not discard the Union. We also need this Europe as a building block for a free world. It's an interesting question whether the European model is ripe and right for emulation. In our policy towards the near East, for example, should we perhaps be encouraging the formation of an Arab Union, as the Americans encouraged the formation of a European Union after 1945?

Whatever we think should happen, I tend to agree with Eric Hobsbawm's historically informed guess as to what will happen. At the end of the short twentieth century, Hobsbawm writes, 'the European Union stood alone and, being the child of a specific and probably unrepeatable historical conjuncture, was likely to remain alone'.[9] Yet even if it remains unique, an enlarged European Union can, constructed with the right mixture of pragmatism and vision, be a formidable component of a free world. Let's imagine, for a moment, Europe in 2025 at its possible best. A political, economic and security community of some forty free countries and 650 million people, embracing all the lands in which two world wars began, and producing, still, a large part of the wealth of the world. A further 650 million people, born in the most explosive parts of the early twenty-first-century globe, but now living in a great arc of partnership with this European Union, from Marrakesh, via Cairo, Jerusalem, Baghdad and Tbilisi, all the way to Vladivostok. That would not be nothing.

Please note that these prescriptions, this vision, this case for a sober European patriotism, are all derived entirely from an examination of Europe's own history, geography, nations and interests. Some comparison with America is inevitable, but it's a disease of current European debate that discussion of what Europe should be always starts, explicitly or implicitly, with America. Thinking about Europe should start with Europe; we must 'think Europe' from Europe outwards. To strive to create a European political identity by making America into Europe's Other, as Britain invented itself by making France its Other, is not European patriotism. It is European nationalism.

It's also bound to fail. I hope the first part of this book has given enough evidence to convince you of that, if nothing else. Of course there are some notable differences between the United States and Europe: about religion, for example, or the welfare state. We can't credibly say that either Europe or America is morally superior. Europe is better in some respects, America in others. Anyway, there are large and growing value divides within both Europe and the US, countries like Canada are somewhere in between, and most of our values are shared. The new old Europe on this side of the Atlantic and the old new Europe on the other are two parts of one extended family. On our landing walls, there hang portraits of the same great-great-grandparents. (My favourite is a beautiful old lady they nicknamed the Enlightenment, but there are other, grimmer-looking ancestors as well.) To try to build a European identity around transatlantic value differences, as Habermas and Derrida have proposed, will split the enlarged European Union, not unite it.

There are also some significant differences between European and American interests; how could there not be? These should be plainly stated. But most of our long-term interests are common, coincident or, at the very least, compatible. Economically, we are more interdependent than ever before. From the need to prevent terrorism, genocide and nuclear, biological or chemical war, through the betterment of the near East, influencing the rise of the far East and helping the poor South, right up to sustaining human life on earth, the global challenges that will determine the well-being of our children are unlikely to be mastered even by America and Europe working together. They surely won't be if we don't work together. Only America, Europe and the other free countries of the post-West, holding between them most of the world's economic and military power, have the resources to try.

Our starting-point should be what John F. Kennedy proposed more than forty years ago: a Declaration of Interdependence. In a constant dialogue, we should look to remove the remaining barriers to free commerce across the Atlantic; to ensure that Nato and the emerging military capacity of the EU don't work against each other; to develop common approaches to aid, debt relief, reducing agricultural subsidies, climate change. Together with other democracies and the UN, we should agree some modernized 'just war' criteria for when it is whose right and duty to intervene in the internal affairs of other states.[10] Institutionally, we need a more permanently structured relationship between the EU, as such, and the US. On difficult issues, however, which may be either themes or countries (eg. Iran), we will also need the well-tried model of 'contact groups' gathering representatives of the states most directly involved. If the political will is there, the institutional forms will be found.

Europe and America bring different strengths and weaknesses to the table. That's because they are themselves ineradicably different. A continent-wide community of more than forty different nation-states, speaking almost as many languages, will never be the same as a single nation of fifty federated states. It is folly for Europe to aspire to be a superpower taking on the American giant. Even in today's world, the most important single dimension of a superpower is military. The Soviet Union demonstrated that a one-dimensional purely military superpower will not endure, but no one has yet seen a superpower that is not militarily strong. The United States would be – and, in recent years, has been – stupid to believe that it can simply ignore Europe because of American military supremacy. Europe, with its economic, diplomatic and cultural power, can practise what has been called 'soft balancing'. In post-war Iraq, America has discovered again the truth of Talleyrand's remark that you can do everything with bayonets except sit on them. But without military power, Europe will not be a superpower in any meaningful sense of the word.

Most Europeans say they want Europe to be a superpower, but when pollsters then ask if they are prepared to increase military spending to make Europe a superpower, half of them say no.[11] As either our economic growth rates or our social welfare provisions, or both, are further reduced, will Europeans spend more on their armies? If you believe that, you'll believe anything. European nations differ considerably in their attitudes to the use of force, but there's a widespread reluctance that flows from Europe's own bitter experience of war. War is one of the things that the whole European project has always defined itself against. We have made a European Union to prevent war, not to wage it. Anyway, a multinational European community is most unlikely to achieve the unity of command, purpose and popular support needed to fight big wars.

To be sure, it would not be healthy for either side if America were to do all the war-fighting on its own, even in a cause that Europe accepted as just, and then expect Europe to do all the peacekeeping and reconstruction afterwards: 'America does the cooking, Europe does the washing-up.' In a just cause, Europe should be ready to do a bit more cooking, America a bit more washing-up. None the less, as in any good partnership, each side has different assets and qualities; not more or less valuable, just different.

Behind Euro-Gaullist fantasies of Europe as a rival to the United States there smoulder the old dreams of former European world powers and empires. But 'world power' is no more morally admirable a goal if pursued by a collectivity called Europe than it is if pursued by a single nation-state. European nationalism is no better than French, German, British or American nationalism; nationalism, in each case, being firmly distinguished from patriotism. With the idealism of the high Enlightenment, Goethe and Schiller once addressed this appeal to their compatriots:

> To become a *nation*, you hope, Germans, in vain;
> Make yourselves rather – you can do it – more freely into
> human beings.*

We hope to become a *superpower*, fellow Europeans, in vain. Let us make ourselves, rather, comrades in a community of free people, working to build a free world.

---

* *Zur* Nation *euch zu bilden, ihr hoffet es, Deutsche, vergebens;*
  *Bildet, ihr könnt es, dafür freier zu Menschen euch aus.* (Xenien, 96)

# 7

# Uncle Sam

What America will do is up to the Americans. If I were them, I'd be getting rather tired of worldly-wise lectures from Europeans in general and the British in particular. These lectures have a characteristic tone of mildly exasperated condescension. 'Now look here, you fellows,' they seem to say, 'we've been playing this game for centuries. We had empires when you were still in short trousers. Just sit quietly and we'll tell you how it's done.' If I were American, I'd reply, 'Thanks, but no thanks.'

Still, it may be helpful to say briefly what I, as an English European, would like America to do. And, in particular, what kind of America would encourage the Europe I've just envisioned. For a start, let's abandon the contested parenthood suit. Historically, America was the daughter of Europe, as de Gaulle said, but the daughter has become an uncle. If I had to summarize my message in a bottle, it would be this: 'So go on then, behave like an uncle. Be Uncle Sam.'

What does that mean? As I write, there's this absurd stand-off between Europe and America. America says: 'We'll support a united Europe so long as it's not anti-American.' Europe says: 'We won't be anti-American so long as you take seriously our uniting Europe.' I would urge America to go first and break the deadlock, both because it is the stronger of the two and because, being a single nation-state, it's easier for America to take clear, decisive action.

Americans should be bold, make a leap of faith, and say: 'We unequivocally, wholeheartedly support a uniting Europe (*sotto voce*: even if some Gaullist French are up there making trouble on the bridge). We've supported it since 1945, and we don't propose to change now. Europe's the first partner we need in building a free world. We wish there really was one telephone number we could call. Let's sign that Declaration of Interdependence. Let's make a transatlantic free trade area. Let's talk about better ways of coordinating the policies of the EU as a whole – not just individual European powers – with those of the US. Let's develop that common project for the near East.'

America should do this with a splash, keep repeating it, and really mean it. This would have a major effect during what is plainly a formative period in Europe's development. Combined with a deeper British involvement in Europe, and the impact of other new and old Euroatlanticist members of the EU, it could swing the great intra-European argument between Euro-Gaullists and Euroatlanticists.

This is a gamble, to be sure. The effects won't be immediately apparent, and there'll be flak along the way. The message would be more easily received if it came from a Democratic president. In recent years, as we've seen, Democrats have been closer to Europeans in their world-view. Yet a moderate Republican, such as the elder President Bush, could be very well respected in Europe, and deservedly so, since his statesmanship was critical to Europe's peaceful emergence from the Cold War. Europeans can hardly expect to tell Americans who to elect. At the moment, America is deeply divided between the 'blue' and the 'red' country. Power will continue to alternate between the two. That's democracy. From time to time, Europeans will therefore have to work with conservative, religious Republican administrations, speaking a political language very different from their own. If we can't manage this, we need to find ourselves another world. But Americans must also see that, after the unilateralism of the younger President Bush's first years in office, after what I've called the 'hubris of the wounded' following 9/11, and after the bruising experience of Washington's 'divide and rule' in Europe, some mistrust is understandable.

In these circumstances, a little more strategic breadth and consistency in American foreign policy would also help. In the first part of this book, I've mentioned some inherent problems of the American system: the country's peculiar habit of changing most of its top civil servants every four years, inter-agency battles that seem to be pre-programmed, the role of Congress, the dictates of the election cycle, a television news agenda that allows only one big story at a time. None the less, the United States managed a higher degree of strategic consistency during the Cold War. Consider, for example, the betterment of the near East. This will not happen in a year or two. In fact, things will probably get worse before they get better, especially if a free or semi-free election in an Arab country brings a radical Islamist party to power. Durable improvement will take at least a decade, probably two. If we Europeans are to sign up to this as one of the big transatlantic projects of the new century, we have to be sure that Americans will also stick with it. Since other problems will inevitably come along, that means Washington being able to sustain several major foreign policy projects at one time, and not giving way to attention deficit disorder.

We fear that America will retreat when the going gets rough, become wholly distracted by another foreign policy crisis, or retreat into America's own 'vast carelessness', absorbed by the domestic economic and social concerns of those heartland Americans for whom almost anywhere else in the world is 'quite a ways across the pond'. Trying to sum up for me his disillusionment with 'the Europeans' over a stately breakfast at a Washington hotel, one senior conservative American commentator said 'they are not serious'.[1] Consciously or unconsciously, this was an exact reprise of what de Gaulle used to say about the Americans: *'ils ne sont pas sérieux'*.[2] But Europeans still have some cause for doubting that the United States is, in this sense, serious.

There's also a difficulty that derives simply from the United States' unique plenitude of power. The British satirical magazine *Private Eye* has an occasional series of front covers on which the Queen is portrayed asking of prominent visitors the standard question that she puts to the people she meets while opening a new hospital, school or factory: 'And what do you do?' When President George W. Bush came on an official visit to Britain in 2003, *Private Eye* showed him standing next to the Queen, in white tie and tails, and answering: 'Whatever I goddam like!'[3] In many respects, the hyperpower can do whatever it goddam likes. And during the early twenty-first-century crisis of the West, Washington seemed to many people around the world set on doing exactly that.

Sitting in the library of Ditchley Park, an English country-house conference centre which is a kind of temple of transatlantic relations, I heard a veteran British historian, much of whose life has been devoted to cultivating those relations, sadly observe that the Bush administration was merely reminding us of the truth of the 'Melian dialogue' in Thucydides' *History of the Peloponnesian War*. Here are the once famous words that the fifth-century BCE Athenian pioneer of contemporary history put into the mouth of his fellow Athenians, as they addressed the much weaker Melians:

We will not make a long and unconvincing speech, full of fine phrases, to prove that our victory over Persia justifies our empire, or that we are now attacking you because you have wronged us, and we ask you not to expect to convince us by saying that you have not injured us, or that, though a colony of Lacedaemon, you did not join her. Let each of us say what we really think and reach a practical agreement. You know and we know, as practical men, that the question of justice arises only between parties equal in strength, and the strong do what they can, and the weak submit.[4]

Is that how Americans would like to be remembered?

Most states aim to maximize and leverage their power. They try, in a phrase which British diplomats use much too often, to 'punch above their weight'. I won't say that the challenge now for America is to punch below its weight – that would be silly, especially when the punch is landed in a good cause. But the challenge for America is to exercise a degree of voluntary self-restraint unusual among states. It would be foolish for the United States to pretend that it does not have the pre-eminent power that it has. It would not be foolish to *act as if* it had somewhat less power. The Romans found a good phrase for this: *primus inter pares*, first among equals. That's strictly a contradiction in terms: if you're first, you're not equal. However, it expresses an attitude of mind, an aspiration to treat other members of the society of states as if they were equals. This is also the advice of the song that Americans sang so movingly after the 11 September 2001 attacks. 'America, the Beautiful' counsels:

> Confirm thy soul in self-control,
> Thy liberty in law.[5]

Self-restraint can be exercised without reference to international organizations and international law. None the less, respect for international organizations and international law, which the United States itself did so much to create and spread after 1945, is an important sign of it. Chief among those organizations is Roosevelt's baby, the UN, with its charter and conventions. I can well understand why American leaders are frustrated with an organization in whose supreme body the world's largest authoritarian regime, China, and a cussed, very partial democracy, Russia, have a permanent veto. I can see why they think that a charter written in 1945 is not adequate to address the new security challenges of sixty years later.

So we need to change them, by consent. That, however, is very difficult. How would we arrive at a better UN Security Council? If we were reshuffling the pack of great powers, Britain and France should give up their permanent seats in favour of a single European Union seat. This would impose the necessity of reaching a common EU position on key foreign policy issues, and encourage France and Britain to make their historic compromise. (Regrettably, it would also increase the already high fudge content in Security Council decisions.) India and Japan would deserve places, on the grounds, respectively, of their demographic and economic weight, but how would you choose the 'great powers' from Africa, Latin America or the Middle East? A Security Council with no permanent members at all would be more universally acceptable – and even less effective. Updating the UN charter for the twenty-first century is equally difficult. Still, we should try.

In the meantime, America can look for sources of international legitimacy short of the full, explicit sanction of a UN Security Council resolution. Nato's military intervention to prevent genocide in Kosovo had less sanction from the UN Security Council than the war in Iraq. However, it had the support of a clear majority of the democracies in the world and a clear majority of Serbia's neighbours. It was illegal but legitimate.[6] The fact that more than half the states in the world are democracies creates a large opportunity. In 2000, US Secretary of State Madeleine Albright and the Polish foreign minister, Bronisław Geremek, convened a founding meeting in Warsaw of a worldwide Community of Democracies, assembling representatives of more than a hundred states. Not much has become of it since, but shouldn't we think of building a caucus of democracies at the UN? It could be the mother of all caucuses.

Ultimately, helping to make international rules and then playing by them will be in America's own interest. This is what the Melians replied to the Athenians:

As you ignore justice and have made self-interest the basis of discussion, we must take the same ground, and we say that in our opinion it is in your interest to maintain a principle which is for the good of all – that anyone in danger should have just and equitable treatment and any advantage, even if not strictly his due, which he can secure by persuasion.[7]

The fact that the weak have an obvious motive for making this argument to the strong does not invalidate the argument. The case has been made by many Americans themselves, arguing that a unilateral use of America's military power, with neither international legality nor international legitimacy, will soon enough diminish America's other two dimensions of power: economic and 'soft'.

The vocal presence of these other American voices suggests that a vigorous, pluralist democracy like the United States is, to some extent, self-righting. And so it is, but only up to a point. The problem with American power is not, as some Europeans believe, that it's American. The problem is simply the power. It would be dangerous even for an archangel to have so much power. 'The strongest poison ever known / Came from Caesar's laurel crown' wrote the poet William Blake.[8] The authors of the US Constitution wisely determined that no single locus of power, however benign, should predominate. Even the best could be led into temptation. The President, the Congress and the Supreme Court must be presumed to share the same basic values, goals and interests, but better let them check and balance each other. Shouldn't the same principle apply in world politics?[9]

If Europe understands that it shares the same basic values, goals and long-term interests as America, then America should want Europe to be a benign check and balance on its own solitary hyperpower. For the reasons I've explored, Europe will always be a very different kind of power from the US. This makes it not more difficult but easier to structure the partnership. Admittedly, to want someone else to balance as well as complement your own power is a very unusual thing for any state to do, but the United States is a very unusual state, the European Union is not a state at all, and both are historic variations of one and the same dream.

Americans might also be in a little less of a hurry to jump up and down crying 'anti-Americanism!' every time someone criticizes what Washington does. That carpet bag of a word obscures more than it reveals. As we've seen, if you press most critical Europeans beyond their first derogatory remark about 'the Americans', they immediately distinguish between a particular administration and the country as a whole. There's a vital difference between disliking what America says or does and hating what America is. Even the most virulent European anti-Americanism is very rarely comparable with anti-Semitism. It is seldom directed against individual, ordinary Americans just because they are Americans; let alone calling for physical acts of discrimination, expulsion or extermination. (I accept that there are a few shocking exceptions, especially among Arabs living in Europe.) Much of what is called 'anti-Americanism' is criticism that comes with the turf of predominant power. The British, the French, the Spanish, the Romans all encountered it in their time. Often it's very unfair: 'The blame of those ye better, / The hate of those ye guard', as Kipling warned in a poem addressed specifically to Americans.[10] Wise uncles react calmly.

Unlike many Europeans, I like the high moral content of American political rhetoric and admire the strain of Wilsonian idealism in American foreign policy. But sometimes the assumption that America is God's own country, equipped by Moses (played by Charlton Heston) with all the answers, can get up even the most sympathetic European nose. At such moments, American presidents sound like a cross between the Puritan governor John Winthrop and a Coca-Cola advertisement. Of course we know where this comes from. I have before me as I write a seventeenth-century English bestseller, William Camden's *Remaines, concerning Britaine: But especially England, and the Inhabitants thereof.* 'The Kingdome of England', writes Camden, 'is God's own Kingdome, and for it God himself will provide.'[11] But we're in the twenty-first century now. In return,

Europeans – and Canadians – should drop their own forms of self-righteousness: the holier-than-thou assumptions of moral superiority in their attachment to international law or social justice, and the unbearable arrogance of Europe's claimed humility.

After Iraq, America should also go to war again. The enemy to be defeated in this war is not a state, a dictator, a terrorist group or an ideology, but extreme poverty and its accompanying plagues of disease, hunger and early death. There is a shocking disparity between what the United States has spent on the war in Iraq, and the subsequent occupation, and what it spends on development aid to the rest of the world. In round figures, at the time of writing, the US is spending some $80 billion a year on the occupation of Iraq and $13 billion a year on development aid to all other countries. Even if one includes a generous estimate for other forms of American government assistance, and allows for the increase which is to come into effect by 2006, the United States is still spending at least five times as much money on one potentially oil-rich country of 25 million people as it is on lifting more than 1 billion people out of an existence that scarcely deserves the name of life.

Let America's next war be the war on want. A country so large in spirit, so religious and so rich can surely be won for such a war. Let a campaign of well-administered aid, medicine, debt relief and trade liberalization be carried to the poorest of the world's poor. Let the world see again, as it saw once after 1945, just how generous America can be – with a great big Stars and Stripes on every packet. Let Europe be challenged to keep pace, matching packet for packet, this time with our own yellow-and-blue star-spangled banner stuck on the side. Why not? Because there are no votes in it? But that's up to us, the thousand million.

A special American responsibility is to reduce its excessive emissions of carbon dioxide. This requires Americans to change their 'way of life' somewhat more than Europeans, putting the long-term interests of the Earth before their own short-term interests. Without American commitment, we shall never reach international agreements that bind emerging industrial giants such as China. And then we'll all be cooked.

I believe that America is capable of taking these steps. If I'd been

born in the Middle East, Latin America or South East Asia, I might
be less inclined to believe this. As a historian, I know that, in the
global competition of the Cold War and in its pursuit of oil and economic advantage, the United States has supported undemocratic
regimes and licensed oppression. This was made worse by the
hypocrisy of fostering unfreedom in the name of 'the free world'. But
as an Englishman who has seen at first hand what the United States
has done for Europe, I still believe it. And when I go to California, as
I do every year, I wonder again at the way in which the sons and
daughters of immigrants from utterly different cultures, from China,
Indonesia, Somalia or Nicaragua, will embrace an ideal that was once
proclaimed in a small church in Putney.

Perhaps this trust comes most naturally to an English European.
Yet I encounter very similar feelings among the young Germans,
Spaniards, Poles and Swedes I deal with almost every day in Europe.
Even Europeans whom many Americans would call 'anti-American'
are often disappointed lovers, measuring America against its own
high ideal of itself. A Europe that likes the idea of America is a better
Europe. Indeed, if we confront America with its own better self, we
are confronting it, historically speaking, with a vision of a better
Europe. And an America that likes the idea of the new Europe is, in
turn, supporting another version of itself. The *New York Times*
columnist Thomas Friedman puts it punchily: 'I support united
Europe because I think two United States are better than one.'[12]

I believe that Americans can do these good things in the world, but
they also need to remember that they don't have unlimited time. A
point the Melians made in reply to the Athenians was that one day
the Athenians might be down and out themselves, and then they'd
want a system of international rules and justice to protect them. In
Thucydides' account, the Athenians contemptuously dismissed this
possibility, and it must seem very remote to today's Americans. But
all powers decline in the end. In 1941, Henry Luce proclaimed in *Life*
magazine the coming of 'the American century'.[13] We can argue
about when the American century began, and how long it might last.
Some would say the 'British century' that preceded the American one
did last exactly a hundred years, from 1814 to 1914, although with a
long epilogue. A humorous parody of British school history, *1066*

*and All That*, famously concluded that after 1918, 'America was thus clearly top nation, and History came to a.'[14] However, it's probably more realistic to date 'the American century' from 1945. This means, if it's to be a full century, that the United States has got about forty years to go; but history is accelerating, and the powers of the far East are coming up fast.

As time goes by – to recall the song from *Casablanca*, a great movie about relations between Americans and Europeans – the power of the United States will fade. As time goes by, Americans will be less and less able to shape the world around them. We cannot know how long this time will be, but it may be no more than twenty years. In those twenty years, however, Americans have a historic chance, working with Europeans, to go beyond 'the free world' of the old West and lay the foundations of a free world. There's a tune there waiting to be played; quite a complicated tune, to be sure, but America has practised it many times before and knows it by heart. Go on, Sam, play it.

# 8

# Towards a Free World

We, the free, face a daunting opportunity. Previous generations, even if they lived in what was called 'the free world', could only dream of a free world. Now we can begin to make it. More people are more free than ever before. Our possibilities of helping the others out of unfreedom are also larger than ever. If Europeans, Americans and free people everywhere don't work together towards this goal, instead remaining sunk in a narcissism of minor differences, it will be impossible to achieve. If we do work together, the task remains daunting, perhaps nearly impossible – but the nearly impossible is what we should demand of our leaders and of ourselves.

I've indicated four key areas in which we are challenged to make a difference: the near East, the far East, the poor South and planet Earth. It would be absurd to sketch any sort of 'action plan' for these vast and complex challenges, each of which requires a fat report written by expert hands. Instead, I want to share a few tentative thoughts about the overall terms on which we in the post-West engage in this larger project, if that's what we agree to do.

In this book, I've talked cautiously about 'a' not 'the' crisis of the West, let alone the 'final crisis' or the 'end' of the West. It is still possible that a new common enemy will sharply revive the geopolitical unity of a slightly enlarged West. Neither rogue states, nor a portmanteau 'Islam', nor even a major terrorist attack on European soil, such as the 11 March 2004 bombings in Madrid, are currently having that effect; but perhaps something will. Yet that's not what we should hope for. What we should hope for is, in a longer perspective, already happening: that the West goes beyond the West, and in so doing, calls itself into question.

For the deepest crisis of the West is a crisis of success. Since the fif-teenth century, ideas, customs and institutions that originated in Europe have spread around the globe. A very sober and far from Eurocentric historian of the world observes that 'the balance sheet of cultural influence is overwhelmingly one-sided . . . The teaching of Marx was long a force throughout twentieth-century Asia; the last non-European whose words had any comparable authority in Europe was Jesus Christ.'[1] In the 'creeping unity' that has seized humankind, writes J. M. Roberts, 'the language of democracy and human rights is now enlisted more widely than ever to pay at least lip service to western notions of what public life should be'. The 'pervasive influence of a civ-ilization originally European' is evident not just in the technologies of modernization but also in 'certain master ideas and institutions'.[2] So – no longer a master race, just master ideas? Europeanization and Americanization are obviously competing variants of Westernization. But is 'globalization' also, at bottom, just a polite euphemism for Westernization? Is Roberts's 'creeping unity' of humankind in fact a creeping imperialism, through which we impose our Western values on others?

'Members of Congress, ours are not Western values, they are the universal values of the human spirit,' Tony Blair declared, to loud applause from his Washington audience in summer 2003.[3] But are they? And what does that mean? 'Western values' as we generally nowadays recognize them – democracy, human rights, free speech, the rule of law, etc – are, historically speaking, just a subset of the val-ues embraced in the lands of the West. Nor has this long been the dominant subset. To be sure, today's 'Western values' have roots that can be traced far back, to ancient Athens, Jerusalem and Rome. The idea of the moral equality of all human beings, for example, appears in Christianity, blending elements from Judaism and Greek philoso-phy.[4] In his speech at St Mary's Church, Putney, in 1647, the Puritan Thomas Rainsborough returned to that Christian source, but made the leap from moral to civic equality. Yet only in the late seventeenth- and eighteenth-century Enlightenment did philosophers systemati-cally elaborate what are recognizably today's Western values.

Our 'Western values' are, in large measure, Enlightenment values; yet throughout the next two centuries these were under fierce challenge inside the West itself. The philosopher Isaiah Berlin spent a good part of his life engaging with these often intellectually formidable enemies of the Enlightenment. For much of the twentieth century, millions of Europeans thought fascism or communism were better alternatives to liberal democracy. Adolf Hitler was also a European, and a Westerner. He was an anti-Western Westerner, but still a product of Western civilization. Like all attempts to harness values to places – 'American values', 'British values', 'central European values', 'European values', 'Asian values' – the claim for 'Western values' deliberately mistakes a part for the whole. In so doing, it mixes description and prescription.

Moreover, as soon as 'Western values' appeared in a shape we would recognize today, they carried the aspiration to go beyond the West, whether in the English Enlightenment universalism of Locke or the German Enlightenment universalism of Kant. All human beings should in principle, as of natural right, be treated as moral equals. So Enlightenment Westerners did claim the universality of human rights. However, it is quite another thing to say that these values were in fact universal, in the sense of being found in the history of all cultures. Rich and cognate notions – tolerance, pluralism, justice, obligations of the ruler to the citizen – can be discovered in the writings of Confucius, the fourth-century BCE Indian political writer Kautilya, or Islamic philosophers. Yet a careful enquiry into the universality of human rights, by Ludger Kühnhardt, finds very little evidence that any recognizable notion of individual human rights was present in these cultures, until it came to them from the West. Kühnhardt notes, for example, that the Chinese language did not have characters for the concept of 'human rights' until the nineteenth century.[5]

In short, what we habitually call 'Western values' are only a few of the values historically embraced in the West, even into very recent times. To associate the West constantly and exclusively with them is, at best, the highly selective claim of a wider Western patriotism. At worst, it's Western nationalism, in the generic, Orwellian meaning of nationalism that I have used in this book. Ever since these values were first articulated systematically, in the Enlightenment, their proponents have staked a claim for them to be accepted as universal. They are not, however, empirically universal. Historically, they were first institutionalized in the West and they came to most other cultures from the West. They go significantly beyond the human universals discovered in all cultures by anthropologists, and the liberal or pluralist elements to be found in most religions. They are now, if you will, just one major offer in the global market for values.

All this may seem rather academic, in the pejorative sense of the term. But for any country that has not always been part of the West – and that's most countries – it is not academic at all. A nice illustration comes from the end of the Cold War, which was also the true beginning of the early twenty-first-century crisis of the West. In December 1989, Soviet President Mikhail S. Gorbachev and American President George H. W. Bush were sitting in a Soviet naval ship, the *Maxim Gorky*, bobbing up and down in stormy seas off Malta. And what were they talking about, the two presidents, while the Soviet empire crumbled and the seas raged around them? About 'Western values'. Bush's secretary of state, James Baker, had raised the prospect of Germany being united on the basis of Western values. According to the Russian transcript, the conversation then went as follows:

*Gorbachev*: Aleksander Yakovlev asks: How come democracy, openness and the market are 'Western' values?
*Bush*: Because the USA and Western Europe have shared them for many years.
*Gorbachev*: But we share them too. These are, after all, values that belong to the whole of humanity.
*Bush*: But that wasn't always true . . .

After some more verbal swordplay, James Baker, the lawyer and consummate deal-maker, suggested cutting the difference:

*Baker*: Perhaps we could agree on the compromise that this positive process is on the basis of 'democratic values'?[6]

The lawyer saves the day. Yet perhaps Baker was wiser than he knew. His improvised suggestion points in exactly the right direction for today. All of us should abandon this muddled, vainglorious talk of 'Western values' or 'universal values', 'American', 'European' or, for that matter, 'Asian' values. Instead, we should say what we actually mean – modestly, plainly, concretely.

What are the basic terms of engagement that we, in the post-West, propose to the rest of the world? At the moment, there are two extreme positions, the Western triumphalist fundamentalist and the Western cultural relativist. The triumphalist fundamentalist posture is well captured in the opening of the Bush administration's 2002 national security strategy. 'The great struggles of the twentieth century between liberty and totalitarianism ended with a decisive victory for the forces of freedom,' it begins, with perfect accuracy and justified satisfaction, but then goes on '– and a single sustainable model for national success: freedom, democracy and free enterprise.' A single sustainable model? What titanic hubris. Even within the present spectrum of democratic capitalism there are many different models, with widely varying roles for the state as against free enterprise. If all the nations of the world successfully imitated today's American model, there would soon be no habitable world. Were America's profligate emissions of greenhouse gases to be matched by China, India, Russia and everyone else, we'd all be fried. 'Sustainable' is what it's not. And even if it were possible for the United Nations to be composed entirely of crypto-Americas, this would be deeply undesirable, on grounds of, so to speak, the biodiversity of world politics – not to mention sheer boredom.

The cultural relativist position is what I call Vulgar Huntingtonism (by analogy with Vulgar Marxism). It says: 'These values and institutions are peculiar to the West; we cannot expect Muslims, Confucians or even Orthodox Christians to share them; therefore we should not expect of them the respect for human rights, free speech, democracy and so forth that we expect among ourselves.' This is equally misguided. Twenty years ago, the West's 'realist' cultural relativists told us the Poles and Hungarians were not ready for democracy, because they had a different 'political culture'. That condescending judgement has been proved wrong since 1989. Then they told us the Orthodox countries of Europe were not ready for it. With truly heroic condescension, Samuel Huntington himself opined that 'Greece is not part of Western civilization', although, he conceded generously, 'it was the home of Classical civilization which was an important source of Western civilization'. Bad luck, Greece. 'In their opposition to the Turks,' Huntington explained, 'Greeks have considered themselves historically spear-carriers of Christianity.'[7] In the meantime, the Greeks, these blighted non-Western anti-Turkish spear-carriers, have been among the most eloquent advocates of largely Muslim Turkey joining the European Union. And Turkey is itself proving that it can consolidate an admittedly still very imperfect democracy with an Islamist party in power. As for Confucian Chinese being quite incapable of democracy: have these cultural relativists never visited Taiwan?

The right way lies between these two extremes. It can be described, without apology, as the path of freedom. Freedom not just for us but for all. However, this freedom we propose to all has to be clearly and even narrowly defined. In the terms popularized by Isaiah Berlin, this is 'negative' liberty: freedom from removable constraints, so long as removing them does not itself constrain the liberty of others.[8] In dealing with other countries and cultures, the constraints on which we should concentrate first are the most obviously acute and burdensome ones – those that no normal man or woman, in any known culture, would gladly endure if he or she had the chance to get rid of them. The more modest and precise is our definition of this freedom we want for others, the more likely it is to be accepted by them, rather than being rejected as arrogant Western imperialism.

Confucius can help here. Most of us – even us secular Europeans – probably know the so-called golden rule of Christian conduct on earth in the shorthand form: 'Do as you would be done by.' Or, in the King James Bible version of the original: 'Therefore all things whatsoever ye would that men should do to you, do ye even so to them; for this is the law and the prophets.'[9] To which George Bernard Shaw made a witty reply, that seems tailor-made for the dilemma of the post-West in today's world. 'Do not do unto others as you would that they should do unto you,' said Shaw. 'Their tastes may not be the same.'[10] Exactly so. But five centuries before Christ, Confucius formulated the injunction in a subtly different way. 'What you do *not* wish for yourself,' wrote Confucius, 'do *not* impose on others'[11] (my italics). Perhaps, taking our lead from Confucius, we can define our purpose thus: we aim to ensure that what other people do not wish for themselves is not imposed upon them.

At a time when Poland was still unfree, a Polish poet wrote this short poem, entitled 'Freedom':

What is freedom, ask the philosophers.
I too sometimes answer that it's
guaranteed liberties in the face of the power
of the state, or else I emphasize the strength
of convictions, the sovereignty of the soul and
loyalty to your own vocation. Yet even when
I'm unable to define the essence of freedom
I know exactly what it is to be unfree.[12]

This makes the essential point. There is always a question, even for wealthy people in free countries, as to how truly free you are as an individual. An American billionaire can still be a slave to convention, fashion, work, or his own desires. Some people in the former communist countries of central Europe have been disoriented and made unhappy by freedom. When the former East German communist party leader Erich Honecker was in prison in West Berlin, he received letters from his former subjects saying they had lived 'more quietly' under his rule.[13] But if you ask most East Germans, they certainly don't want his old regime back. There are also exceptional people who can find spiritual freedom in captivity. One of the most moving conversations I have ever had was with a young woman in Rangoon who told me how, in the miserable, overcrowded, half-starved conditions of a Burmese prison cell, she had found her way, through intensive Buddhist meditation, to *nirvana*. 'I thanked my jailers,' she recalled. 'I thanked them for helping me to reach *nirvana*.' But she didn't want to return to prison.

Freedom is elusive, difficult, risky, hard to define, let alone to achieve; but those who are unfree know exactly what unfreedom is. A Confucian no more enjoys having his nails pulled out under torture than a Christian. To see your daughter raped in front of your eyes by a militia gang is as soul-rending for a Muslim mother as for a Jewish mother. To feel your son slowly dying in your arms from hunger or AIDS is as unbearable for an African father as for an Indian father. So many people in the world still live, and die, in an unfreedom which we can be quite sure they do not want, simply because they are human and we are human.

What is now the most widespread form of basic unfreedom? Sixty years ago, when Roosevelt spelled out his 'four freedoms', and even thirty years ago, at the height of the Cold War, most of us would probably have answered 'dictatorships and the wars they cause'. Today, the answer must be extreme poverty. The first freedom towards which we should now work, if we want a free world, is Roosevelt's 'freedom from want'. This is also the field in which it is clearest what we – the thousand million rich and free – have to do.

Two large but very simple steps can lift hundreds of millions of our fellow human beings out of this kind of unfreedom. The first step is to practise what we preach: free trade. We should open our markets to their goods and cut our agricultural subsidies. This can only happen if America and Europe do it together. The second step is to increase aid. All rich and free countries should catch up with the exemplary Scandinavians and reach the target of giving 0.7 per cent of GDP, suggested by Lester Pearson, back in 1969, in a truly worthwhile Canadian initiative. But what states do is only half the story. All rich and free individuals should also donate more in private aid. Peter Singer, in his inspiring book *One World*, suggests that we should each aim to give 1 per cent of our annual income towards providing clean water, basic sustenance, shelter and medical care for the poorest of the poor. Anyone whose income is more than the average wage in a rich country can well afford that 1 penny from each pound we earn, or 1 cent from each Euro or dollar. Why don't we?

Some obvious reservations apply. We need to make sure our own farmers will not go to the wall in order to save the lives of African farmers. We have to see that aid is skilfully administered and doesn't stick to the wrong fingers along the way. The Great Aid Hike cannot and should not happen overnight. Yet in principle, the means to spread 'freedom from want' are right in front of our noses.

Working towards what Roosevelt called 'freedom from fear' is more complicated. Fear, unlike want, is a constituent part of all human lives. So what we're confronting here are only the causes of particularly acute fear, threatening basic human dignity and the most elementary human right: the right to life. Where do such threats now mainly come from? In the twentieth century, we spent most of our time worrying about states that were too strong: the 'Big Brother' regimes. There are still quite a few of them about – in Burma, in

North Korea, in several parts of Africa, and, in some respects, still the Chinese communist party-state.

In the early twenty-first century, however, we spend as much time worrying about states that are too weak. It's in failed states, such as Somalia and Rwanda, that people are murdered in large numbers just because of their ethnicity. It's in failed states, such as Afghanistan, that militant extremists and international terrorists find a congenial home. Then there's the danger of dictators, extremists or terrorists getting hold of the weapons of mass destruction which, thanks to the Western-led arms industry and arms trade, are ever more deadly and ever more widely available.

In a breathtaking example of American 'can-do' idealism, a former American ambassador, Mark Palmer, has proposed a campaign by the world's democracies to get rid of the world's last forty-four dictators over the next twenty years. 'The Community of Democracies', he writes, 'must adopt this common goal: All Dictators Out by 2025.'[14] It was actually forty-five dictators by his count when he started writing his book, but, while he wrote, Saddam Hussein was deposed by American and British military force. One down, forty-four to go? Palmer's work is mainly devoted to an admirable programme of non-violent means for encouraging the fall of dictators, and he says these should have been explored more thoroughly in the case of Iraq. However, he adds, in a slightly embarrassed formulation, 'I did personally favour invasion over a failure to act at all to oust Saddam Hussein'[15] – which, as he has himself just pointed out, is to pose a false alternative.

Palmer's contortions reflect the dilemma of many who care for other people's freedom as well as their own. We now face this question: is Western military intervention justified simply to remove a brutal dictatorship? If so, we should, logically, be urging our governments to prepare an invasion of Burma. Burma suffers under a military dictatorship at least as brutal as Saddam's, facing an opposition which already has the legitimacy of an overwhelming victory in democratic elections.[16] Now there are few things in the world that I would like more than to see the end of that loathsome Burmese junta, and Aung San Suu Kyi at last taking the place to which she was elected, at the head of a free Burma. But I'm afraid the answer to the question has to be 'no'. 'No' for Burma, and 'no' altogether.

Military intervention – preferably with explicit UN sanction, failing that with the support of a double majority (of democracies and of the country's neighbours), and, in very exceptional cases, even with a smaller coalition – can be justified a) where there is genocide taking place, as in Bosnia, Kosovo, Rwanda, and Iraq in 1988 but not Iraq in 2003; or b) where there is a real and present danger of a regime or terrorist group acquiring weapons of mass destruction which they are likely to use against us, their neighbours or their own people. How on earth we establish whether there is such a real and present danger is something we shall all have to wrestle with – especially after this claim was made about Saddam's Iraq, on the authority of secret intelligence, and turned out to be untrue. What qualifies as genocide is also a matter for the most serious debate.[17] But intervention is not justified simply to end a dictatorship.

There are good reasons why statesmen from the signatories of the Peace of Westphalia in 1648 to the authors of the UN Charter in 1945 set such store by respect for state sovereignty and non-intervention. If I think I'm justified in invading your country, you may equally well feel you're justified in invading mine. Or someone else's. President Putin plainly felt encouraged by America's unilateral action over Iraq to continue his oppression of Chechnya; and China felt it had a freer hand in Tibet. The road back to international anarchy is a short one.

Moreover, even if intervention is justified, for one of the reasons I've just given, what do we do when we're there? You may say: 'just give the country back to the people!' But which people, and how? What if, as often happens, there are several peoples in an ethnically fractured state? And so we enter the strange business of early twenty-first-century international occupations: Bosnia, Kosovo, East Timor, Afghanistan, Iraq. 'Nation-building' was the oddly nineteenth-century term first given to this enterprise; now the more modern and accurate 'state-building' is gaining ground. But are we any good at it? We're not. Of course it's early days, but I don't yet see a single example of a post-intervention international occupation which has successfully 'built' a self-governing free country. The two precedents usually quoted – Germany (West) and Japan – are the exceptions that prove the rule. Both were functioning nation-states before they were occupied. Both were occupied by just a few leading Western powers, which assumed total control following the unconditional surrender of regimes that had launched wars of aggression against them.

In our modern crypto-colonies, non-functioning, ethnically fractured states or parts of states are occupied by a multiplicity of national forces and international organizations, who rush to share power with hastily appointed or elected local elites. Power and legitimacy are hopelessly fragmented. Different international organizations pass the buck to each other; the locals pass the buck to the internationals, and the internationals back to the locals. The internationals keep changing, and half the participating governments want to get out as soon as they can. Corruption is rife, confusion endemic. Where we really had to intervene, in Bosnia, Kosovo, East Timor and Afghanistan, we must now stick with it, keep trying, and not sullenly withdraw, leaving the job half done. In Iraq, where we did not have to intervene, we none the less have promises to keep, and Europe has an even more vital interest than America in the outcome. But these are not good roads to freedom.

No, whether we look at its causes or its consequences, we conclude that military intervention must remain a last resort, only to be tried when all other means have failed. Armed intervention is, in itself, already a confession of failure. Both in principle and in practice it's better that people find their own path to freedom, in their own countries, in their own time, and, wherever possible, peacefully. But should we help these people as they fight freedom's battle? Most emphatically we should, by every non-violent means at our disposal. For we hold this truth to be self-evident: that those who love freedom must also want it for others.

We should urge our governments and companies to link trade and investment to respect for human rights, and other political and legal conditions which will vary from case to case. We should urge our parliaments to give more money to organizations like the American National Endowment for Democracy, the German party foundations and Britain's Westminster Foundation for Democracy, as they support those working for democracy in countries that do not yet have it. We can also give our own money or time to some of the myriad non-governmental organizations that help independent media, lawyers, women's groups, trades unions, students and political parties in places that are still unfree, or only partly free. Nor should we hesitate to expose these places to the full magnetism of our own freedom, through the internet, international broadcasting and scholarships for foreign students to study in our schools and colleges.

There's no room here for the false modesty of exaggerated cultural relativism. The Chinese students on Tiananmen Square gave pride of place to a model of the Statue of Liberty. One day, as the poet James Fenton prophesied soon after their demonstration was crushed by tanks, 'they'll come again / to Tiananmen'.[18] In the Chinese film *Balzac and the Little Chinese Seamstress*, a student banished to a remote mountain region during the Cultural Revolution approaches a doctor to ask him to perform an abortion on a friend. Instead of cash, he promises the doctor a volume of Balzac, in a classic Chinese translation. He shows him some sample lines he has written on the inside of his sheepskin jacket: 'My dear Christophe, you cannot know the delights of being free. To feel that all minds are free around you, yes, even the dunces, is an indescribable pleasure, as if the soul were swimming in endless skies.'[19] As the doctor reads these lines, he is moved almost to tears. It's good to be reminded by the Chinese that French is one of the great languages of liberty.

There is, however, a place for the true modesty of realism about our possibilities of influence. When we support the oppressed, dictators will always cry 'foul' and protest that this is 'intervention in our internal affairs'. The truth is that so long as the rulers of a state control their own frontiers, army, riot police and secret police, even the most powerful free countries in the world cannot topple them. All we can do is to give their own people the chance of toppling them or, preferably, negotiating them out of power. By our external assistance we are, as it were, just levelling up the playing field. By military intervention, we may bring an oppressed people freedom from the barrel of a gun. By these non-military forms of intervention, using our economic and 'soft' power, we do something slower and more open-ended, but in the end much better: we give them the chance to win it for themselves. It is, so to speak, not freedom itself we bring, merely the freedom to seize the possibility of freedom.

We also need to be modest about our ability to find all the right answers for other societies. What is it we want them to build? The shorthand answer generally given, especially by Americans, is Democracy with a capital D. Now liberal democracy is the best form of government yet discovered. But if you rush to a multi-party election without having first developed the underpinnings of liberal democracy – the rule of law, habits of good government, civil society, private property, independent media – you can end up with what Fareed Zakaria has called 'illiberal democracy'.[20] And if extremists win that election, you may find yourself with 'one man, one vote, once'. Some writers then leap to an opposite conclusion: that you have first to build the economic, legal and other foundations before 'topping out' with democracy. As with Spain under Franco, first make your bourgeoisie, then it's an easy step to bourgeois democracy. So the Chinese communists were right to put economic modernization before democratization, Gorbachev wrong to do it the other way round. But this is not self-evident. Actually, much of post-communist Europe has built the house of democracy from the roof downwards. A rather wonky building results, but it's still a freedom house.

The wiser conclusion, surely, is that it's not for us to say in what order others should do things. We can, and should, offer a toolbox of experiences in all aspects of transition, from how to write a constitution to how to deal with a difficult past, from demolishing nuclear silos to building a welfare system. But then it's up to them to decide. They should know best what is best for them. And if they don't, they must have the right to make their own mistakes. The Chinese house in 2025 will be different from an American house, and that is good – provided always that the essential moral and political minima are observed. And one further, vital task for the post-West is to lead the international debate about the definition of these universal minima of inalienable human dignity, on which there can be no compromise.

Democracy, like European union, is not an end in itself. It is a means to higher ends. What are these higher ends? Free people will differ about them too. My own shortlist comes from a prayer I chanced upon in one of my sons' old schoolbooks. It asks for 'freedom, good government, just laws and happy homes'. The first three

– freedom, good government and just laws – seem to me at once a more precise and a more inspiring formulation of our political goals than the blank Democracy. The fourth – happy homes – reminds us of the limits of politics:

> How small, of all that human hearts endure,
> That part which laws or kings can cause or cure.[21]

The recipe for human happiness is mysterious and cannot be purchased at Wal-Mart.

As I conclude this modest yet also hair-raising programme for a free world, I will confess to a nagging voice of doubt. This doubt, this Tiresias twinge, concerns the insatiable power of Western-style consumerism. If you visit a country like Burma, you see a miserable dictatorship but you also see a society which conserves in dress, custom and religion a very different, more traditional way of life. Only here and there do you notice the reversed baseball cap creeping in. Now Burma's dictators must go; but when they fall, the armies of Western-style consumerism will be waiting at the frontier, with their container-loads of tawdry goods, their cheap cigarettes called 'London', their sex shops, ready-made lifestyle packages and state-of-the-art techniques for the unceasing manufacture of new consumer desires. This invasion force is more irresistible than the Red Army, or even today's US Army, for it advances by asking what people want – and giving it to them. Then it makes them want more, and more, and more. This manufacturing of consumer desires is the exact opposite of the Buddhist ideal of transcending human desires. Which of the two will make more happy homes?

In any case, Western-style consumerism is unsustainable on a global scale. The earth cannot for ever bear more and more people demanding more and more. Yet how can economies grow without demand? If this is the underlying reality of the 'single sustainable model' then it will turn out to be not a model and not sustainable. All that remains will be the 'single', but that is itself undesirable, because humankind evolves through diversity. In this respect, too, as the West goes far beyond the West, it calls itself into question – as it often has before, and always should. Not only must we expect that the models of a free society that China, India, Africa or Latin America produce will differ from our own; we must actively hope that they will. An 'open society' inside a Western country does not mean the predominance of a single model; it means the constant, peaceful, regulated competition of many models. In this sense, we also need an open society of states.

So our ultimate objective is not that in 2047, on the four-hundredth anniversary of the Putney debates, some preppy Rainsborough from Boston should stand crowing from a hilltop: 'All dictators gone; world free; mission accomplished!' It's that a young woman in Teheran, Mombasa or Shanghai should adapt the old words of Thomas Rainsborough, in her own way, in her own country, in her own tongue, and say

For really I think that the poorest she that is on earth has a life to live, as the greatest he; and therefore truly, sir, I think it's clear, that every woman that is to live under a government ought first by her own consent to put herself under that government; and I do think that the poorest woman on earth is not at all bound in a strict sense to that government that she has not had a voice to put herself under.

# What Can We Do?

A crisis of the West has revealed a great chance. Shall we seize it? Or will Europe half-heartedly pursue a half-baked dream of being a rival superpower to the United States, and frustrate its own better purposes as a result? Will Britain go on dithering, like a pensioner Hamlet? Will America yield to the temptations of predominant power, the rich go on living high and letting the poor die, the free remain indifferent to the misery of the unfree?

There's a wise motto for freeworlders: 'pessimism of the intellect, optimism of the will'.[1] Observe that its author did not say 'optimism of the heart'. The *will* is something active, defiant, striving. We expect the worst but work for the best.

One of the oddest things about our age of unparalleled democracy is that so many people feel so disillusioned with conventional politics that they don't even bother to vote. They say: 'We can't really influence what our politicians do and it doesn't matter that much anyway.' Wrong and wrong. It matters a lot. Most of us, the lucky thousand million, live relatively peaceful, comfortable private lives, in which, from day to day, we can happily ignore politics or ideologies; but in the meantime, our rulers are steadily demolishing the possibility that our children will do the same. Not that the people who govern us are generally scoundrels. Well, not utter scoundrels anyway. But half the time they really don't know what they're doing. The world is not safe in their hands. We must not leave it to them.

And we can influence them. In fact, there's never been a time when politicians tried so often and assiduously to find out, through opinion polls and focus groups, what the people really desire – and then to offer it, at least in slogans and promises. What is this 'public opinion' to which they are so nervously attentive? It's us.

Lenin's question 'What is to be done?' somehow suggests that, whatever the 'what', it's 'to be done' by someone else, by impersonal parties, governments or classes. Our question should be: 'What can *we* do?' The answer is: a lot. For a start, every time we hear someone holding forth, in the bar, office or family living room, about '*the* Europeans' or '*the* Americans' we can stop them and ask: '*Which* Europeans? *Which* Americans?' I hope this book has supplied ammunition for a good round or two. Every time we do this, we deflate just a little the dangerous myths of nationalism – British, French and American nationalism, but also what I've described as European nationalism. And we swing, if only by a thousandth of 1 per cent, that anonymous 'public opinion' recorded in the polls.

Those who write, broadcast or teach may even hope to swing a hundredth of 1 per cent. While I've been writing this book, many others have been arguing against the stupidity of Europe and America squabbling while the world burns. Political writing is, in this respect, unlike other kinds of writing. As a novelist or a poet, you always hope to be a unique voice. As a political writer, you also hope to express things differently, better, more vividly, but you are – or at least, should be – pleased, not distressed, when others are saying something similar; for what matters is that the right cause will prevail. When I listen to the chorus of fellow spirits on both sides of the Atlantic, I think it may. It's like hearing other people hacking away at the Berlin Wall to left and right of you – very heartening.

If we think our politicians are corrupt and useless, we can go into politics and get rid of them: locally, nationally or internationally. If we don't like old-fashioned party politics, which require us to live in half-truth, other forms of direct action are available. For example, we can give our time or money to pressure groups, charities and non-governmental organizations – the 'NGOs'. We have to pick with care: some are excellent, others useless. The best have a huge impact. What has been done to relieve the debt burden of the poorest countries was in large part a response to an NGO campaign. So was the international treaty to ban landmines. When Jody Williams, who won the

Nobel Peace Prize for her work in bringing that about, was asked how she did it, she replied 'e-mail'.

E-mail and the internet can empower us in ways that we've only just begun to explore. What I've called the democratization of political knowledge is one of the great advances of our time. With the erosion of official secrecy, and the genius of Google, we can know what our rulers are up to almost before they know themselves. And then, using e-mail, we can do something about it.

Not everything passes through virtual reality. I've argued that the future of civilized political life in Europe depends on making it possible for immigrants, especially Muslim immigrants, to feel at home in our post-Christian societies. At the moment, we're doing very badly. When an American Jewish friend talks of the 'moral incompetence' of Europeans in this respect, I wish I could disagree. Part of the answer is to change government policies but another part comes in the everyday reality of our human contacts with neighbours or colleagues. This is what determines whether people really feel at home. For the non-immigrant European there are multiple pitfalls. Offensive racism is one danger, but so is excruciating kindness: talking very slowly and clearly to the Indian or Moroccan postman as we tell him how glad we are to have him in our country. *Our* country? His country too. That matter-of-fact acceptance is increasingly the norm in cities like London, but elsewhere there is still a long way to go. And a little more cross-cultural knowledge would do no harm. How many non-Muslims know when or what Eid-ul-Fitr is?

Then there's development aid. I've said it before, but it bears repeating: if we want to be able to look ourselves in the face every morning, anyone who earns more than the average wage in a rich country should aim to give 1 per cent of his or her annual income to charities with a good track record in the developing world. We can afford it.

Meanwhile, who's for another demonstration? Whatever our view on the pros and cons of the Iraq War, we can surely agree that the massive anti-war protests on Saturday, 15 February 2003, in many of the capitals of Europe – but also in New York, San Francisco and Sydney – created a remarkable moment of popular political participation.

Right or wrong, this was better than apathy. But why is it that virtually all the large demos we see on international issues are against American-led wars or arms deployments? Isn't there anything else we need to shout against, or *for*? How about a simultaneous march, across the whole of the post-West, against terrorism of all kinds? Or another, organized at a critical moment in world trade negotiations, to demand the kind of free trade that will benefit the world's poor?

These are just a few thoughts about what we can do. Freeworldweb.net is a website for us to exchange ideas. We have plenty of other places where we can talk and act. The main thing is to refuse the illusion of impotence. There are many divisive walls in today's world. There's the wall being built between Israelis and Palestinians, which in places looks uncannily like the Berlin Wall. There are the high walls of trade protectionism around both Europe and the United States. But behind them are the biggest walls of all: the mind-walls. If we raise our voices, these walls will come down. We are many, and we have not spoken yet. It's up to us.

# *Postscript: Progress Report 1*

It's a freezing winter's night in the capital of Ukraine. Standing between the tents of the revolutionary encampment on Kiev's equivalent of Regent Street is Svyatoslav Smolin, a tough-looking, pasty-faced man in a khaki jacket, whose usual job is checking the radiation levels at Chernobyl. He tells me that when, on Monday 22 November, he heard the news that the opposition candidate had supposedly lost the presidential election, he turned to his wife and said: 'I just have to go.' He came to Kiev, joined the vast protesting crowds on Independence Square and, seeing the tents going up, offered his services. Now he's in charge of the guards in this well-organized section of the 'tent city', which stretches for perhaps half a mile down the broad city boulevard.

Warming himself by one of the braziers of burning timber is Vasil Khorkuda, a stocky, clear-eyed countryman from a rural area near the Carpathian mountains, where he runs a travel agency. He has never, he says, been active in politics before. But that Monday he, too, decided he simply must go to Kiev. He's been here ever since and he'll stay until 'success', which, he explains, means a president chosen in a free and fair election.

Further on, giggling by an all-orange synthetic Christmas tree, is Elena Mayarchuk. Decoratively clad in fur and the obligatory orange scarf, she's the owner of a beauty shop in a small town in central Ukraine. Again, the same story: she heard the news of the stolen election. She knew she had to come. She'll stay till the end. And then there's Vova, a worker from an industrial city in the north-east, who, striking a heroic pose with both black-gloved, ham-sized hands raised in V-for-victory signs, declares: 'The country called me!'

That was Kiev on the night of Tuesday 7 December 2004. Sometimes there are heartwarming surprises in the struggle for the expansion of human freedom. Despite all the poverty, corruption, violence and manipulation of Ukrainian political life, here were so-called ordinary people doing an extraordinary thing. Ukraine's 'orange revolution' joined the growing list of Europe's new-style, largely peaceful, evolutionary revolutions, stretching back thirty years to the 'revolution of the carnations' in Portugal in 1974. And the response, as I have argued in this book, should be a strategic 'yes' from Brussels to a democratic Ukraine eventually taking its proper place as a member of the European Union.

A few weeks earlier, and half way across the world, I witnessed another presidential election. Unlike the ballot-rigged Ukrainian fiasco, which sparked the orange revolution, monitors from the Organization for Security and Cooperation in Europe found this one to be 'mostly' free and fair. Yet the result was less encouraging. At 11.39 p.m. Washington time on Tuesday 2 November, when ABC called Florida for George W. Bush, I felt in my bones that he had won. The gloom that settled on many Europeans was as nothing compared with the despair of liberal Americans I encountered over the next fortnight, travelling from Washington to other cities of the so-called 'blue' (i.e. liberal) United States. They talked of emigration to Canada or New Zealand. A somewhat overheated American contributor to the FreeWorldWeb.net website, which grew out of this book and has become a lively forum for debate, even called on Europeans to invade the United States and save it from 'Christian theocratic fascism'.

It's no use pretending that Bush's re-election was good news for the agenda proposed in the second part of this book. It wasn't. Whether on global warming, trade and aid for the world's poor, or the prospect of Europeans and Americans working together for the amelioration of the near and far East, a President John F. Kerry would have had a better chance of making a new beginning. But we have to start from where we are.

True to type, Jacques Chirac and Tony Blair reacted in very different ways to Bush's re-election. Restating a classic Euro-Gaullist position, Chirac said, 'It is clear that Europe, now more than ever, has the need, the necessity, to strengthen its dynamism and unity when faced with this great world power.' Fresh from a recent visit to Beijing, he talked again about 'multipolarity'. Meanwhile, Blair hurried off to Washington, to be the first ever-supportive ally to congratulate and consult with President Bush. He also urged him to re-engage, following Yasser Arafat's death, in peace talks between Israel and the Palestinians. But how much influence did Blair have, speaking for Britain alone?

Now more than ever we require the historic compromise that I advocate in this book between the competing French and British poles of our divided Europe. What we need is not the current policies of the French president Chirac or the British prime minister Blair, but the combined approach of a European president Blairac. Blair is right about the futility of Europe trying to constitute itself as a rival superpower, an alternative 'pole' to the United States; Chirac correctly concludes that only a stronger, more united Europe, speaking with one voice, will have the weight to be taken seriously in Washington. In politics as in business, you listen to a partner because you want to but also because you have to.

There are signs that the Bush administration, at the beginning of its second term, may be prepared to start treating the European Union as a serious partner, rather than continuing its first-term 'cherry-picking' of individual European allies in a politics of 'divide and rule'. We shall see how long this lasts. It also seems that the Wilsonian element in President Bush's thinking about how to win the 'war on terror' has grown stronger. In his Washington press conference with Tony Blair, he talked repeatedly of democracy as the key to transforming the wider Middle East. 'The reason why I'm so strong on democracy,' he said, 'is . . . democracies don't go to war with each other.' And again: 'I've got great faith in democracies to promote peace.' Had the American president suddenly become a disciple of the Enlightenment philosopher Immanuel Kant? Certainly, Bush was here articulating a classic neo-Kantian position. Yet Kant is considered by the American neo-conservative Robert Kagan to be the patron saint of a distinctively European way of thinking about international affairs.

Europeans could and did react to this apparent conversion in several different ways: ridicule, incredulity, or cautious, sceptical engagement. Such an engagement has two premisses: 1. this is the only American president we've got for the next four years; 2. the modernization, liberalization and eventual democratization of the wider Middle East is an even more vital interest for us in Europe than it is for the United States. If we can not help our neighbours, especially our younger Arab neighbours, to find more hope in their own countries, they will come to us in such overwhelming numbers, and with such an explosive cocktail of economic hopes and cultural resentments, that the consequences will tear our own societies apart. After the Madrid bombing, done by disaffected Moroccan immigrants, we have now seen the murder in Amsterdam of the Dutch filmmaker Theo van Gogh. The Netherlands, one of the most tolerant, liberal countries in Europe, has been dragged into a downward spiral of revenge attacks between Muslim extremists on the one hand and Christian or secularist extremists on the other. Is this the face of Europe's future?

In our own interest, we Europeans should take up the Wilsonian part of Washington's new agenda but respond to it in our own way. 'Yes,' we should say, 'we share the same goal, but we disagree about some of the means you have chosen to pursue it' – above all, the invasion of Iraq. 'Here,' we should continue, 'is what we in the European Union can do to help our neighbours move gradually in the right direction.' And what we can do in countries so close to us is as important as anything the United States can do from far away. In fact, the EU's bold, high-risk decision to open membership negotiations with Turkey is a much larger contribution to 'winning the war on terror' (to express it in Bushspeak) than the American-led occupation of Iraq.

Iraq is currently a bloody playground for existing groups of Islamist terrorists, and probably a breeding ground for new ones. The EU offer to Turkey, by contrast, sends a clear signal that Europe is not an exclusive 'Christian club', that the West is engaged in no new 'crusade' (as Osama bin Laden alleges it is), and that a largely Islamic society can be reconciled with the rules and customs of modern liberal democracy. For these are the membership requirements of the EU. Moreover, the offer has been made to a Turkish government headed by a devout muslim, Recep Tayyip Erdogan, who just a few years ago was jailed for publicly reciting a poem containing the memorable lines, 'The mosques are our barracks/ the domes our helmets/ the minarets our bayonets/ and the faithful are our warriors.' Now he's doing everything in his power to meet what Turks call 'European standards'. Even if Turkey will not have such a direct effect on its Arab and Persian neighbours in the Middle East as is sometimes claimed, the broader message of peace and openness to the Islamic world is worth ten divisions of the US marines.

'Pessimism of the intellect' is still very much in order. Faced with another terrorist attack, or a rogue state threatening to aquire weapons of mass destruction, a second Bush administration could revert to the unilateralist, bellicist and nationalist responses of its first term. The European Union may become bogged down in introverted debates about its constitutional treaty, its new budget, and so on. History is full of surprises and no one is more surprised by them than historians. By the time you read this, you will know more.

Yet we must not lose sight of the larger picture. Presidents, prime ministers and chancellors come and go: the great challenges identified in this book endure. How we address them over the next twenty years will determine whether our children live in more free and civilized societies or in increasingly fractured, intolerant ones. And that depends, to a significant degree, on us, the citizens.

Think again of Ukraine. Ukraine in the autumn of 2004 was a poor, deeply divided society, with a massively corrupt state controlled by a gangsterish regime. It had only been an independent country for thirteen years, and many of its Russian-speaking citizens were still not sure it was a proper country at all. It had a weak civil society and almost no tradition of peaceful civic activism. Yet the Vasils and Svyatoslavs, the Elenas and Vovas, came to Kiev and camped out night after night, in temperatures that plunged to minus 10 degrees, to make a velvet revolution.

If they could take their fate into their own hands, so can we. We don't need to go and camp out in the rain on Regent Street – or the Champs Elysées, las Ramblas, Nowy Świat, the Kurfürstendamm. We just need to raise our voices through all the formal and

informal channels available in a functioning democracy. I repeat:
It's up to us.

*TGA*
*Oxford*
*14 January 2005*

# *Maps*

Money

Arms

People

Values

Freedom

# Money

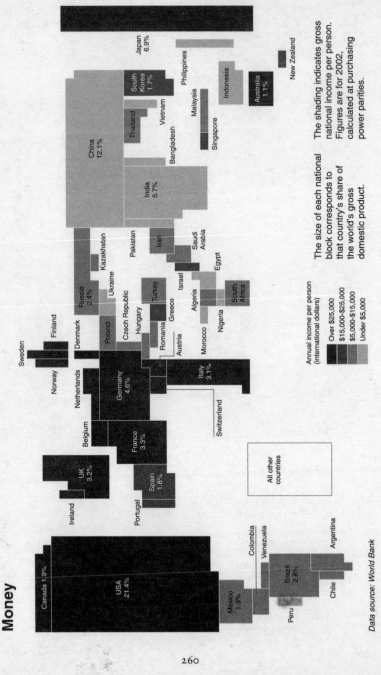

The size of each national block corresponds to that country's share of the world's gross domestic product.

The shading indicates gross national income per person. Figures are for 2002, calculated at purchasing power parities.

Annual income per person (international dollars)

Over $25,000
$15,000-$25,000
$5,000-$15,000
Under $5,000

All other countries

Canada 1.9%
USA 21.4%
Mexico 1.9%
Colombia
Venezuela
Brazil 2.8%
Peru
Chile
Argentina

Ireland
UK 3.2%
Portugal
Spain 1.8%
France 3.3%
Belgium
Germany 4.6%
Netherlands
Norway
Sweden
Finland
Denmark
Switzerland
Italy 3.1%
Austria
Poland
Czech Republic
Hungary
Romania
Greece
Turkey
Ukraine
Russia 2.4%
Kazakhstan

Israel
Algeria
Morocco
Nigeria
South Africa
Egypt
Saudi Arabia
Iran
Pakistan
China 12.1%
India 5.7%
Bangladesh
Thailand
Vietnam
South Korea 1.7%
Japan 6.9%
Philippines
Malaysia
Singapore
Indonesia
Australia 1.1%
New Zealand

*Data source: World Bank*

260

# Arms

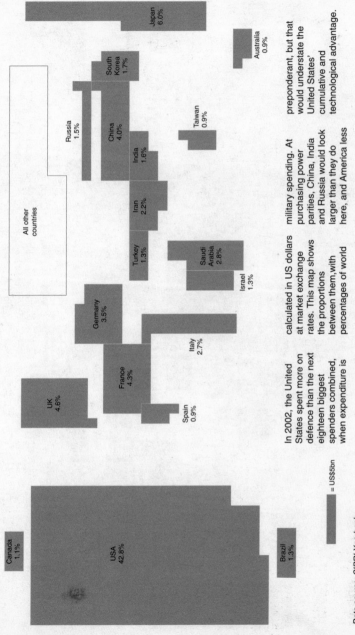

**Canada** 1.1%

**USA** 42.8%

**Brazil** 1.3%

**UK** 4.6%

**France** 4.3%

**Spain** 0.9%

**Germany** 3.5%

**Italy** 2.7%

**Saudi Arabia** 2.8%

**Israel** 1.3%

**Turkey** 1.3%

**Iran** 2.2%

**India** 1.6%

**China** 4.0%

**Russia** 1.5%

**South Korea** 1.7%

**Taiwan** 0.9%

**Japan** 6.0%

**Australia** 0.9%

All other countries

= US$5bn

In 2002, the United States spent more on defence than the next eighteen biggest spenders combined, when expenditure is calculated in US dollars at market exchange rates. This map shows the proportions between them, with percentages of world military spending. At purchasing power parities, China, India and Russia would look larger than they do here, and America less preponderant, but that would understate the United States' cumulative and technological advantage.

*Data source: SIPRI Yearbook*

261

# People

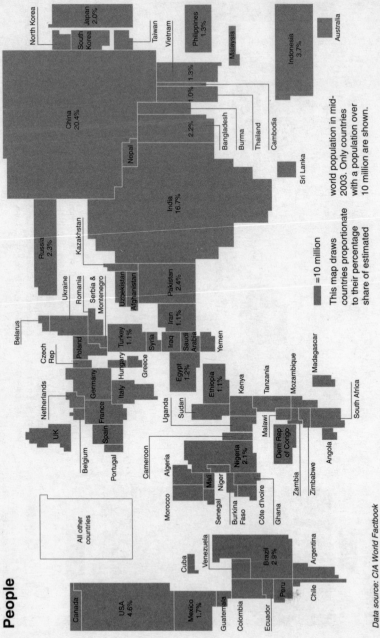

This map draws countries proportionate to their percentage of estimated world population in mid-2003. Only countries with a population over 10 million are shown.

■ =10 million

Data source: CIA World Factbook

North Korea

South Korea

Japan 2.0%

Taiwan

Vietnam

Philippines 1.3%

Malaysia

Indonesia 3.7%

Australia

China 20.4%

1.3%

1.0%

Bangladesh

Burma

Thailand

Cambodia

2.2%

Nepal

India 16.7%

Sri Lanka

Russia 2.3%

Kazakhstan

Belarus

Ukraine

Romania

Serbia & Montenegro

Uzbekistan

Afghanistan

Pakistan 2.4%

Czech Rep.

Poland

Hungary

Turkey 1.1%

Syria

Iraq

Iran 1.1%

Saudi Arabia

Yemen

Netherlands

Germany

Italy

Greece

Egypt 1.2%

Ethiopia 1.1%

Kenya

Tanzania

Mozambique

Madagascar

UK

Belgium

France

Spain

Portugal

Uganda

Sudan

Malawi

Dem Rep of Congo

South Africa

Angola

Cameroon

Algeria

Mali

Niger

Nigeria 2.1%

Zambia

Zimbabwe

Morocco

Senegal

Burkina Faso

Côte d'Ivoire

Ghana

All other countries

Canada

USA 4.6%

Mexico 1.7%

Guatemala

Colombia

Ecuador

Peru

Chile

Cuba

Venezuela

Brazil 2.9%

Argentina

# Values

This map shows findings of the World Values Survey along two key axes, from traditional values to secular-rational values, and from survival values to self-expression values.

Sometimes known as the Inglehart Values Map, after its author, Ronald Inglehart, it summarizes responses from interviews conducted in 1999–2001 with more than 120,000 people in eighty-one countries. The designated clusters, including Catholic Europe, Protestant Europe, Ex-Communist (marked by a dotted line) and English-Speaking, are part of his map.

Inglehart reports that the basic pattern has changed little over three successive rounds of the World Values Survey, covering the 1990s, although there is a tendency for all richer countries to move somewhat towards the upper right-hand corner of the map.

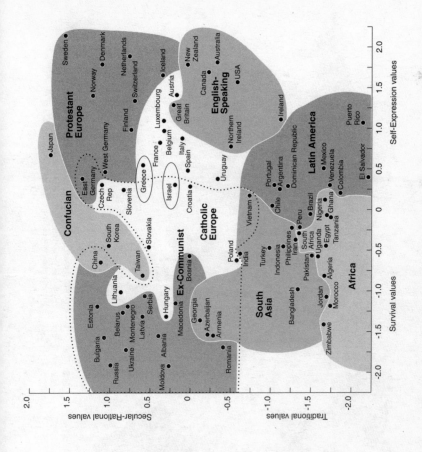

Source: Ronald Inglehart et al. (eds).,
Human Values and Beliefs:
A Cross-Cultural Sourcebook
(Mexico City: Siglo XXI, 2004)

# Freedom

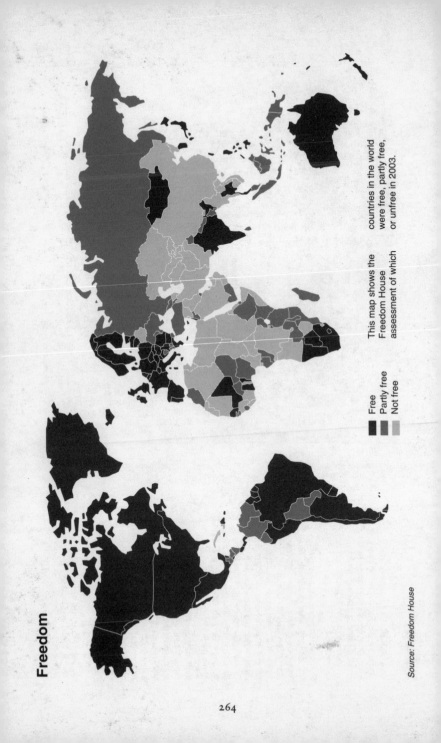

This map shows the Freedom House assessment of which countries in the world were free, partly free, or unfree in 2003.

Free
Partly free
Not free

264

# *Freeworldweb.net*

The end of a book is only the beginning of a conversation. Or, in this case, the continuation of a conversation which is already in progress along millions of different lines of communication across the world. The age of the physical book is very far from over, but websites can respond faster to change. Freeworldweb.net is a website where readers of this book in different countries, and anyone interested in its subject, can exchange reactions, information and ideas. I shall also post new material there from time to time.

TGA

# Notes

*These notes only give references for direct quotations in the text, numerical claims, and points where I have drawn very directly on other people's work. They occasionally make small but significant qualifications to statements in the text. They don't give references for non-attributable remarks made in private conversations. What use is it for you to read 'personal information' or 'conversation with the author' if I can't tell you who said it and when?*

## A CRISIS OF THE WEST

1. *Life's Picture History of Western Man* (New York: Time Inc., 1951), quotations from pp. 1–2 and 290.

2. Jean-Marie Colombani, 'Nous sommes tous Américains', *Le Monde,* 13 September 2001.

3. Quoted by Martin Walker, UPI's Chief International Correspondent, in a UPI report from Washington, 4 February 2003.

4. Charles A. Kupchan, 'The End of the West', *Atlantic Monthly,* 1 November 2002.

5. Robert Kagan, *Of Paradise and Power: America and Europe in the New World Order* (New York: Alfred A. Knopf, 2003), p. 3.

6. Note that these rankings are based on purchasing power parities. See the table, based on 2002 World Bank figures, in *Strategic Audit: Discussion Document, November 2003*, prepared by the British government's Strategy Unit, and available on <http://www.strategy.gov.uk> At market exchange rates, it would be first (America) and fourth (Britain) against third (Germany) and fifth (France).

7. *Libération,* 11 February 2003.

8. George Orwell, *Collected Essays* (London: Secker & Warburg, 1961), p. 281.

# 1 JANUS BRITAIN

1. Quoted from the original manuscript in A. S. P. Woodhouse (ed.), *Puritanism and Liberty: Being the Army Debates from the Clarke Manuscripts, with Supplementary Documents* (London: Dent, 1938), p. 53. I have modernized the spelling of Rainsborough, sometimes given as Rainborough or Rainborow.

2. John Winthrop's 1630 'Model of Christian Charity', quoted in Daniel J. Boorstin, *An American Primer* (New York: Mentor, 1966), pp. 26–43, at p. 40.

3. Information on his younger brother and his sister from Richard L. Greaves and Robert Zaller (eds), *Biographical Dictionary of British Radicals in the Seventeenth Century* (Brighton: Harvester Press, 1982–4), entries on Thomas and William Rainsborough.

4. According to a search on <http://mapquest.com>

5. On the 350th anniversary of the Putney Debates, in-church speeches were delivered by the left-wing Labour politician Tony Benn and the Marxist historian Christopher Hill. The anniversary was also marked by a large conference in Washington, DC.

6. Figures from VSO Annual Report 2003, on <http://www.vso.org.uk>

7. Quoted from their website, <http://www.longview.com/ourcompany/>, accessed on 26 August 2003.

8. William Shakespeare, *King Richard II*, Act II, Scene 1.

9. I saw this in a German newspaper in the 1970s. I have unfortunately been unable to retrace it.

10. Quoted by Leszek Kołakowski in his *Main Currents of Marxism* (Oxford: Clarendon Press, 1978), vol. 1, p. 1.

11. John Major quoted in Jeremy Paxman, *The English* (London: Penguin, 1999), p. 142. What Orwell actually wrote was 'the old maids biking to Holy Communion through the mists of the autumn mornings', see George Orwell, *The Lion and the Unicorn: Socialism and the English Genius* (London: Secker & Warburg, 1941), p. 11.

12. Jeremy Black, *A History of the British Isles* (London: Macmillan, 1997), p. 325.

13. This is the conclusion of Robert Colls, *Identity of England* (Oxford: Oxford University Press, 2002), pp. 380–81. The location of Brunanburh has apparently not been established.

14. The 2001 Census put minority ethnic groups at 7.9 per cent of the total population, or one in twelve and a half. If one allows for subsequent growth, immigrants not covered by the Census, and asylum-seekers, one in twelve seems a fair conservative estimate.

15. See the results of the April 2001 Census on <http://www.statistics.gov.uk/cci/nugget.asp?id=273>

16. BBC News report, 29 January 2001, on <http://news.bbc.co.uk/1/hi/uk/1142546.stm>

17. As reported by Andrew Gimson in a fascinating series of articles in the *Evening Standard* on multi-ethnic London, this on 10 July 2001.

18. Philip Baker and John Eversley (eds), *Multilingual Capital* (London: Battlebridge Publications, 2000).

19. *Daily Express*, 8 May 2002.

20. Figures from the British Beer and Pub Association, *Facts 2003*. See <http://www.beerandpub.com>

21. John Major on the BBC *Today* programme, 18 September 2002.

22. William Shakespeare, *King Henry V*, Act IV, Scene 3.

23. Estimates from the Foreign Office website <http://www.fco.gov.uk> and *Social Trends 2000* (London: The Stationery Office, 2002). Official Spanish statistics record 105, 479 British citizens registered as resident in Spain on 31 December 2003, (<http://dgei.mir.es/en/general/balance_DGEI2003.pdf>). The real number of British people spending a large part of the year there is certainly larger.

24. A figure of 1.2 million is given in *The Observer*, 16 November 2003. The 2000 US Census puts the number of UK-born US residents at just over 600,000. The estimate for Americans living in the UK was given to me by the then Minister at the US Embassy in London, Glyn Davies, on 1 July 2003.

25. *Social Trends No. 32, 2002 Edition* (London: The Stationery Office, 2002), p. 217.

26. Estimate by the then Minister at the US Embassy in London, Glyn Davies, 1 July 2003.

27. *Newsweek*, 13 November 2001.

28. Intelligence[2] debate on 24 April 2003. The final vote was 188 for, 115 against, 26 don't knows.

29. Raymond Seitz, *Over Here* (London: Phoenix, 1998), p. 9.

30. Quoted from Trevelyan's hugely influential *English Social History* by Philip Bell in 'A Historical Cast of Mind: Some Eminent English Historians and Attitudes to Continental Europe in the Middle of the Twentieth Century', *Journal of European Integration History*, 1996, vol. 2, no. 2, pp. 5–19, at p. 12. Bell notes that Trevelyan's book sold nearly 400,000 copies between 1944 and 1949. J. H. Plumb commented in 1951: 'In many homes it must be the one and only history book. This work is not only a social history but a social phenomenon.' Scottish, Irish and, to a lesser degree, Welsh schoolchildren were taught rather different histories.

31. See J. C. D. Clark, *The Language of Liberty 1660–1832: Political*

*Discourse and Social Dynamics in the Anglo-American World* (Cambridge: Cambridge University Press, 1994).

32. See Norman Davies, *The Isles: A History* (London: Macmillan, 1999), pp. 7–8.

33. See Jeremy Black, *Convergence or Divergence? Britain and the Continent* (London: Macmillan, 1994), pp. 261ff.

34. Trade and foreign investment figures for 2001 in *UK International Priorities: A Strategy for the FCO* (London: The Stationery Office, 2003), pp. 37–8.

35. The Treasury estimates that 3 million jobs in the UK are linked, directly or indirectly, to the export of goods and services to the European Union. This figure is based on the assumption that the share of total UK employment associated with UK exports to the EU is equal to the total UK value added (GVA) generated by UK exports to the EU. Joseph P. Quinlan, *Drifting Apart or Growing Together? The Primacy of the Transatlantic Economy* (Washington: Center for Transatlantic Relations, 2003), calculates that 1.3 million British jobs depended on American affiliates in 2000.

36. See <http://www.lakenheath.af.mil/home.html>

37. Stated with some authority by a former head of the Joint Intelligence Committee, Sir Rodric Braithwaite, in *Prospect*, May 2003, pp. 20–23, at p. 21.

38. Reported on the BBC's *Today* programme, 31 October 2002.

39. Admiral James Woolsey, quoted on the BBC's *Today* programme and in *The Economist*, 26 April 2000.

40. The fourth largest at market exchange rates, but only the seventh using purchasing power parities. See the table, based on 2002 World Bank figures, in *Strategic Audit: Discussion Document, November 2003* prepared by the British government's Strategy Unit, and available on <http://www.strategy.gov.uk>

41. 'Aber dieses groteske Österreich ist nichts anderes als ein besonders deutlicher Fall der modernen Welt.' Robert Musil, *Tagebücher: Band 1* (Reinbek bei Hamburg: Rowohlt, 1983) p. 354. I am grateful to Malcolm Spencer for this reference.

42. Cartoon of 18 June 1940, see David Low, *Years of Wrath: A Cartoon History 1932–1945* (London: Victor Gollancz, 1986), p. 117.

43. *The Sun*, 15 May 2003.

44. Letter from John Church in *Daily Mail*, 3 January 1997. I owe the reference to Edwin Jones, *The English Nation: The Great Myth* (Stroud: Sutton Publishing, 2000).

45. William Shakespeare, *King John*, Act V, Scene 7.

46. Conrad Black, *Britain's Final Choice: Europe or America?* (London: Centre for Policy Studies, 1998).

47. Ibid., p. 27.

48. Robert Conquest, 'Toward an English-Speaking Union' in *The National Interest*, Fall 1999, pp. 64–70.

49. This is the definition by one of the main promoters of the idea of the Anglosphere, James C. Bennett. See his 'An Anglosphere Primer' from <http://www.pattern.com/bennettj-anglosphereprimer.html>

50. Gerard Baker, *Financial Times*, 20 March 2003.

51. The combined readership figure of 22.4 million is from the 2003 National Readership Survey, for the broadly 'Eurosceptic' *Sun*, *Daily Mail*, *Daily Telegraph*, *Times*, *Daily Express* and *Daily Star*, as against a total of 30.8 million for all national dailies. See <http://www.nrs.co.uk/open_access/open_topline/newspapers/newspapersJan03-Dec03_print.htm>

52. Ibid. For comparison, some 8.4 million read the broadly 'Europhile' *Daily Mirror*, *Guardian*, *Independent* and *Financial Times*.

53. Hugo Young, *This Blessed Plot: Britain and Europe from Churchill to Blair* (London: Papermac, 1999), p. 1.

54. *Guardian*, 16 September 2003.

55. William Shakespeare, *Richard II*, Act II, Scene 1. 'Pelting' means paltry.

56. Will Hutton, 'We must be at the heart of Europe,' in *The Observer*, 10 June 2001.

57. Will Hutton, *The World We're In* (London: Little Brown, 2002), p. 271 and *passim*.

58. Jonathan Freedland, *Bring Home the Revolution: The Case for a British Republic* (London: Fourth Estate, 1998).

59. Harold Macmillan, *Pointing the Way, 1959–1961* (London: Macmillan, 1972), p. 316.

60. Headlines in *The Sun*, 27 May 2003, *Daily Mail*, 16 May 2003, *Sunday Express*, 19 October 2003, *Daily Telegraph*, 15 May 2003.

61. See Eugene L. Rasor, *Winston S. Churchill 1874–1965: A Comprehensive Historiography and Annotated Bibliography* (Westport, CT: Greenwood Press, 2000).

62. Speech of 4 June 1940, in Robert Rhodes James (ed.), *Winston S. Churchill: His Complete Speeches 1897–1963* (New York and London: Chelsea House, 1974), pp. 6225–31, at p. 6231. (Subsequently referred to as: Rhodes James, *Churchill Speeches*.)

63. 'Let us therefore brace ourselves to our duty and so bear ourselves that if the British Commonwealth and Empire lasts for a thousand years men will still say "This was their finest hour"', speech of 18 June 1940, in Rhodes James, *Churchill Speeches*, pp. 6231–8, at p. 6238.

64. Entry for 4 December 1943, *Chips: Diaries of Sir H. Channon* (London: Weidenfeld & Nicolson, 1967), p. 381.

NOTES TO PAGES 38-43

65. Speech of 3 April 1939 in Rhodes James, *Churchill Speeches*, p. 6094.
66. Speech of 19 May 1939 in Rhodes James, *Churchill Speeches*, p. 6126.
67. H. V. Morton, *Atlantic Meeting* (London: Methuen, 1943), p. 98.
68. Ibid., pp. 152–5.
69. See D. C. Watt, *Succeeding John Bull* (Cambridge: Cambridge University Press, 1984).
70. This remark, made to Clark Clifford, is quoted by Paul Addison in 'Churchill in the Twenty-First Century', a special issue of *Transactions of the Royal Historical Society*, 6th series, xii (2002), at p. 198.
71. Simon Jenkins in *The Times*, 30 October 2002.
72. Minute of the Roosevelt–Stalin meeting on 4 February 1945 by Charles Bohlen in *Foreign Relations of the United States: The Conferences at Malta and Yalta* (Washington: Department of State, 1955), p. 572.
73. Rhodes James, *Churchill Speeches*, p. 7381.
74. Rhodes James, *Churchill Speeches*, p. 7842.
75. Rhodes James, *Churchill Speeches*, p. 7836.
76. Rhodes James, *Churchill Speeches*, p. 7382 and, for 'France and Britain', p. 7485.
77. Quoted in Roy Jenkins, *Churchill* (London: Pan Books, 2002), p. 855.
78. Ibid., p. 855.
79. Konrad Adenauer, *Erinnerungen 1945–1963* (Stuttgart: DVA, 1987), p. 512.
80. 'I believe myself to be what is called a good European', broadcast, 21 March 1943, in Rhodes James, *Churchill Speeches*, p. 6758.
81. See David Reynolds, 'Rethinking Anglo-American Relations' in *International Affairs*, vol. 65, no. 1, pp. 89–111.
82. Eisenhower's diary, 6 January 1953, quoted in Anthony Seldon, *Churchill's Indian Summer: The Conservative Government 1951–55* (London: Hodder & Stoughton, 1981), p. 391.
83. Roy Jenkins, *Churchill* (London: Pan Books, 2002), p. 864, quoting Churchill's doctor Lord Moran. Jenkins notes that Moran is 'not always verbally reliable', but there is ample evidence that Churchill practised self-censorship in this respect while preparing for publication the final volume of *The Second World War*.
84. Ivan Krastev in *Die Zeit*, 14 August 2003.
85. Speech of 17 July 2003, available at <http://www.number-10.gov.uk/output/Page4220.as>
86. Quoted in Peter Riddell, *Hug Them Close: Blair, Clinton, Bush and the 'Special Relationship'* (London: Politicos, 2003), p. 137.
87. Quoted with phonetic accuracy in John Kampfner, *Blair's Wars* (London: Free Press, 2003), p. 121.

88. *New Labour: Because Britain Deserves Better* (London, 1997), p. 36. I owe this reference to Anne Deighton.

89. For example, in his speech to the Confederation of Indian Industry in Bangalore, 5 January 2002. <http://www.number-10.gov.uk>

90. As reported by a usually reliable source.

91. Speech on receiving the Charlemagne Prize in Aachen, 13 May 1999. <http://www.number-10.gov.uk>

92. Hugo Young, *This Blessed Plot: Britain and Europe from Churchill to Blair* (London: Papermac, 1999), p. 482.

93. Speech delivered at the Warsaw Stock Exchange, 6 October 2000. <http://www.number-10.gov.uk>

94. Speech to a joint session of both houses of Congress, 17 July 2003, <http://www.number-10.gov.uk/output/Page4220.as>

95. Remarks by the president on accepting the bust, 13 July 2001, quoted from 17 July 2001 news story on <http://www.ananova.com>

96. Peter Riddell, *Hug Them Close: Blair, Clinton, Bush and the 'Special Relationship'* (London: Politicos, 2003), p. 161.

97. He listed this as the top priority of British foreign policy in a meeting with British ambassadors on 7 January 2003. Text on <http://www.number-10.gov.uk> There also 'broadening its agenda'.

98. Diary entry for 7 March 2002, in Robin Cook, *The Point of Departure* (London: Simon & Schuster, 2003), p. 116.

99. The reference was to Colin Powell, US Secretary of State, not Jonathan Powell, Blair's Chief of Staff.

100. A witticism I first heard from the BBC's political editor, Andrew Marr.

101. The aide was Alistair Campbell, quoted in Peter Stothard, *30 Days: A Month at the Heart of Blair's War* (London: HarperCollins, 2003), p. 106.

102. Quoted in John Kampfner, *Blair's Wars* (London: Free Press, 2003), p. 350.

103. See the various drafts in Warren F. Kimball, *Churchill and Roosevelt: The Complete Correspondence*. Volume I (Princeton: Princeton University Press, 1984), pp. 86–109, at p. 94.

104. US Department of State, *Foreign Relations of the United States: The Conference at Quebec 1944* (Washington, DC: US Government Printing Office, 1972), p. 348.

105. *Wall Street Journal Europe*, 5/6 October 2001.

106. Remarks at the Cheltenham Literary Festival, 19 October 2003.

107. The parallel is sharply pointed out by Peter Riddell in his *Hug Them Close: Blair, Clinton, Bush and the 'Special Relationship'* (London: Politicos, 2003), p. 231. For Adenauer and de Gaulle's Placentia Bay in Reims, see Hans-Peter Schwarz, *Adenauer: Der Staatsmann 1952–1967* (Stuttgart: DVA, 1991), p. 755ff.

108. Tony Blair, conversation with the author, London, 3 September 2003.

109. The political editor of *The Sun*, Trevor Kavanagh, emphasizes that their readership has a large number of floating voters, by contrast with the solidly Conservative readership of the *Daily Mail* (conversation with the author, London, 1 July 2003). According to the 2003 National Readership Survey, the average daily readership of *The Sun* is just under 9 million. See <http://www.nrs.co.uk/open_access/open_topline/newspapers/newspapersJa no3-Deco3_print.htm>

110. Philip Gould, *The Unfinished Revolution: How the Modernisers Saved the Labour Party* (London: Abacus, 2001), p. 375.

111. Interview on BBC *Newsnight*, 14 November 2003.


## 2 EUROPE AS NOT-AMERICA

1. *Le Monde*, 26 February 2003.

2. Letter to the author from Dominique Strauss-Kahn, 23 July 2003, and background papers of the Round Table.

3. *Frankfurter Allgemeine Zeitung*, 31 May 2003. All following quotations also come from this source.

4. Oxford Union debate, 12 June 2003. My notes.

5. Claus Koch in *Merkur*, Sonderheft 9/10, September/October 2000, pp. 980–90, at p. 990.

6. In a television discussion on *Das philosophische Quartett*, ZDF, 30 March 2003.

7. At a press conference on 22 January 2003. For the full reference, see note 83 below.

8. One of many indignant responses by European intellectuals to Rumsfeld's 'old Europe' remark in the *Feuilleton* of the *Frankfurter Allgemeine Zeitung*, 24 January 2003.

9. Robert Kagan, *Of Paradise and Power: America and Europe in the New World Order* (New York: Knopf, 2003), p. 3. The book's US publication date was 5 February 2003. The original article appeared in *Policy Review* No. 113, June/July 2002.

10. Quoted in Tony Judt, *Past Imperfect: French Intellectuals 1944–1956* (Berkeley: University of California Press, 1992), p. 188.

11. According to the notes of the Italian journalist Paolo Valentino, who was present at the press conference where Berlusconi made these remarks, what Berlusconi said was: 'The Western world is bound to westernize and conquer people: we did it with the communist world and with parts of the Islamic world. Unfortunately, there is part of the Islamic world which is still 1400

years backwards. From this point of view, we must be conscious of the strength of our civilization, of its superiority and supremacy.' E-mail from Paolo Valentino to the author, 13 November 2001.

12. Oriana Fallaci, *The Rage and the Pride* (New York: Rizzoli, 2002), translated from the Italian in Fallaci's own inimitable English. 'Moslem invaders' on p. 177; 'Reverse Crusade' on p. 83.

13. See Denys Hay, *Europe: The Emergence of an Idea* (Edinburgh: Edinburgh University Press, 1957) p. 25. The battle is variously described as being of Tours or Poitiers, in 732 or 733.

14. Ibid., p. 83ff.

15. The preamble, drafted by Valéry Giscard d'Estaing, refers only to 'the cultural, religious and humanist inheritance of Europe', see *Draft Treaty Establishing a Constitution for Europe* (Brussels: European Convention, 2003), p. 5.

16. Estimates from *The Economist*. 6 March 2004.

17. See the reconstruction of his map in John Goss, *The Mapmaker's Art: An Illustrated History of Cartography* (New York: Rand McNally, 1993), p. 24. Eratosthenes appears to have placed the eastern frontier of Europe on the River Don. Only in the eighteenth century did the Urals come to be accepted as the conventional eastern frontier of the geographer's Europe.

18. Quoted by Giuliano Amato in Mark Leonard (ed.), *The Future Shape of Europe* (London: Foreign Policy Centre, 2000), p. 32.

19. Quoted in Jeremy Black, *Convergence or Divergence? Britain and the Continent* (London: Macmillan, 1994), p. 164.

20. The suggestive sub-title of Linda Colley's outstanding study of the formation of British national identity is 'forging the nation'; see *Britons: Forging the Nation 1707–1837* (New Haven: Yale University Press, 1992).

21. Rudolf von Thadden at a conference of the Collège d'Europe in Warsaw, 10/11 May 2003, drawing on remarks about French identity by Fernand Braudel.

22. Henry Kissinger, 'America at the Apex: Empire or Leader?' in *The National Interest*, Summer 2001, pp. 9–17, at p. 12.

23. Jean Lacouture in *Le Débat*, no. 125, May–August 2003, and Douglas Johnson in *Prospect*, April 2003.

24. See his article '1940: Fulcrum of the Twentieth Century?' in *International Affairs*, vol. 66, no. 2, pp. 325–50.

25. Quoted in Jean Lacouture, *De Gaulle: The Ruler, 1945–1970* (London: Harvill, 1991), p. 359.

26. I owe this reference originally to Robert Darnton, 'A Euro State of Mind', *New York Review of Books*, 28 February 2002.

27. Harold Macmillan, *Pointing the Way: 1959–1961* (London: Macmillan, 1972), p. 427.

28. De Boissieu's formal position was Deputy Secretary-General of the Council of the European Union.

29. Jacques Delors and Clisthène, *La France par l'Europe* (Paris: Bernard Grasset, 1988), p. 60. I owe this reference originally to Tony Judt, *A Grand Illusion? An Essay on Europe* (London: Penguin, 1996).

30. Dominique Noguez, 'Une langue si "easy"', in *Le Monde*, 8 August 2002.

31. Speech to the UN Security Council, 14 February 2003, on <http://www.france.diplomatie.fr.>

32. Dominique de Villepin, *Le cri de la Gargouille* (Paris: Albin Michel, 2002), pp. 9–10.

33. Allensbach poll reported in *Frankfurter Allgemeine Zeitung*, 19 March 2003.

34. This was the clear gist of an evening's conversation that I and another historian had with him about 'German identity' on 19 February 2002.

35. Quoted by William Horsley in a BBC report dated 17 September 2002.

36. Quoted by Michael Naumann in *Die Zeit*, 6 February 2003.

37. Peter Pulzer, by whom I originally heard this quoted, suggests it may be part of political folklore, like so many of the best political quotations. I would be grateful to any reader who can produce a source.

38. Peter Struck in the *Berlin Mitte* talkshow on ZDF, 13 February 2003.

39. Quoted in Timothy Garton Ash, *In Europe's Name: Germany and the Divided Continent* (London: Jonathan Cape, 1993), p. 114.

40. For 'colony' see, for example, the jacket copy of Egon Bahr, *Der deutsche Weg: Selbstverständlich und normal* (Munich: Blessing, 2003); for 'vassal', Christoph Bertram in *Financial Times*, 28 May 2003.

41. This and other quotations from my notes of our conversation in Berlin, 1 June 2003.

42. Angela Merkel, after-dinner remarks at a dinner in London, 10 June 2003.

43. Allensbach poll reported in *Frankfurter Allgemeine Zeitung*, 19 March 2003.

44. Ipos poll reported in *Le Monde*, 13 November 2003.

45. German Marshall Fund et al., *Transatlantic Trends* (Washington, DC, 2003), p. 9.

46. Figures from the Gallup International Millennium Survey of 1999 on <http://www.gallup-international.com>. Note that figures are for 'North America', presumably including Canada.

47. Pew Global Attitudes Project, *Views of a Changing World: June 2003*

(Washington, DC: The Pew Research Center for the People and the Press, 2003), p. 115.

48. Figures from a 1996 survey quoted in Andrew Kohut et al., *The Diminishing Divide: Religion's Changing Role in American Politics* (Washington, DC: Brookings Institution Press, 2000), p. 27.

49. Pew Global Attitudes Project, *Views of a Changing World: June 2003* (Washington, DC: The Pew Research Center for the People and the Press, 2003), p. 105.

50. Ibid., p. 108. However, the proportion of people who blame failure on the individual rather than 'society' is only a few percentage points lower in Britain and West Germany than in the US, ibid., p. T-53.

51. OECD figures quoted in *Financial Times*, 23 October 2003.

52. See Lawrence Mishel et al., *The State of Working America 2002–3* (Ithaca: Cornell University Press, 2003), pp. 411–16.

53. Here I follow Will Hutton, *The World We're In* (London: Little Brown, 2002), p. 149.

54. Quoted by Minxin Pei in 'The Paradoxes of American Nationalism', *Foreign Policy*, May/June 2001, based on figures from the World Values Survey.

55. Estimates for 2000 put gun ownership in the US at 83–96 per 100 inhabitants, compared to around 30 for France and Germany and 10 in Britain. Report by Stephen Castle in *The Independent*, 2 July 2003.

56. These figures are based on a British Home Office comparative study for the years 1998–2000, see <http://www.homeoffice.gov.uk/rds/pdfs2/hosb502.pdf> (Tables 1.1, 1.2).

57. Seymour Martin Lipset, *American Exceptionalism: A Double-Edged Sword* (New York: Norton, 1996).

58. See our co-authored response to Habermas and Derrida, 'Die Erneuerung Europas' in *Süddeutsche Zeitung*, 5/6 July 2003. This insight came from Dahrendorf.

59. See the fascinating Introduction to Peter A. Hall and David Soskice, *Varieties of Capitalism: The Institutional Foundations of Comparative Advantage* (Oxford: Oxford University Press, 2001), pp. 1–68.

60. Ibid., p. 21.

61. In 2001, the tax burden was 50.8 per cent in Sweden and 37.4 per cent in the UK. Data from OECD Revenue Statistics 2002, see <http://www.oecd.org/dataoecd/30/37/2401707.pdf>

62. See Minxin Pei, 'The Paradoxes of American Nationalism', *Foreign Policy*, May/June 2001, based on figures from the World Values Survey. Against 72 per cent of Americans, the figures were 74 per cent of the Irish, 71 per cent of Poles and 20 per cent of the Dutch.

63. Pew Global Attitudes Project, *Views of a Changing World: June 2003* (Washington, DC: The Pew Research Center for the People and the Press, 2003), p. 115.

64. All estimated demonstration numbers from the BBC, 17 February 2003. As usual, estimates of demonstration numbers varied widely.

65. The figure of half is taken from a poll reported in *The Australian* on 25 March 2003. Obviously the figures fluctuated.

66. Examples can be found in Peter A. Hall and David Soskice, *Varieties of Capitalism: The Institutional Foundations of Comparative Advantage* (Oxford: Oxford University Press, 2001), p. 22, and Adair Turner, *Just Capital: The Liberal Economy* (London: Macmillan, 2001), pp. 261–3.

67. See Peter A. Hall and David Soskice, *Varieties of Capitalism: The Institutional Foundations of Comparative Advantage* (Oxford: Oxford University Press, 2001), pp. 19–21 and *passim*.

68. Seymour Martin Lipset, *American Exceptionalism: A Double-Edged Sword* (New York: Norton, 1996), p. 289.

69. This and following figures from the excellent OECD website, <http://www.oecd.org>

70. Larry Lindsey in the *Financial Times*, 28 August 2003, quotes a 2003/4 figure of $311 billion for Medicaid against $105 billion for the NHS.

71. All figures from Budget of the United States Government, 'Table 3.1 – Outlays by Superfunction and Function: 1940–2009', accessed via <http://frwebgate5.access.gpo.gov/cgi-bin/waisgate.cgi?WAISdocID= 532133420880+8+0+0&WAISaction=retrieve>

72. I am most grateful to Ronald Inglehart for letting me have early sight of the latest version of the map, and for checking my account of it. He notes that the results are quite consistent over successive surveys. The results of the 1999–2001 surveys are published and analysed in Ronald Inglehart et al. (eds), *Human Values and Beliefs: A Cross-Cultural Sourcebook* (Mexico City: Siglo XXI, 2004).

73. Again, I am drawing on the authoritative work in Peter A. Hall and David Soskice, *Varieties of Capitalism: The Institutional Foundations of Comparative Advantage* (Oxford: Oxford University Press, 2001).

74. Article II-15 of the Charter of Fundamental Rights of the European Union, conveniently reprinted in *Draft Treaty Establishing a Constitution for Europe* (Brussels: European Convention, 2003), p. 82.

75. See John M. Evans et al., 'Trends in Working Hours in OECD countries', *OECD Labour Market and Social Policy – Occasional Papers*, 45 (29 March 2001), pp. 7–30.

76. The figures for 2001 were USA 73.1 per cent, Germany 65.9 per cent, France 62 per cent, but note that Britain was close to the USA with 71.3 per

cent. See OECD, *Employment Outlook 2002; Statistical Annex*, p. 304.

77. OECD figures for 2000, Table B2 in 'Education at a Glance 2003', available via <http://www.oecd.org>

78. Ralf Dahrendorf has estimated the rough ratio of private giving as 100 for the US to 10 for the UK to 1 for continental Europe. Others argue that British and European giving is significantly higher than that.

79. According to *The Indian Programmer*, September 2001, 'a couple of thousand' programmers took up the German offer of 2000. See <http://www.theindianprogrammer.com/issues/germany revisited.htm>

80. Pew Global Attitudes Project, *Views of a Changing World: June 2003* (Washington, DC: The Pew Research Center for the People and the Press, 2003), p. 112.

81. German Marshall Fund et al., *Transatlantic Trends* (Washington, DC, 2003), p. 4. Note that 83 per cent of Americans agreed.

82. See, for example, his essay 'Warum braucht Europa eine Verfassung?' in *Die Zeit*, 28 June 2001.

83. Quoted from the transcript of his press conference on <http://www.defenselink.mil/transcripts/2003/t01232003_sdfpc.html>

84. Article entitled 'United We Stand' in *Wall Street Journal Europe*, 30 January 2003.

85. 'New Allies back US Iraq Policy', *New York Times*, 6 February 2003. The forceful advocate and drafter was Bruce Jackson, a Republican activist for Nato enlargement. For a critical account of his role see <http://www.prospect.org/print-friendly/print/V14/5/judis-j.html>

86. Report by Nicholas Watt in *The Guardian*, 15 February 2003. Straw later told me that he had initially thought of saying something like 'invaded' or 'occupied' in 1066 by the French, but *politesse* prevailed.

87. 34.3 million Americans claim Irish ancestry, almost nine times the population of Ireland (3.9 million). See <http://www.census.gov/Press-Release/www/releases/archives/facts for features/001687.html>

88. *Snění o Evropě*, written in 1986 and published in samizdat.

89. Jiří Dienstbier, *Od snění k realitě: vzpomínky z let 1989–1999* (Prague: Lidove Noviny, 1999).

90. Oswald Spengler, *Der Untergang des Abendlandes: Umrisse einer Morphologie der Weltgeschichte* (Munich: Beck, 1979) p. 3.

91. *Granta*, No. 11, 1984. The full title given there to Kundera's seminal essay on the fate of central Europe was 'A Kidnapped West or a Culture Bows Out'. The version published in *New York Review of Books*, 26 April 1984, bears a more cautious title, 'The Tragedy of Central Europe'.

92. Quoted from TCDS Bulletin, Graduate School, New School University (June 2003), p. 6. I owe this reference to Jacques Rupnik's excellent chapter

in Denis Lacorne and Tony Judt (eds), *Antiamericanism* (London: Hurst, forthcoming).

93. For example, 'I deem it very important that there should be clear functional links between the CSCE and the other existing European or *Euro-atlantic structures*', speech to Foreign Ministers Council of the Conference on Security and Cooperation in Europe, Prague, 30 January 1992. <http://old.hrad.cz/president/Havel/speeches/index uk.html>

94. Quoted in an article by Steven Erlanger in the *New York Times*, 4 June 2000.

95. Report by Laurent Zecchini in *Le Monde*, 19 February 2003.

96. In *International Herald Tribune*, 22 February 2003.

97. André Glucksmann, *Ouest contre Ouest* (Paris: Plon, 2003).

98. Nicolas Bavarez, *La France qui tombe: Un constat clinique du déclin français* (Paris: Perrin, 2003), Alain Duhamel, *Le désarroi français* (Paris: Plon, 2003), Romain Gubert and Emmanuel Saint-Martin, *L'arrogance française* (Paris: Balland, 2003).

99. Quoted from my notes of the Intelligence[2] debate in London on 29 October 2003.

100. Jean-François Revel, *L'obsession anti-américaine: Son fonctionnement, ses causes, ses inconséquences* (Paris: Plon, 2002), Philippe Roger, *L'ennemi américain: Généalogie de l'antiaméricanisme français* (Paris: Seuil, 2002).

101. Conversation with the author, Washington, DC, 31 May 2001.

102. See Joseph P. Quinlan, *Drifting Apart or Growing Together? The Primacy of the Transatlantic Economy* (Washington, DC: Center for Transatlantic Relations, 2003). Unless otherwise indicated, all figures in the next three paragraphs are taken from that invaluable study.

103. Ibid., Executive Summary, p. iii.

104. See Pew Global Attitudes Project, *What the World Thinks in 2002* (Washington, DC: The Pew Research Center for the People and the Press, 2002), p. T-57.

105. Ibid., p. 22.

106. Ibid., p. 21.

107. German Marshall Fund et al., *Transatlantic Trends* (Washington, DC, 2003), p. 9.

108. Article II-11.4 of the *Draft Treaty Establishing a Constitution for Europe* (Brussels: European Convention, 2003), p. 17.

109. Hubert Védrine, 'The Europe of the Future', *Newsweek*, Special Davos edition, December 2002/February 2003, p. 34.

110. See above, note 5.

111. In the *Feuilleton* of the *Frankfurter Allgemeine Zeitung*, 24 January 2003.

112. In his introductory speech to the Convention on 26 February 2002, available on <http://european-convention.eu.int>

113. Quoted in Jean Lacouture, *De Gaulle: The Ruler, 1945–1970* (London: Harvill, 1991), p. 393.

114. Calculations for 2001 by Marton Benedek from figures provided by OECD Development Assistance Committee.

115. *Gazeta Wyborcza*, 8/9 February 2003.


## 3 AMERICA, THE POWERFUL

1. From my notes of that meeting, 31 May 2001.

2. Will Hutton, *The World We're In* (London: Little Brown, 2002), p. 365.

3. See Walter Russell Mead, *Special Providence: American Foreign Policy and How it Changed the World* (New York: Routledge, 2002), p. xvii and *passim*.

4. The point is made forcefully by Michael Lind in his *Made in Texas: George W. Bush and the Southern Takeover of American Politics* (New York: Basic Books, 2003), p. 145 and *passim*.

5. James Madison, Alexander Hamilton and John Jay, *The Federalist Papers* (London: Penguin, 1987), p. 113. This comes in Paper VIII, by Hamilton.

6. Quoted in Arthur M. Schlesinger, *The Disuniting of America: Reflections on a Multicultural Society* (New York: Norton, 1998), p. 29.

7. Entry on Steven Udvar-Hazy, founder of the aircraft leasing business ILFC, in <http://www.forbes.com/global/1999/1011/0220093a.html>

8. Irving Howe, *Celebrations and Attacks: Thirty Years of Literary and Cultural Commentary* (London: André Deutsch, 1979), p. 243.

9. Merrill D. Peterson (ed.), *Thomas Jefferson: Writings* (New York: Literary Classics of the United States, 1984), p. 98.

10. Quoted by Wolf Lepenies, in *La vie des idées dans le monde*, No. 4, June–July 2003. I'm more broadly indebted to Lepenies's article for this thought about the first European Union.

11. Goethe, 'Den Vereinigten Staaten'.

12. Rudyard Kipling remembered peeking through the eyes of the statue as a child, when it was exhibited in Paris before being shipped across the Atlantic. See Julian Barnes, 'Sentimental Journeys' in *Guardian Review*, 11 January 2003.

13. William H. McNeill, 'What we mean by the West' in *Orbis*, Fall 1997, pp. 513–24, at p. 520.

14. Ibid., p. 520.

15. *Life's Picture History of Western Man* (New York: Time Inc., 1951), p. 290.

16. Notes from a trip in December 2002. I drew on this material for my 'Anti-Europeanism in America', *New York Review of Books*, 27 March 2003.

17. The exact figure was 18 per cent. Quoted by Bruce Cole in *Wall Street Journal*, 24 November 2003.

18. Address at Independence Hall, Philadelphia, 4 July 1962, from <http://www.jfklibrary.org/jfk-independencehall-1962.html> The following quotation is from the same source.

19. See his *An Essay towards the Present and Future Peace of Europe*, first published in 1693.

20. Desmond King, *Making Americans: Immigration, Race and the Origins of the Diverse Democracy* (Cambridge, MA: Harvard University Press, 2000), p. 252.

21. For 1.5 million, ibid., p. 251; the 2000 Census counted 11.89 million Asian Americans, see <http://www.awib.org/content_frames/census2000.html>

22. The term used by the American scholar Richard Alba; see Desmond King, *Making Americans: Immigration, Race and the Origins of the Diverse Democracy* (Cambridge, MA: Harvard University Press, 2000), p. 261.

23. Projection from the *Statistical Abstracts of the United States, 1994*, cited in Stephen M. Walt, 'The Ties That Fray', *The National Interest*, Winter 1998/99, pp. 3–11, at p. 7.

24. As opposed to Rome, Georgia, or Rome, Iowa, or any of the ten American Romes that can be found on <http://mapquest.com>

25. E-mail to the author from Thomas W. Simons, 16 May 2002, quoted with his kind permission.

26. See Alistair Horne, *Macmillan: 1894–1956* (London: Macmillan 1988), p. 160.

27. See Joseph S. Nye, *The Paradox of American Power: Why the World's Only Superpower Can't Go It Alone* (New York: Oxford University Press, 2002), pp. 8ff. and *passim*.

28. Max Boot, 'America Acts the Grown-up', *International Herald Tribune*, 26 November 2002.

29. Quoted, without a reference, in two slightly different forms in Brendan Simms, *Unfinest Hour: Britain and the Destruction of Bosnia* (London: Penguin, 2001), p. 53 and p. 339. I have been unable to trace this back to an original source.

30. Poos is often quoted as having said 'the hour of Europe' had dawned during an EC 'troika' diplomatic mission to Yugoslavia on 28 June 1991. Like so many famous quotations in recent history, this one proves very difficult to trace back to a reliable source. Brendan Simms, *Unfinest Hour: Britain and the Destruction of Bosnia* (London: Penguin, 2001), p. 54, quotes it without giving a source. Mark Almond, *Europe's Backyard War: The War in the*

*Balkans* (London: Heinemann, 1994), p. 32, gives his source as ITV *News at Ten* on 27 June 1991, but no such news item appears on the ITN archive website, and the words Almond goes on to quote appear, in a slightly different form, in an item for 28 June (see note 31, below), where, however, Poos does not say 'the hour of Europe'. Laura Silber and Alan Little, *The Death of Yugoslavia* (London: Penguin, 1995), p. 175, have him saying 'the age of Europe has dawned', also without a source.

31. Transcript from ITN *News*, 28 June 1991. I owe this reference originally to Mark Almond, *Europe's Backyard War: The War in the Balkans* (London: Heinemann, 1994), p. 32.

32. Quoted in Brendan Simms, *Unfinest Hour: Britain and the Destruction of Bosnia* (London: Penguin, 2001), p. 54.

33. Quoted in Ivo H. Daalder, *Getting to Dayton: The Making of America's Bosnian Policy* (Washington, DC: Brookings Institution Press, 2000), p. 34.

34. Madeleine Albright, *Madam Secretary: A Memoir* (London: Macmillan, 2003), p. 382. The reference was of course to Neville Chamberlain's notorious 'Munich Agreement' with Adolf Hitler.

35. Richard Holbrooke, *To End a War* (New York: Random House, 1998), p. 364.

36. Sidney Blumenthal, *The Clinton Wars* (London: Viking, 2003), p. 667.

37. Both quotations in ibid., p. 670.

38. Gertrude Himmelfarb, *One Nation, Two Cultures* (New York: Vintage, 2001), p. 120. The book was first published in 1999.

39. Goldberg File, *National Review Online*, 31 July 2002.

40. Conversation with author, Washington, DC, 9 December 2002.

41. This and subsequent quotations from his acceptance speech at Aachen on 2 June 2000. The text can be found at <http://www.karlspreis.de>

42. Ipsos US Express poll, 3–5 December 2002. I am most grateful to Michael Petrou for arranging for the inclusion of these questions.

43. My notes of that meeting, Washington, DC, 31 May 2001.

44. See Colin Powell's article with that title in *Foreign Affairs*, January/February 2004.

45. Quoted from David Frum's lively portrait of *The Right Man: The Surprise Presidency of George W. Bush* (New York: Random House, 2003), p. 70.

46. For what they found, see the *Climate Change Review*, released by the White House on 11 June 2001, as the president left for Europe. See <http://www.whitehouse.gov>

47. See <http://www.whitehouse.gov/news/inaugural-address.html>

48. *Weekly Defense Monitor*, 28 June 2001, available at <http://www.cdi.org/weekly/2001/issue25.html#2>

49. *Washington Post*, 8 June 2001.

50. Quoted in Bob Woodward, *Bush at War* (New York: Simon & Schuster, 2002), p. 37.

51. Ibid., p. 46.

52. I owe this comparison to Michael Hirsh's illuminating *At War with Ourselves: Why America is squandering its chance to build a better world* (New York: Oxford University Press, 2003). Obviously this capacity did not – at this writing – extend to catching Osama bin Laden.

53. Bob Woodward, *Bush at War* (New York: Simon & Schuster, 2002), p. 176.

54. Ibid., pp. 179–80.

55. Quoted in Sidney Blumenthal, *The Clinton Wars* (London: Viking, 2003), p. 780.

56. Charles Krauthammer, *Washington Post*, 26 April 2002.

57. Issued on 17 September 2002. All quotations are from the version on the official White House website, <http://www.whitehouse.gov>

58. Partially declassified Presidential Decision Directive of 21 June 1995, available on <http://www.fas.org/irp/offdocs/pdd39.htm> I owe this reference to Melvyn P. Leffler, in his 2003 Harmsworth Inaugural Lecture at Oxford, entitled '9/11 and the Past and Future of American Foreign Policy'.

59. Conversation with a senior administration official, Washington, DC, 11 December 2002.

60. The letter, dated 26 January 1998, can be found on the Project's website, <http://www.newamericancentury.org>

61. This account, based on the recollections of former Treasury Secretary Paul O'Neill, comes from Ron Suskind, *The Price of Loyalty: George W. Bush, the White House and the Education of Paul O'Neill* (New York: Simon & Schuster, 2004), pp. 72–3.

62. Bob Woodward, *Bush at War* (New York: Simon & Schuster, 2002), pp. 49, 83–5.

63. Bush to Woodward, looking back on the Afghan war, ibid., p. 45.

64. And one of the six refers to Uzbekistan's desire to have immediate membership in Nato as its reward for supporting the war on terror. Ibid., p. 172.

65. Richard Perle, in *The Guardian*, 13 November 2002.

66. I explore this at greater length in 'Anti-Europeanism in America', *New York Review of Books*, 27 March 2003.

67. See Charlemagne, 'Divide and Rule', *The Economist*, 26 April 2003, quoting a senior administration official. Subsequently, when out of office, Richard Haass acknowledged that he was the source. E-mail to the author, 6 March 2004.

68. Richard Haass at a Ditchley Conference, 27–29 June 2003, quoted with his kind permission.

69. See John C. Hulsman, 'Cherry-picking as the future of the transatlantic alliance', in the web magazine *Open Democracy* (<http://www.opendemocracy.net>), 20 February 2003.

70. Editorial in *Wall Street Journal Europe*, 30 May/1 June 2003.

71. Draft Defense Planning Guidance, quoted in *New York Times*, 8 March 1992.

72. This particular formulation comes from his remarks at a Center for Security Policy 'Keeper of the Flame' award dinner, 6 November 2001, see <http//:www.defenselink.mil/speeches/2001/s20011106-secdef.html> He used the formula many times.

73. Conversation with a senior administration official, Washington, DC, 10 December 2002.

74. For the text of his triumphant remarks on the deck of the USS *Abraham Lincoln* see <http://usinfo.state.gov/topical/pol/terror/texts/03050112.htm>

75. Quoted in Ron Suskind, *The Price of Loyalty: George W. Bush, the White House and the Education of Paul O'Neill* (New York: Simon & Schuster, 2004), p. 96.

76. Pierre Hassner, *The United States: the empire of force or the force of empire?* Chaillot Papers No. 54 (Paris: Institute for Security Studies, 2002), p. 43.

77. This and following quotations from speech by George W. Bush in the Banqueting House, London, 19 November 2003. Text at <http://www.whitehouse.gov>

78. Alistair Horne, Macmillan's biographer, believes this often quoted remark to have been made at the time of the Profumo affair, but has never found an exact context. Letter to the author, 25 February 2004.

79. Quoted in *The Guardian*, 2 December 2003.

80. This is based on 2002 expenditure calculated at market exchange rates, in *SIPRI Yearbook 2003: Armaments, Disarmament and International Security* (Stockholm: SIPRI, 2003), pp. 305, 345–50. When using purchasing power parities, the United States only exceeds the next five powers, with China, India and Russia now coming before France and Britain (ibid., p. 305) but such a reckoning clearly understates its cumulative and technological advantage. I am most grateful to Marrack Goulding for drawing my attention to these careful calculations.

81. See Dana Priest, *The Mission: Waging War and Keeping Peace with America's Military* (New York: Norton, 2003), p. 70.

82. See, for example, the projections in Goldman Sachs, *Dreaming with BRICs: The Path to 2050*, Global Economics Paper No 99, on <http://www.gs.com>

83. See the British Foreign Office projections, based on Economist Intelligence Unit data, in *UK International Priorities: A Strategy for the FCO* (London: The Stationery Office, 2003), p. 16.

84. Thomas Jefferson writing to William Short, 28 July 1791, in *The Writings of Thomas Jefferson* (Washington, DC: Taylor & Maury, 1853), vol. III, pp. 273–9.

85. The nearest parallel one can find is early twentieth-century British liberal imperialism. This is trenchantly explored by Niall Ferguson in his *Colossus: The Price of America's Empire* (London: Penguin, 2004).

86. These words are spoken by Pastor Lorenzen in Chapter 23 of *Der Stechlin*.

87. Quoted in Niall Ferguson, *Colossus: The Price of America's Empire* (London: Penguin, 2004), p. 49.

88. Report by Frank Bruni in *New York Times*, 22 September 2001, quoted in Ivo H. Daalder and James M. Lindsay, *America Unbound: The Bush Revolution in Foreign Policy* (Washington, DC: Brookings Institution Press, 2003), p. 88.

89. Richard Perle, writing in Robert Kagan and William Kristol (eds), *Present Dangers: Crisis and Opportunity in American Foreign Policy* (San Francisco: Encounter Books, 2000), p. 335.

90. German Marshall Fund et al., *Transatlantic Trends* (Washington, DC, 2003), p. 7.

91. Pew Global Attitudes Project, *Views of a Changing World: June 2003* (Washington, DC: The Pew Research Center for the People and the Press, 2003), p. 27. There also the 76 per cent figure.

92. Figures quoted by the retiring Nato Secretary-General, George Robertson, on the BBC *Today* programme, 9 December 2003.

93. This and the following figures are from the Executive Summary in Joseph P. Quinlan, *Drifting Apart or Growing Together? The Primacy of the Trans-atlantic Economy* (Washington, DC: Center for Transatlantic Relations, 2003).

94. Walt Whitman, 'Song of Myself'.

## 4 THE NEW RED ARMIES

1. Introduction by Ambassador Francis X. Taylor to US Department of State, *Patterns of Global Terrorism 2001* (May 2002), available on <http://www.state.gov>

2. Quoted from section 2, 'Definitions' in US Department of State, *Patterns of Global Terrorism 2002* (April 2003), available on <http.//www.state.gov> The report notes that the US government has employed this definition 'for statistical and analytical purposes' since 1983.

3. The graph to 2001 is drawn as Figure 2 to an article, to which I am also otherwise indebted, by Charles Tilly, 'Violence, Terror and Politics as Usual', originally published in the *Boston Review*, summer 2002, and available on <http://www.bostonreview.net>

4. This and other 2002 figures in section 4, 'The Year in Review', of US Department of State, *Patterns of Global Terrorism 2002* (April 2003), available on <http://www.state.gov>

5. Attributed to an unnamed statistician by E. L. Jones, *The European Miracle: Environments, Economies and Geopolitics in the History of Europe and Asia* (Cambridge: Cambridge University Press, 1987), p. xii.

6. Speech at the UN Financing for Development Conference in Monterrey, Mexico, 22 March 2002, available on <http://www.whitehouse.gov>

7. National security strategy issued on 17 September 2002, section III. All quotations are from the version on <http://www.whitehouse.gov>

8. In his State of the Union address to Congress on 6 January 1941.

9. In *Newsweek*, special Davos edition 'Issues 2004', dated December 2003–February 2004.

10. The list in Francis Fukuyama, *The End of History and the Last Man* (London: Penguin, 1992), p. 49 seems to me arbitrarily short. I am most grateful to Jonathan Keates, and his disintegrating *Almanach de Gotha*, for help in augmenting it.

11. This and the following figures follow Larry Diamond, 'A Report Card on Democracy' in *Hoover Digest*, 2000, no. 3, pp. 91–100, at p. 91.

12. This covers the period from January to November 2003. Information from Freedom House, to be published in Adrian Karatnycky et al. (eds), *Freedom in the World: The Annual Survey of Political Rights and Civil Liberties 2004* (New York: Freedom House, forthcoming).

13. The difference is spelled out clearly by Larry Diamond, 'Universal Democracy?', *Policy Review*, June/July 2003, pp. 3–25, esp. p. 8.

14. Figures for 2003 from Freedom House. The methodology is explained in Adrian Karatnycky et al. (eds), *Freedom in the World: The Annual Survey of Political Rights and Civil Liberties 2003* (New York: Freedom House, 2003), pp. 691ff.

15. See the discussion later in this chapter, 'Rich North, Poor South', pp. 164–73.

16. See his *Development as Freedom* (Oxford: Oxford University Press, 1999).

17. This correlation was famously demonstrated historically by Adam Przeworski et al., *Democracy and Development: Political Institutions and Well Being in the World, 1950–1990* (Cambridge: Cambridge University Press, 2000), following an earlier suggestion by Seymour Martin Lipset. I

have increased their per capita threshold figures slightly, to take account of 2002 per capita GDP in purchasing power parity (PPP), as shown in Adrian Karatnycky et al. (eds), *Freedom in the World: The Annual Survey of Political Rights and Civil Liberties 2003* (New York: Freedom House, 2003), pp. 703–4.

18. National security strategy issued on 17 September 2002. All quotations are from the version at <http://www.whitehouse.gov>

19. Francis Fukuyama, *The End of History and the Last Man* (London: Penguin, 1992), pp. 39ff. The original article appeared in *The National Interest*, Summer 1989, pp. 3–18, entitled 'The End of History?' Note the question mark.

20. Kofi A. Annan, '*We the Peoples . . .*' *Nobel Peace Message* (New York: Ruder Finn Press, 2001), p. 43.

21. Samuel P. Huntington, *The Clash of Civilizations and the Remaking of World Order* (London: Touchstone Books, 1997), pp. 83ff. and *passim*.

22. Ibid., p. 209.

23. Joseph Stiglitz, *Globalization and its Discontents* (London: Penguin, 2002), p. 9.

24. Peter Singer, *One World: The Ethics of Globalization* (New Haven: Yale University Press, 2002), p. 10.

25. I owe this (real) example to Anthony Giddens, *Runaway World: How Globalization is Reshaping our Lives* (London: Profile Books, 2002), p. 6.

26. For 'post-modern' see Robert Cooper, *The Breaking of Nations: Order and Chaos in the Twenty-first Century* (London: Atlantic Books, 2003); for 'neo-medieval' see Jan Zielonka, (ed.), *Europe Unbound: Enlarging and Reshaping the Boundaries of the European Union* (London: Routledge, 2002), p. 13.

27. See his *Longitudes and Attitudes: Exploring the World before and after September 11* (London: Penguin, 2003), pp. ix–x.

28. See his *The Shield of Achilles: War, Peace and the Course of History* (London: Penguin, 2002).

29. See the quotation from Bernard Lewis's 1990 article 'The Roots of Muslim Rage' in Samuel P. Huntington, *The Clash of Civilizations and the Remaking of World Order* (London: Touchstone Books, 1997), p. 213.

30. Alfred Stepan and Graeme B. Robertson, 'An "Arab" more than a "Muslim" electoral gap' in *Journal of Democracy*, vol. 14, no. 3, July 2003, pp. 30–44.

31. United Nations Development Programme/Arab Fund for Economic and Social Development, *The Arab Human Development Report 2002* (New York: UNDP, 2002), p. 27. See also the 'freedom score'. No source is given for the freedom score, but it is clearly based on the Freedom House assess-

ments, as subsequently acknowledged in *The Arab Human Development Report 2003* (New York: UNDP, 2003), p. 28.

32. Ibid., p. 1.

33. Ibid., p. 2.

34. *The Arab Human Development Report 2003* (New York: UNDP, 2003), p. 25.

35. United Nations Development Programme/Arab Fund for Economic and Social Development, *The Arab Human Development Report 2002* (New York: UNDP, 2002), p. 85.

36. Ibid., p. 44.

37. Ibid., p. 52.

38. Albert Hourani, *A History of the Arab Peoples* (London: Faber & Faber, 2002), p. 449 and *passim*.

39. Thomas Friedman, *Longitudes and Attitudes: Exploring the World before and after September 11* (London: Penguin, 2003), p. 197.

40. Quoted by Clyde Prestowitz, *Rogue Nation: American Unilateralism and the Failure of Good Intentions* (New York: Basic Books, 2003), p. 14.

41. 'Strengthening the EU's Partnership with the Arab World', Memorandum to the Italian Presidency of the European Council from Javier Solana, Romano Prodi and Chris Patten, dated Brussels, 4 December 2003, section 3, 'Objectives'. <http://europa.eu.int/>

42. From the final version of the European Security Strategy adopted by the European Council in Brussels on 12 December 2003, and available on the EU website, <http://europa.eu.int/>

43. Régis Debray in *International Herald Tribune*, 24 February 2003.

44. United Nations Development Programme/Arab Fund for Economic and Social Development, *The Arab Human Development Report 2002* (New York: UNDP, 2002), pp. 37–8. According to estimates by the UN Economic Commission for Europe (Population Activities Unit, Indicators) the population of the EU of twenty-five countries in 2020 would be around 446 million.

45. Ibid., p. 30.

46. Lecture at St Antony's College, Oxford, 18 November 2003.

47. Quoted in Marc Lynch, 'Taking Arabs Seriously', *Foreign Affairs*, September/October 2003, p. 86.

48. Interview in *Muslim Democrat*, vol.5, no.1, November 2003, p. 8, downloaded from <http://www.islam-democracy.org>

49. See, for example, Pew Global Attitudes Project, *Views of a Changing World: June 2003* (Washington, DC: The Pew Research Center for the People and the Press, 2003), pp. 33–41.

50. Quoted in Marc Lynch, 'Taking Arabs Seriously', *Foreign Affairs*, September/October 2003, p. 93.

51. See the table compiled on the basis of data supplied by Ronald Inglehart from the World Values Survey in *The Arab Human Development Report 2003* (New York: UNDP, 2003), p. 19.

52. In fact, nearly two thirds of those living on less than $1 a day in 1999, according to World Bank figures. But the proportion is declining due to Asia's economic development.

53. Gerald Segal gives a figure of 33 per cent for China compared to 28 per cent for Europe and 0.8 per cent for the US, in his 1999 *Foreign Affairs* article, 'Does China Matter?', reprinted in Barry Buzan and Rosemary Foot (eds), *Does China Matter? A Reassessment. Essays in Memory of Gerald Segal* (London: Routledge, 2004), pp. 11–20, at p. 12. I'm grateful to Rosemary Foot for letting me have early sight of this volume.

54. Alice Amsden, *The Rise of "The Rest": Challenges to the West from Late-Industrializing Economies* (New York: Oxford University Press, 2001).

55. Quoted in David Hale and Lyric Hughes Hale, 'China Takes Off', *Foreign Affairs*, November/December 2003, pp. 36–53, at p. 46.

56. For China, see the chapter by Stuart Harris in ibid., pp. 54–70, at pp. 55–7. For India, see Stephen P. Cohen, *India: Emerging Power* (Washington, DC: Brookings, 2001), p. 27.

57. See the discussion by Stuart Harris in Barry Buzan and Rosemary Foot (eds), *Does China Matter? A Reassessment. Essays in Memory of Gerald Segal* (London: Routledge, 2004), pp. 57–8.

58. Henry Kissinger, *Does America Need a Foreign Policy? Toward a Diplomacy for the 21$^{st}$ Century* (New York: Free Press, 2002), p. 110.

59. See, for example, President Jiang Zemin, quoting Deng Xiaoping, in Orville Schell and David Shambaugh (eds), *The China Reader: The Reform Era* (New York: Vintage, 1999), p. 497.

60. Thus Avery Goldstein in G. John Ikenberry and Michael Mastanduno (eds), *International Relations Theory and the Asia-Pacific* (New York: Columbia University Press, 2003), pp. 57–106.

61. Quoted by Evan S. Medeiros and M. Taylor Frevel, 'China's New Diplomacy', *Foreign Affairs*, November/December 2003, pp. 22–35, at p. 32.

62. Henry Kissinger, *Does America Need a Foreign Policy? Toward a Diplomacy for the 21st Century* (New York: Free Press, 2002), p. 110.

63. Thus Barry Buzan in Barry Buzan and Rosemary Foot, (eds), *Does China Matter? A Reassessment. Essays in Memory of Gerald Segal* (London: Routledge, 2004), p. 159.

64. Henry Kissinger, *Does America Need a Foreign Policy? Toward a Diplomacy for the 21st Century* (New York: Free Press, 2002), p. 160.

65. Part of a presidential address made at the 'Voice of America' in October

1997, quoted in Orville Schell and David Shambaugh (eds), *The China Reader: The Reform Era* (New York: Vintage, 1999), pp. 479–87, at pp. 480–82.

66. See the European Commission's paper, dated 10 September 2003, on 'A maturing partnership – shared interests and challenges in EU–China relations', p. 16, on EU website <http://europa.eu.int/>

67. The figure for the US is cited by David Hale and Lyric Hughes Hale, 'China Takes Off', *Foreign Affairs*, November/December 2003, pp. 36–53, at p. 49. The EU figure of €47 billion is given in the paper cited in note 66 above, also for 2002.

68. This is the thrust of the argument made by Henry S. Rowen in an incisive paper, *The Growth of Freedoms in China* (Stanford University: Asia/Pacific Research Center, 2001).

69. Simon Leys, Introduction to his edition of *The Analects of Confucius* (New York: Norton, 1997), p. xxv.

70. See Henry S. Rowen, *The Growth of Freedoms in China* (Stanford University: Asia/Pacific Research Center, 2001), pp. 10–14.

71. I count *The Economist* and *Financial Times* as international rather than purely British or European papers.

72. The story is well told in Chris Patten, *East and West* (London: Macmillan, 1998), pp. 303–305.

73. See the European Commission's paper, dated 10 September 2003, on 'A maturing partnership – shared interests and challenges in EU-China relations', available on the EU website, <http://europa.eu.int/>

74. I follow here the assessment of Jeff Sachs, Director of the Earth Institute at Columbia University. See his 'Visiting Global Public Policies for Sustainable Development: A Transatlantic Dialogue', speech at the Atlantic Conference, 26 May 2003, on <http://www.earthinstitute.columbia.edu.>

75. UN Food and Agricultural Organization, *The State of Food Insecurity in the World 2003*, quoted in *International Herald Tribune*, 26 November 2003.

76. This figure is given in the *Human Development Report 1999* (New York: UNDP, 1999), p. 38. My attention was drawn to it by Peter Singer, *One World: The Ethics of Globalization* (New Haven: Yale University Press, 2002), p. 81, from whom I take the population figure of 600 million.

77. My notes of a panel discussion at the World Economic Forum, Davos, 2001.

78. I owe this thought to Peter Singer, *One World: The Ethics of Globalization* (New Haven: Yale University Press, 2002), at p. 151, drawing on the UNICEF 2001 report on *The State of the World's Children*.

79. I take this figure from the 2003 *Report of the Commission on Human*

*Security*, available on <http://www.humansecurity-chs.org/finalreport/index.html>

80. See *Human Development Report 1999* (New York: UNDP, 1999), p. 38.

81. See *Globalization, Growth and Poverty: Building an Inclusive World Economy* (Washington, DC/Oxford: World Bank/Oxford University Press, 2002), p. 2 and *passim*. This incisive report was written by Paul Collier, of St Antony's College, Oxford, and the aptly named David Dollar.

82. See *Human Development Report 2003* (New York: UNDP, 2003), pp. 1–3.

83. Conversation with Dov Zakheim, then in effect the chief financial officer of the Pentagon, Washington, DC, 25 July 2003.

84. See *Foreign Aid in the National Interest: Overview* (Washington, DC: US Agency for International Development, 2002), pp. 27–9.

85. See, for example, *Global Civil Society 2002* (Oxford: Oxford University Press, 2002), a yearbook launched by the London School of Economics in 2001.

86. Speech at the UN Financing for Development Conference in Monterrey, Mexico, 22 March 2002, available on <http://www.whitehouse.gov>

87. See *Foreign Aid in the National Interest: Overview* (Washington, DC: US Agency for International Development, 2002), pp. 29–30.

88. Report in *International Herald Tribune*, 10 September 2003. In April 2003, Congress approved $79 billion (a good part of which had already been spent by the Pentagon) for the Iraq War and initial post-war expenses; it approved a further $87 billion in September 2003.

89. Calculations for 2001 by Marton Benedek from figures provided by OECD Development Assistance Committee.

90. This and the figures in the next two paragraphs are taken from *Human Development Report 2003* (New York: UNDP, 2003), pp. 145–7.

91. The group was headed by Jeff Sachs. He summarizes their findings in a lecture on 'The Millennium Compact and the End of Hunger', Des Moines, Iowa, 16 October 2003, available on <http://www.earthinstitute.columbia.edu/about/director/index.html>

92. See *Globalization, Growth and Poverty: Building an Inclusive World Economy* (Washington, DC/Oxford: World Bank/Oxford University Press, 2002), p. 9.

93. *Human Development Report 2003* (New York: UNDP, 2003), pp. 155–6.

94. See *Make Trade Fair* (Oxford: Oxfam, 2002), p. 98ff. Available on <http://www.maketradefair.com>

95. *Human Development Report 2003* (New York: UNDP, 2003), p. 155.

96. There are two qualifications that need to be made here. First, where a

poor country has tariff-free access to the EU market, its agricultural producers can in principle benefit from the higher food prices inside the EU which result from the CAP. Second, where poor countries are net food importers, they benefit in the short term from the lower prices of subsidized food exports from the West. However, the much more damaging long-term effect of those subsidized exports is to undermine those countries' farm sectors. I am most grateful to Alex Duncan for drawing these points to my attention.

97. In practice, some import restrictions remain on bananas, rice and sugar. For the details, see <http://europa.eu.int/comm/trade/issues/global/gsp/eba/index_en.htm>

98. As reported in the Charlemagne column in *The Economist*, 21 June 2003.

99. Report in *New York Times*, 27 June 2002.

100. Fareed Zakaria, *The Future of Freedom: Illiberal Democracy at Home and Abroad* (New York: Norton, 2003), p. 174, gives a figure of $2 billion.

101. This figure is given by Joseph Stiglitz, *Globalization and its Discontents* (London: Penguin, 2002), p. 269.

102. See Adrian Karatnycky et al., (eds), *Freedom in the World: The Annual Survey of Political Rights and Civil Liberties 2003* (New York: Freedom House, 2003), p. 93.

103. Debt service to social spending figures are given by the Worldwatch Institute on <http://www.worldwatch.org/press/news/2001/04/26/>

104. Debt and cotton export figures are from the September 2003 Jubilee Research, *Real Progress Report on HIPC*, country entry on Benin. Available on <http://www.jubileeplus.org/analysis/reports/realprogressHIPC.pdf>

105. The BBC *Today* programme, 10 June 2003, reported a specific case of a Ghanaian tomato farmer forced out of business by EU-subsidized exports.

106. For this first Commitment to Development Index (CDI) see 'Ranking the Rich' in *Foreign Policy*, May/June 2003.

107. Fareed Zakaria, *The Future of Freedom: Illiberal Democracy at Home and Abroad* (New York: Norton, 2003), p. 173, gives a figure of 20,000 for 1990. I'm assuming their number has not decreased.

108. See *United Nations Chronicle*, on-line edition, vol. XXXVI, no. 3, 1999.

109. See <http://www.unfpa.org/6billion/ccmc/thedayofsixbillion.html> and UNPD, *World Population Prospects: The 2002 Revision*, on <http://www.un.org/esa/population/unpop.ht>

110. See <http://www.unfpa.org/6billion/> Every two fifths of a second is my timing of that counter.

111. *World Population Prospects: The 2002 Revision*, p. 1, available on <http://www.un.org/esa/population/unpop.ht>

112. Ibid., p. vii.

113. Thomas Malthus, *Essay on Population*, quoted in Amartya Sen, *Development as Freedom* (Oxford: Oxford University Press, 1999), p. 205. I follow Sen's argument.

114. Ibid., Table 9.1 on p. 206.

115. *Human Development Report 2003* (New York: UNDP, 2003), p. 227.

116. Ibid., p. 125. 'Water stress' is defined as consuming more than 20 per cent of your renewable water supply every year.

117. See Marq de Villiers, *Water Wars: Is the World's Water Running Out?* (London: Phoenix, 2001)

118. International Energy Agency, *World Energy Outlook 2002*, on <http://www.worldenergyoutlook.org/weo/pubs/weo2002/weo2002.asp>, p. 33.

119. See International Energy Agency, *World Energy Outlook 2002*, <http://www.worldenergyoutlook.org/weo/pubs/weo2002/weo2002.asp> and US International Energy Administration, *International Energy Outlook 2003*, <http://www.eia.doe.gov/oiaf/ieo/>

120. I say 'modern' because a primitive form of steam power was used earlier in China, but not in the piston-to-wheel form that contributed to the industrial revolution. I am grateful to David Faure for enlightening me on this point.

121. See World Bank, *Entering the 21st Century: World Development Report 1999/2000* (New York: OUP, 2000), pp. 87ff.

122. See the revealing account in ibid., pp. 94–7.

123. Here I follow Bjorn Lomborg, *The Skeptical Environmentalist: Measuring the Real State of the World* (Cambridge: Cambridge University Press, 2000), p. 261.

124. I follow the authoritative Intergovernmental Panel on Climate Change report, *Climate Change 2001*, available on <http://www.ipcc.ch/pub/reports.htm>

125. BBC news report, 5 March 2004, citing a report in the journal *Science*.

126. Munich Re, as reported on <http://news.bbc.co.uk/2/hi/americas/3308959.stm>

127. World Bank, *Entering the 21st Century: World Development Report 1999/2000* (New York: OUP, 2000), p. 100.

128. Quoted in Dinyar Godrej, *The No-Nonsense Guide to Climate Change* (London: Verso, 2001), p. 90.

129. Intergovernmental Panel on Climate Change, *Climate Change 2001: Synthesis Report,* <http://www.ipcc.ch/pub/reports.htm>, p. 5.

130. Ibid., p. 8.

131. Ibid., p. 9.

132. International Energy Agency, *World Energy Outlook 2002*, <http://

www.worldenergyoutlook.org/weo/pubs/weo2002/weo2002.asp>, p. 30.

133. *Globalization, Growth and Poverty: Building an Inclusive World Economy* (Washington, DC/Oxford: World Bank/Oxford University Press, 2002), p. 17.

134. Ibid., p. 17. These were 1998 figures, so may now be higher. 'European' presumably refers to the 1998 EU of fifteen countries.

135. Peter Singer, *One World: The Ethics of Globalization* (New Haven: Yale University Press, 2002), p. 21. A BBC report dated 29 September 2003 gives a figure of 16 per cent above 1990 levels, see <http://news.bbc.co.uk/2/hi/science/nature/3143798.stm>

136. John Steinbeck, *America and Americans* (New York: Penguin, 2002), pp. 377–8.

137. As reported in *Time* (international edition), 1 June 1992.

138. Sir John Houghton, quoted in the *New Statesman*, 1 December 2003.

139. See the table in Bill Emmott, *20:21 Vision: The Lessons of the 20th Century for the 21st* (London: Penguin, 2003), p. 267.

140. Presidential announcement on 14 February 2002, available on <http://www.whitehouse.gov/news>

141. US International Energy Administration, *International Energy Outlook 2003*, <http://www.eia.doe.gov/oiaf/ieo/>, pp. 162–3. For the 7 per cent commitment level, see the table in Dinyar Godrej, *The No-Nonsense Guide to Climate Change* (London: Verso, 2001), p. 107.

142. Tony Blair, speech on sustainable development, 24 February 2003, available on <http://www.number-10.gov.uk>

143. See the report in *The Observer*, 22 February 2004.

144. Quoted in Dinyar Godrej, *The No-Nonsense Guide to Climate Change* (London: Verso, 2001), pp. 114–15.

145. See the exploration and extension of Freud's idea in Michael Ignatieff, *The Warrior's Honour: Ethnic War and the Modern Conscience* (London: Chatto & Windus, 1998), pp. 48ff.

146. Robert Cooper, *The Breaking of Nations: Order and Chaos in the Twenty-first Century* (London: Atlantic Books, 2003), p. 138ff.

147. Thomas Aquinas, *Summa Theologiae. Secunda Secundae.*

## CRISIS AS OPPORTUNITY

1. As reported in *The Observer*, 22 February 2004.

2. See Chapter 25 of Niccolò Machiavelli, *The Prince* (London: Penguin, 1961), at p. 130.

3. See chapter 1 above, p. 28.

## TWENTY YEARS AND A THOUSAND MILLION CITIZENS

1. Ian Buruma and Avishai Margalit, 'Seeds of Revolution', in *New York Review of Books*, 11 March 2004, summarizing the argument of their book *Occidentalism* (New York: Penguin, 2004).

2. These well-known lines appear in the poem 'To Althea, From Prison' by the seventeenth-century English poet Richard Lovelace.

3. The title of the autobiography of Ken Livingstone: *If Voting Changed Anything, They'd Abolish It* (London: HarperCollins, 1987). Livingstone was subsequently elected Mayor of London.

## 5  BRITAIN FINDS ITS ROLE

1. See Douglas Brinkley, 'Dean Acheson and the "Special Relationship": The West Point speech of December 1962', *The Historical Journal*, vol. 33, no. 3 (1990), pp. 599–608. Later, contemplating the resulting storm, Acheson commented ruefully, 'the first requirement of a statesman is that he be dull'.

2. Dictated by Bismarck on 9 November 1876; see Johannes Lepsius et al. (eds), *Die grosse Politik der europäischen Kabinette 1871–1914*, vol. 2 (Berlin: Deutsche Verlagsgesellschaft für Politik und Geschichte, 1922), no. 256, p. 88.

3. The story is told in my *In Europe's Name: Germany and the Divided Continent* (London: Jonathan Cape, 1993).

4. BBC News report, 11 February 2002, see <http://news.bbc.co.uk/2/hi/uk_news/education/1815073.stm>

5. Rudyard Kipling, 'The English Flag'.

6. I am treating the *Financial Times* as an international rather than a British daily paper.

7. Quoted in P. Williamson, *Conservative Leadership and National Values* (Cambridge: Cambridge University Press, 1999), p. 234.

8. Conversation with the author, London, 22 September 2003.

9. See Jennifer Jenkins, *The Phonology of English as an International Language* (Oxford: Oxford University Press, 2000), p. 1.

10. Václav Havel, conversation with the author.

11. Gisela Stuart, conversation with the author.

12. William Wordsworth, lines from 'It Is Not to Be Thought of, that the Flood' in *Poems Dedicated to National Independence and Liberty*.

13. George Orwell, *The Lion and the Unicorn: Socialism and the English Genius* (London: Secker & Warburg, 1941), p. 127.

## 6 WHAT EUROPE CAN BE

1. I owe this splendid formulation to my colleague Kalypso Nicolaïdis. She develops the notion in Kalypso Nicolaïdis and Robert Howse (eds), *The Federal Vision: Legitimacy and Levels of Governance in the United States and the European Union* (Oxford: Oxford University Press, 2001), p. 474.

2. The essay is reprinted in P. J. O'Rourke, *Holidays in Hell* (London: Picador, 2002), pp. 211–31, at p. 212.

3. I owe this imagery of induction to my colleague Adam Roberts, who explores it further in his forthcoming book on liberal international order.

4. See Helen and William Wallace (eds), *Policy-Making in the European Union* (Oxford: Oxford University Press, 2000), p. 33ff.

5. In *Frankfurter Allgemeine Zeitung*, 31 May 2003.

6. Quoted above, p. 111.

7. Quoted from the transcript, republished in facsimile as *Congress of Europe: The Hague 7–11 May 1948* (Strasbourg: Council of Europe, 1999), p. 16.

8. Bertolt Brecht, 'Kriegsfibel', Verse 69.

9. Eric Hobsbawm, *The Age of Extremes 1914–1991* (New York: Pantheon, 1994), p. 578.

10. See below, p. 242 and the report of the International Commission on Intervention and State Sovereignty, *The Responsibility to Protect* (Ottawa: International Development Research Centre, 2001).

11. German Marshall Fund et al., *Transatlantic Trends* (Washington, DC, 2003), p. 10. Of the 71 per cent who said they wanted the EU to become a superpower, 49 per cent changed their mind if this would involve greater military expenditure. In other words, only 36 per cent of all those asked supported the EU becoming a superpower with greater military expenditure.

## 7 UNCLE SAM

1. The speaker was George F. Will, Washington, DC, 10 December 2002.

2. De Gaulle's biographer, Jean Lacouture, confirms that de Gaulle almost certainly did make this often quoted remark, but cannot point to an exact source for it.

3. *Private Eye*, 28 November–11 December 2003.

4. Thucydides, *The History of the Peloponnesian War*, edited and translated by R. W. Livingstone (London: Oxford University Press, 1943), p. 267.

5. The full text is given in Caroline Kennedy, *A Patriot's Handbook: Songs,*

*Poems, Stories and Speeches Celebrating the Land we Love* (New York: Hyperion, 2003), pp. 644–5.

6. I owe this crisp formulation to the Independent International Commission on Kosovo, *The Kosovo Report: Conflict. International Response. Lessons Learned* (Oxford: Oxford University Press, 2000), p. 4. It is justified in detail in that report.

7. Thucydides, *The History of the Peloponnesian War*, edited and translated by R. W. Livingstone (London: Oxford University Press, 1943), p. 267.

8. William Blake, 'Auguries of Innocence'.

9. Here I am plagiarizing my own article, 'The Peril of Too Much Power', in the *New York Times*, 9 April 2002.

10. Rudyard Kipling, 'The White Man's Burden' (1899), a poem addressed to the United States on the annexation of the Philippines.

11. William Camden, *Remaines, concerning Britaine: But especially England, and the Inhabitants therof* (London: printed by Nicholas Okes for Simon Waterson, 1623), p. 5.

12. Conversation with the author, Washington, DC, 24 July 2003.

13. *Life*, 17 February 1941.

14. W. C. Sellar and R. J. Yeatman, *1066 and All That* (London: Methuen, 1999), p. 123. The book was first published in 1930.

## 8 TOWARDS A FREE WORLD

1. J. M. Roberts, *The New Penguin History of the World* (London: Penguin, 2002), p. 797.

2. Ibid., pp. 1174–6.

3. Speech to a Joint Session of Congress, 17 July 2003, <http://www.number-10.gov.uk/output/Page4220.asp>

4. This is eloquently explored by Larry Siedentop, *Democracy in Europe* (London: Penguin, 2000), p. 193f.

5. Ludger Kühnhardt, *Die Universalität der Menschenrechte* (Bonn: Bundeszentrale für politische Bildung, 1987), pp. 190, 300f. and *passim*.

6. Michail S. Gorbatschow (*sic*), *Gipfelgespräche: Geheime Protokolle aus meiner Amtszeit* (Berlin: Rowohlt, 1995), pp. 128–9.

7. Samuel P. Huntington, *The Clash of Civilizations and the Remaking of World Order* (London: Touchstone Books, 1997), p. 162.

8. See Isaiah Berlin, *Liberty* (Oxford: Oxford University Press, 2002), edited by Henry Hardy.

9. Matthew 7:12.

10. George Bernard Shaw, 'Maxims for Revolutionists: The Golden Rule', in

*Man and Superman: a Comedy and a Philosophy* (London: Penguin, 2004), p. 251.

11. *The Analects of Confucius* (New York: Norton, 1997), translated by Simon Leys, p. 55.

12. '*Wolność*' in Adam Zagajewski, *List. Oda do Wielości* (Paris: Instytut Literacki, 1983). The last word of the poem, '*niewola*', is more usually translated as 'captivity', but 'to be unfree' seems to me closer to the meaning in this poem.

13. See my *History of the Present: Essays, Sketches and Despatches from Europe in the 1990s* (London: Penguin, 2000), pp. 101–104.

14. Mark Palmer, *Breaking the Real Axis of Evil: How to Oust the World's Last Dictators by 2025* (Lanham: Rowman & Littlefield, 2003).

15. Ibid., p. 283.

16. See my 'Beauty and the Beast in Burma', *New York Review of Books*, 25 May 2000.

17. See the report of the International Commission on Intervention and State Sovereignty, *The Responsibility to Protect* (Ottawa: International Development Research Centre, 2001).

18. 'Tiananmen' in James Fenton, *Out of Danger: Poems* (London: Penguin, 1993), p. 41.

19. I am citing the lines as quoted (and retranslated) in the film, directed by Dai Sijie. They do not appear in the original book version, Dai Sijie, *Balzac and the Little Chinese Seamstress* (London: Vintage, 2002).

20. See Fareed Zakaria, *The Future of Freedom: Illiberal Democracy at Home and Abroad* (New York: Norton, 2003).

21. Samuel Johnson, lines added to Goldsmith's 'The Traveller'.

## WHAT CAN WE DO?

1. This motto is often ascribed to the Italian Marxist Antonio Gramsci, who used it on the masthead of his journal *Ordine Nuovo*. In fact, Gramsci was popularizing words originally coined by the French author and pacifist Romain Rolland.

# Acknowledgements

This book was made possible by an intellectual free world of colleagues and friends. I can name only some of them here, but I am profoundly grateful to them all.

At St Antony's College, Oxford, I would like to acknowledge first and foremost my colleagues at the European Studies Centre, for intellectual stimulation and congeniality, and, in the case of Janet Pearson and Ulli Parkinson, for invaluable administrative support. Marrack Goulding, Avi Shlaim, Rosemary Foot, David Faure, Robert Mabro, Steve Tsang, Eugene Rogan, Paul Collier, Alex Duncan, Alistair Horne and Dennis Anderson have commented on particular sections or enlightened me on specific points. I am also grateful to the Zeit Foundation Gerd and Ebelin Bucerius for its generous financial support. In the wider Oxford community, I owe specific thanks to Adam Roberts, Jennifer Welsh, Peter Pulzer and Mark Freedland.

My understanding of the United States has been deepened by my annual sojourns as a Senior Fellow at the Hoover Institution, Stanford University. I thank John Raisian, the Director, for getting me there in the first place, and all my Stanford friends for sharing with me their widely differing Americas.

A third source of regular stimulus has been my fortnightly commentary in *The Guardian* and an informal syndicate of newspapers across Europe and the Americas. I thank particularly Alan Rusbridger, and my confrères, too numerous to name, on all those papers. The *New York Review of Books* – arguably not just America's but Europe's finest intellectual journal – enabled me to make an illuminating trip exploring attitudes to Europe in the United States. My thanks go once again to Robert Silvers and Rea Hederman. On that trip, John and Leslie Earle arranged a memorable evening with their students in Lawrence, Kansas.

A major source for this book was conversations with leading politicians and officials. A few of them are identified in the notes. However, most of these conversations were on a non-attributable or private basis. I can therefore only offer a blanket vote of thanks to all who talked to me, discreetly and indiscreetly.

The typescript was read in first draft by this potent array of critical intelligences: Arnulf Baring, David Cornwell, Ralf Dahrendorf, John Fox, Pierre Hassner, Ian McEwan, Michael Mertes, Kalypso Nicoläidis, Aleksander Smolar, Timothy Snyder, Michael Taylor, Maurice Thompson, Tobias Wolff, my brother Christopher, my father and my wife. I believe it's a better book as a result, and I owe a very special debt of gratitude to each and every one of them.

For assistance on individual topics, I am grateful to Ronald Asmus, Dan Clark, Anne Deighton, Giles Fraser, Richard Haass, Judith Herrin, Trevor Kavanagh, Jonathan Keates, Jean Lacouture, Melvin P. Leffler, Noel Malcolm, Jacques Rupnik, Thomas W. Simons, Malcolm Spencer, Gisela Stuart and Paulo Valentino. Andrew Kohut was an incisive guide through the polling riches of the Pew Research Center for the People and the Press.

I enjoyed working closely with students from many countries on the research for this book. Glyn Prysor hunted down historical and political sources with a passion for accuracy that promises much for his future work as a historian. Marton Benedek was endlessly ingenious and helpful, particularly in his pursuit of American–European comparisons. As a Canadian, Michael Petrou took a sharply critical look at both Europe and America. Julia de Clerck-Sachsse surveyed the German debate, and shared with me some of her generation's views. John Crouch, Seth Green, Rachel Ziemba, Eric Weaver, Stefan Szwed and Dimitar Bechev participated in lively student debates, and helped me with specific points.

For the Values map, and its interpretation, I thank its begetter, Ronald Inglehart; for the Freedom map, Adrian Karatnycky and Christopher Walker at Freedom House. The idea for the proportional block maps originally came from a *Financial Times* version of a map in the *World Bank Atlas*, relating only to Money. It was my idea to do the same for Arms and People. Russell Birkett expertly translated the idea into graphic reality.

At Penguin, I am once again indebted to Stuart Proffitt for his meticulous and supportive editing, and to an impressive editorial and production team. At Rogers, Coleridge & White, Gill Coleridge has seen this book through every stage from idea to reality, with a calm and experienced eye.

*Free World* was chewed over most often and most enjoyably at a kitchen table. Deepest thanks to my wife, Danuta, for her patience and support, and to my frankest and warmest critics, my sons, to whom it is dedicated and for whom, in several different senses, it is written.

# Index

# PENGUIN HISTORY

**HISTORY OF THE PRESENT: ESSAYS, SKETCHES AND DESPATCHES FROM EUROPE IN THE 1990S**
TIMOTHY GARTON ASH

'The best Anglophone observer of contemporary Europe' Niall Ferguson, *Evening Standard*

'*History of the Present* is the natural sequel to his compelling, indispensable eyewitness writings about the season of revolutions around the year 1989 ... Timothy Garton Ash holds a mirror that magnifies ... He writes masterfully and with compassion about the dilemmas of coming to terms with bad pasts' Neal Ascherson, *Observer*

'Journalism, history and literature come together ... with elegance, erudition and skill. Garton Ash is a fine historian, journalist and raconteur ... He has been at one time or another in most of the places that mattered during these turbulent times – Prague, Warsaw, Belgrade, Pristina, Berlin, Zagreb ... in his essays he explores all of the ideas and the pressures to which these Europeans have been subjected since the fall of the wall – ethnicity as well as ethnic cleansing, nationalism, justice, memory and much more besides' William Shawcross, *Sunday Times*

'The most eloquent reporter of post-Cold War Europe ... He has the vivid intelligence of a Tocqueville and the unassumingly informed authority of a John Hersey...We'll still be reading Timothy Garton Ash in fifty years, not for what he predicted, but for what he saw' Brian Morton, *Glasgow Sunday Herald*

'In *History of the Present* we find him chatting with Helmut Kohl, strolling with Václav Havel, in discussions with Lech Walesa. His great theme is the "surreal, almost grotesque discrepancy" between the shells falling on the marketplace in Sarajevo and the economically integrated West, whose leaders proclaimed that "war in Europe has become unthinkable"' Tom Karshan, *Moscow Times*

'Catches history on the hop...the presiding spirit in this engrossing book is George Orwell...[It] will prove invaluable to anyone attempting to put the 1990s in Central and Eastern Europe in perspective' Paul Bailey, *Daily Telegraph*

# PENGUIN POLITICS

**THE END OF POVERTY**
JEFFREY SACHS

FOREWORD BY BONO

'The ideas in this book have a hook you won't forget: the end of poverty ... In Jeff's hands, the millstone of opportunity around our necks becomes an adventure, something doable and achievable' Bono

## WE CAN END POVERTY BY 2025 ... AND CHANGE THE WORLD FOREVER.

For the first time in history, our generation has the opportunity to end extreme poverty in the world's most desperate nations. But how can we stop the cycle of bad health, bad debt, and bad luck that holds back more than a billion people?

Jeffrey D. Sachs, Special Advisor to UN Secretary-General Kofi Annan and 'probably the most important economist in the world' (*The New York Times*) has the answers. He has visited and worked in over 100 countries across the globe – from Africa to India, Poland to Bolivia – advising leaders on economic development and poverty reduction. Here he lays out how poverty has been beaten in the past, how – in realistic, attainable steps – we can make a real difference for the one-fifth of humanity who still live in extreme poverty, how they can find partnership with their wealthy counterparts, how little it will actually cost, and how everyone can help.

*The End of Poverty* is a roadmap to a more prosperous and secure world.

# PENGUIN CURRENT EVENTS

## LONGITUDES AND ATTITUDES: EXPLORING THE WORLD BEFORE AND AFTER SEPTEMBER 11
THOMAS FRIEDMAN

The Number One International Bestseller

**Thomas Friedman, three times winner of the Pulitzer Prize, on the most momentous news story of our time.**

*Longitudes and Attitudes* brings together reportage and reflections by one of the world's most admired journalists about the state of the world leading up to and after September 11, 2001. Travelling throughout the Middle East and Europe, Thomas Friedman talks to men and women in bazaars, schools and alleyways, as well as the world's leading political figures, developing and refining his unique perspective on the new kind of war the West finds itself fighting.

Friedman gives voice to our awakening sense of a radically new world and our own complex place in it. His commentary provides a trenchant perspective on international affairs, setting the terms of debate for the most complex and contentious issues of today.

'When the world changed last September, it was Friedman, more than any other journalist, who was there to explain what happened and why … To read [*Longitudes and Attitudes*] is to relive an anguishing year in world history but also to witness a more human-size drama: Through these dispatches, you see a man trying to explain the unthinkable not only to his readers but to himself' *Rolling Stone*

'The country's best newspaper columnist, period. The horrors of September 11 snapped him into focus, compelling him to write heartfelt, readable, often personal essays … he treats the perilous state of global affairs with an energized earnestness' *Vanity Fair*

# PENGUIN POLITICS

## GLOBALIZATION AND ITS DISCONTENTS
JOSEPH STIGLITZ

'A massively important political as well as economic document ... we should listen to him urgently' Will Hutton, *Guardian*

**Our world is changing. Globalization is not working. It is hurting those it was meant to help. And now, the tide is turning ...**

Explosive and shocking, *Globalization and Its Discontents* is the bestselling exposé of the all-powerful organizations that control our lives – from the man who has seen them at work first hand.

As Chief Economist at the World Bank, Nobel Prize-winner Joseph Stiglitz had a unique insider's view into the management of globalization. Now he speaks out against it: how the IMF and WTO preach fair trade yet impose crippling economic policies on developing nations; how free market 'shock therapy' made millions in East Asia and Russia worse off than they were before; and how the West has driven the global agenda to further its own financial interests.

Globalization *can* still be a force for good, Stiglitz argues. But the balance of power has to change. Here he offers real, tough solutions for the future.

'Compelling ... This book is everyone's guide to the misgovernment of globalization' J. K. Galbraith

'Stiglitz is a rare breed, an heretical economist who has ruffled the self-satisfied global establishment that once fed him. *Globalization and Its Discontents* declares war on the entire Washington financial and economic establishment' Ian Fraser, *Sunday Tribune*

'Gripping ... this landmark book ... shows him to be a worthy successor to Keynes' Robin Blackburn, *Independent*

# PENGUIN POLITICS/HISTORY

**DEMOCRACY IN EUROPE**
LARRY SIEDENTOP

'At last, a proper book on Europe' Denis MacShane, *Independent*

'A thrilling, compulsively readable book about constitutional reform in the European Union? Come on, you must be joking. Yet that is exactly what Larry Siedentop provides. Compulsive, because brisk, erudite and full of intellectual fireworks. Thrilling, because he manages to recast the entire European debate ... This is a book for every chancellory across our continent' Peter Preston, *Observer*

'Were the ghost of Tocqueville to fly into Brussels, he would probably produce something like this stimulating analysis of the dilemmas currently facing the European Union ... A first-rate piece of political analysis and a clear sense of the difficulties that lie ahead for Europe' Mark Mazower, *Financial Times*

'If you feel you need straightening out on Europe but can't bear another word of the partisan blustering and cajoling that passes for debate, this is the book for you' George Walden, *Evening Standard*

'Full of provocative thoughts and ideas. Above all, it brings to a supremely political enterprise the analysis of a political thinker, not that of a political scientist or economist. Europe has waited far too long for this kind of scrutiny' *The Economist*

'Required reading in the chancellories of Europe...Siedentop is brave enough to assess the political health of all Europe...hailed for breaking a deadlock that has held for nearly fifty years...his book is a clarion-call for Europe to get its act together – before it is too late' Jonathan Freedland, *Guardian*

'The most original political book of the year' Simon Jenkins

# PENGUIN HISTORY

**THE UNCONQUERABLE WORLD: POWER, NON-VIOLENCE
AND THE WILL OF THE PEOPLE**
JONATHAN SCHELL

International bestselling author of *The Fate of the Earth*

'Perhaps the most impressive argument ever made that there exists a viable and desirable alternative to a continued reliance on war' *The New York Times*

'Passionate and polemical ... An ambitious study of Western civilization's predisposition to military action as the means by which to resolve differences ... The benchmark against which many 9/11 books will be set' *Observer*

After a century of unprecedented devastation, are we embarking on another cycle of bloodshed in the twenty-first century? Is there a peaceful alternative to war?

Jonathan Schell, one of the most eloquent voices in the debate about global warfare, argues that war has become dysfunctional as a political instrument. There is, he says, another path humankind can follow. Examining the history of violent action against the emergence of peaceful protest movements – Gandhi, Martin Luther King Jr, the collapse of Soviet power – he shows how the battle for the hearts and minds of the people can be as powerful and effective as war. Optimistic, pragmatic and compelling, *The Unconquerable World* uses the lessons of our violent past to try to lead us to a peaceful future.

'An important contribution in our quest to make sense of this new era ... Schell is excellent at laying bare the emergence of the new America and describing the character of its new imperial policy' *Guardian*

'Schell, in this profoundly important book, wants us to begin thinking about how we can use democracy – the actions of people, rather than governments – to bring about a peaceful world' *Boston Globe*

# PENGUIN POLITICS

## THE RIGHT NATION: WHY AMERICA IS DIFFERENT
JOHN MICKLETHWAIT & ADRIAN WOOLDRIDGE

'Conservatism's 40-year climb to dominance receives an examination worthy of its complexity in *The Right Nation*, the best political book in years' George Will, *Washington Post*

**What makes America seem so different from the rest of the world?** *The Right Nation* **is the definitive portrait of a United States that few outsiders understand: the nation that votes for George Bush, that supports the death penalty and gun rights, that believes in minimal government and long prison sentences, that pulled out of the Kyoto Protocol.**

America, argue John Micklethwait and Adrian Wooldridge, award-winning journalists at the *Economist*, has always been a conservative country; but over the past fifty years it has built up a radical conservative movement unlike any other. The authors examine how these right-wing radicals took over the Republican Party, and deconstruct the Bush White House, examining its many influences from neo-conservatism to sun-belt entrepreneurialism. Their quest to understand the mindset of the overlooked and often disdained, but crucial, Middle America takes them from young churchgoers in Colorado Springs to gay gun clubs in Massachusetts to black supporters of school vouchers in Milwaukee.

*The Right Nation* drives to the heart of a question that is relevant to us all: why is America – increasingly, and often frighteningly – different, and what does this mean for the world?

'A remarkable achievement … *The Right Nation* is authoritative, entertaining and astonishing in its breadth and objectivity.  It can perhaps make claim to an extraordinary boast as the best book on modern America in print'
Graham Stewart, *Spectator*